PUBLICATIONS

OF THE

NAVY RECORDS SOCIETY

VOL. LXXI.

THE SANDWICH PAPERS

VOL. II.

JOHN MONTAGU, FOURTH EARL OF SANDWICH
from the portrait by
THOMAS GAINSBOROUGH, painted in 1783 at the order of SIR HUGH PALLISER
for presentation to Greenwich Hospital, and now in the Painted Hall,
Greenwich.
By permission of the Lords Commissioners of the Admiralty.

[*Frontispiece*

THE PRIVATE PAPERS OF
JOHN, EARL OF SANDWICH

FIRST LORD OF THE ADMIRALTY

1771–1782

EDITED BY

G. R. BARNES AND J. H. OWEN

VOLUME II

MARCH 1778 – MAY 1779

PUBLISHED BY ROUTLEDGE FOR THE NAVY RECORDS SOCIETY
1933

First published 1933 for the Navy Records Society

Published 2019 by Routledge
2 Park Square, Milton Park, Abingdon, Oxon OX14 4RN
52 Vanderbilt Avenue, New York, NY 10017

Routledge is an imprint of the Taylor & Francis Group, an informa business

ISBN 13: 978-1-911248-99-6 (pbk)
ISBN 13: 978-0-85354-054-0 (hbk)

CONTENTS

CONTENTS

PLATES

LIST OF AUTHORITIES CITED

(Italics indicate manuscripts)

A. GENERAL

Abstract of Progress. (Admiralty Library.)

' A Short Account of the Naval Actions of the Last War." Anon. (London : J. Murray, 1788.)

[The Admiralty Librarian has learnt from Col. John Murray that Captain John Nicholson Inglefield was the only person the firm dealt with. Presumably he was the author.]

Barrow, Sir John, Bart., F.R.S., ' The Life of Richard, Earl Howe, K.G., Admiral of the Fleet and General of Marines.' (London : John Murray, 1838.)

Bridport Papers. (British Museum.)

Corbett, Sir Julian, ' England in the Seven Years' War.' (London : Longmans, 1907.)

Fortescue, the Hon. Sir John, ' The Correspondence of King George the Third,' Vol. IV. 1778–1779. (London : Macmillan, 1928.)

Historical Manuscripts Commission. Appendix to 9th Report, Part II. (London : 1884.)

—— Rutland MSS., III. (London : 1894.)

—— Dartmouth MSS., II. (London : 1895.)

—— Various Collections. Vol. VI., Cornwallis Wykeham-Martin MSS. (1909.)

Hunt, Robert M., ' The Life of Sir Hugh Palliser, Bart., Admiral of the White and Governor of Greenwich Hospital.' (London : Chapman and Hall, 1844.)

Keppel, the Hon. and Rev. Thomas, ' The Life of Augustus Viscount Keppel, Admiral of the White, and First Lord of the Admiralty in 1782–3.' 2 vols. (London : Henry Colburn, 1842.)

Lacour-Gayet, G., ' La Marine militaire de la France sous le règne de Louis XVI.' (Paris : 1905.)

Navy Records Society.—III, ' Letters written by Sir Samuel Hood.' (1895.)

—— XIX, ' Journals and Letters of Sir T. Byam Martin,' III. (1901.)

—— XXXV, ' Signals and Instructions, 1776–1794.' (1908.)

—— XXXII and XXXVIII, ' Letters and Papers of Charles, Lord Barham,' I. (1906.) II. (1910.)

—— LXIX, ' The Private Papers of John, Earl of Sandwich,' I. (1932.)

Public Record Office :

Admiralty : 1 *In letters from Secretary of State.*
          Admirals' Dispatches.
          Reports of Courts Martial.
        2 *Orders and Instructions.*
          Secret Orders and Instructions.
        8 *List Books.*
       36 *Muster Books.*
       50 *Admirals' Journals.*
       51 *Captains' Logs.*
       52 *Masters' Logs.*

State Papers, Domestic, naval.

' Some Seasonable Advice from an honest sailor, to whom it might have concerned, for the service of the C——n and C——y.' [Admiral Edward Vernon.] 8vo. (London : 1746.)

B. THE TRIALS

[*Note*.—The Official Minutes of the Trials are not so complete as the other editions, since matters ruled out of court are not printed therein. Palliser drew attention to this in his speech of 4 December 1780. Almon's edition is probably the fullest in this respect, but it is difficult to compare the editions because no library possesses them all.

Nos. 10 and 11 are simple records of Palliser's speeches ; but John Stevenson's ' Address to Admiral Keppel ' and the other pamphlets are all controversial. There are numerous references to the quarrel in contemporary literature, and daily paragraphs in the Press ; but in our opinion no satisfactory explanation has yet been given of the Battle of Ushant, of the misunderstanding nor of the quarrel.]

1. ' Minutes of the Proceedings at a Court-Martial, assembled for the trial of the Honourable Admiral Augustus Keppel, on a charge exhibited against him by Vice-Admiral Sir Hugh Palliser, Baronet. As taken by George Jackson, Esq., Judge-Advocate of his Majesty's Fleet. Published by order of the Right Honourable the Lords Commissioners of the Admiralty. With an Appendix, containing all the Letters and Papers that have any relation to the Trial.' (London : printed for W. Strahan and T. Cadell, 1779. Folio, pp. iv + 182. Price 6s.)

2. ' The Proceedings at large of the Court-Martial, on the Trial of the Honourable Augustus Keppel, Admiral of the Blue. Held on board his Majesty's ship the Britannia, on Thursday, January 7th, 1779. And adjourned to the House of the Governor of Portsmouth, and held there till Thursday, February 11th, when the Admiral was honourably acquitted. Taken in Short Hand, by W. Blanchard, for the Admiral, and published by his permission.' (London : printed for J. Almon, 1779. Folio, pp. 11 + 184 + 10. Price 6s.)

3. ' The Trial of the Honourable Augustus Keppel, Admiral of the Blue Squadron, at a Court Martial, held on board his Majesty's ship Britannia, in Portsmouth Harbour, on Thursday, January 8, 1779, before Admiral Sir Thomas Pye, President, upon a charge exhibited against him by Vice-Admiral Sir

Hugh Palliser, for Misconduct and Neglect of Duty. To which is annexed several interesting Letters and Papers relative to the subject. Together with a Glossary of the Technical Terms and Sea Phrases, used in the course of the Trial. Faithfully taken down in Court by Thomas Blandemar, for the Gentlemen of the Navy.' (Portsmouth : printed by Wilkes, Breadhower and Peadle, 1779. 8vo. (Feb. 23), pp. xxxii + 384. Price 4s.)

4. 'An authentic and impartial copy of the Trial of the Honourable Augustus Keppel, Admiral of the Blue. Held at Portsmouth on the 7th of January, 1779, and continued by several adjournments to the 11th day of February, 1779. Taken in Shorthand, by a person who attended during the whole Trial. And printed by the desire of a Society of Gentlemen. With several interesting Papers.' (Portsmouth printed. 1779. 12mo, pp. 416.)

5. 'Minutes of the Proceedings at a Court-Martial, assembled for the Trial of Vice-Admiral Sir Hugh Palliser, Bart. As taken by George Jackson, Esq., Judge-Advocate of his Majesty's Fleet. Published by order of the Right Honourable the Lords Commissioners of the Admiralty.' (London : printed for W. Strahan, and T. Cadell, 1779. Folio, pp. iv + 96. Price 4s.)

6. 'The Trial of Sir Hugh Palliser, Bart., Vice-Admiral of the Blue, at a Court-Martial held on board his Majesty's ship Sandwich, in Portsmouth Harbour on Monday, April 12th, 1779, before Vice-Admiral George Darby, President, upon a charge exhibited against him for Neglect and Disobedience of Orders, on 27th and 28th July, 1778. To which is annexed a list of all the Witnesses called at the Trial.' (Portsmouth : printed for Wilkes, Breadhower and Peadle, 1779. 8vo, pp. vi + 178. Price 2s. 6d.)

7. 'An authentic and impartial copy of the Trial of Sir Hugh Palliser, Vice-Admiral of the Blue, held on board his Majesty's ship the Sandwich in Portsmouth

Harbour on Monday, April 12, 1779, and continued
by several adjournments to Wednesday the 5th of
May 1779. Taken in Short Hand by a person who
attended during the whole Trial. And published
by order of his Friends.' (Portsmouth printed.
1779. 8vo, pp. 276.)

8. 'An Address to the Lords of the Admiralty on
their conduct towards Admiral Keppel.' (London :
printed for J. Almon, 1778.) 8vo., 48 pp.

9. 'An Address to the Hon. Admiral Augustus Keppel.
Containing Candid Remarks on his Defence before
the Court-Martial ; To which are added Impartial
Observations on the late Trial and Acquittal of Vice-
Admiral Sir Hugh Palliser. With an Explanation
of Sea-Phrases, and a Letter to the Monthly Re-
viewers. By a Seaman [John Stevenson.]' Three
editions. (London : printed for William Nicoll.
8vo, 120 pp. Price 2s. [1779].)

10. 'The Defence of Vice-Admiral Sir Hugh Palliser, Bart.,
at the Court-Martial lately held upon him, with the
Court's Sentence.' (London : printed for T. Cadell
in the Strand, 1779.) 8vo, pp. iv + 72.)

[Contains his Address to the Court, when called upon
for his Defence ; his Address to the Court, on the Close
of the Evidence ; the Court's Sentence.]

11. 'The Speech of Sir Hugh Palliser, Bart., in a Committee of the House of Commons, on Monday the
4th of December, 1780.' ([No printer or publisher.]
8vo, pp. ii + 34.)

12. 'Thoughts on the Conduct of Admiral Keppel.
Together with reasons for restoring Sir Hugh Palliser
into the full confidence and good opinion of his
country.' The second edition. (London : printed
for Richardson and Urquhart, 1780. 8vo, 24 pp.)

13. 'A Candid Defence of the Character and Conduct of
Sir Hugh Palliser, Bart., Vice-Admiral of the White.'
(London : printed for W. Nicoll, 1781. 8vo,
pp. iv + 96. Price 2s.)

14. 'Ode to the Naval Officers of Great Britain,' written immediately after the trial of Admiral Keppel. By William Mason, M.A. (London: T. Cadell, 1779. 4to. 10 pp. Price 6*d*.)

15. 'A Congratulatory Ode to the Honourable Augustus Keppel, Admiral of the Blue.' By the author of the Ode to the Warlike Genius of Great Britain [William Tasker]. (London: 2nd edition. 4to. 1779.)

16. 'Considerations on the Principles of Naval Discipline, and Naval Courts-Martial; in which the Doctrines lately laid down in the House of Commons upon those Subjects, are examined, and the Conduct of the Courts-Martial on Admiral Keppel and Sir Hugh Palliser, are compared.' Anon. (London: J. Almon and J. Debrett, 1781. 8vo. 190 pp.)

[In the Annual Register of 1822 this pamphlet is credited to the Right Rev. Dr. Thomas Lewis O'Beirne, Bishop of Meath, 'a chaplain in the fleet under Lord Howe,' and author of *A Candid and Impartial Narrative of the Transactions of the Fleet, under the command of Lord Howe . . . with observations by an Officer then serving in the Fleet.* Anon. (2nd ed. London: 1779.)]

CHAPTER I

HOME WATERS, 1778

3

INTRODUCTION

ADMIRAL THE HON. AUGUSTUS KEPPEL was born in 1725. His reputation was made in the Seven Years' War: first as captain of the Torbay in the Western squadron and especially at Quiberon; afterwards as commodore commanding the sea forces in the expedition against Belleisle, where at one time he had a score of great ships under his broad pendant; lastly at the capture of Havana. He was half way down the list of vice-admirals when the King, in November 1776, chose him to command the main fleet in the event of war with France. One of his seniors, James Young, was then at sea in the minor command of the Leeward Islands station; after Keppel struck his flag in 1779, three others, Sir Charles Hardy, Francis Geary, and Sir George Rodney, hoisted theirs for the first time in the American war. It was more than politeness, therefore, that prompted the form of Lord Sandwich's congratulations. The choice was very popular at sea and in the country at large; whether it was wise is less certain. The Admiral was an active follower of the Marquis of Rockingham, who led the most uncompromising branch of the Opposition. He promised to keep away from politics, but that was against nature. He had refused to serve against the Colonists, and he could not refrain from pointing out to the King the large number of ships and men that were tied up in America and therefore lost to his command at home. Lord Weymouth reported him ' very ready to do his duty at sea, but not so much to give advice.' [1]

[1] Fortescue, *Correspondence of King George III*, iv. 2312 and 2263. This volume is henceforward referred to as *Corr.* followed by the letter number.

In this, however, Lord Weymouth was wrong, as the long and friendly correspondence between Keppel and Lord Sandwich proves. At the same time, the Admiral's position was far from easy, for his third in command at sea, Vice-Admiral Sir Hugh Palliser, was the senior professional member of the Board of Admiralty. It was common in those days for a commander-in-chief at sea to be also a member of the Board. But however good their personal relations and however hard they tried to keep their politics under control, difficulties were bound to arise if a junior admiral in the fleet was at the Admiralty, and therefore of the ministerial party in politics, while the commander-in-chief was prominent in opposition. Keppel's letters show that he was generous both to Palliser and to Lord Mulgrave, who commanded the Courageux and was also at the Admiralty. Palliser too was loyal, though he may have thought himself, and very likely was, an abler man than his commander-in-chief. In the end, however, their political differences made the situation impossible.

As we have seen in Volume I, war with France had long been expected, and after Saratoga it was obvious that a European war would break out before the American rebellion had been suppressed. The Cabinet did not wish to precipitate matters by appearing the aggressor, so that in spite of Lord Sandwich's warnings the Navy was not put upon a war footing until March, when France, by recognising the independence of the United States and by concluding an alliance with them, made war with Great Britain inevitable. Mobilization, then as now, was a delicate matter; and balanced against the fear of being the aggressor was the wish to have a force ready to strike. Throughout the 18th century it was our policy to let our enemies take the initiative: thus we were late in 1740; Minorca was attacked in 1756 before Byng reached the Mediterranean; and in 1793 only the disorganized state of the French navy allowed us to escape without punishment.

The letters in this chapter form an almost daily record of the preparation of the main fleet, and of the

commander-in-chief's anxieties and doubts when he got
to sea. Whatever he was led to say afterwards in the
House of Commons, Keppel freely acknowledged at the
time the efficiency and good order of those ships of
the line which had cruised for the protection of the trade
during the previous year. He complained with good
reason of the want of frigates and smaller vessels, and of
the lack of men, faults due to the traditional policy of the
country rather than to inefficiency at the Admiralty.

In 1778 this was partly due to the abnormal demands
of the squadron in North America ; but it was a common
state of affairs. When war came small ships could be
built quickly, and in many yards that could not cope
with great ships ; it was therefore the usual practice in
time of peace to spend the bulk of the money voted on
ships of the line, which took longer to build and
incidentally seemed to show Parliament a better return
for their money. For all that the practice was not
altogether sound, either economically or in preparation
for war : as Lord Sandwich pointed out towards the end
of his administration, frigates were wanted as much as
larger ships in all stages of war, and they were built of
the small timber that was left over from ships of the
line.[1]

A greater difficulty was the early provision of
seamen, without whom the ships newly commissioned
could not be fitted for sea. It was not merely a question
of putting stores on board: rigging must be rove and
gun gear fitted, and this needed the services of trained
seamen. Landsmen would volunteer in fair numbers
and marines were permanently enrolled (though at this
time many were serving on shore in America) ; but
thoroughbred seamen were reluctant to serve in the
Navy in time of war because they could always count on
far higher pay in merchant ships, and on better chances
of prize money in privateers. The only ways to procure

---

[1] According to a tabular statement at Hinchingbrooke the
following ships were in commission at the end of 1777 : of the line
53, frigates 89 (including 50-gun ships), and 122 smaller vessels.
At the end of 1778 the numbers were 79, 96, 142.

them in sufficient numbers were by means of impressment, an embargo on merchant shipping, and loudly advertised bounties ; and those Government hesitated to employ until the last moment lest it should seem an act of aggression and spoil the chances of peace. The result was delay in the preparation of the fleet and great hardship to the seamen already in the Navy, who were turned over from one ship to another, sometimes after long service abroad, without the rest and recreation on shore that their health needed or the opportunity of seeing their families. In fact, as Admiral Vernon said, the men upon whom depended the liberties of our country were the only people who had no liberty at all.[1]

The faults of this method were recognised. Schemes for manning the fleet, most of them copied from the French *Inscription maritime* which was founded in the reign of Louis XIV, were offered to Parliament or the Admiralty throughout the eighteenth century and earlier (there are several at Hinchingbrooke) ; but none was satisfactory. They were either too costly or too slow in action to answer the purpose. It was not until the middle of the following century that press gang and bounty gave way to continuous service with a regular reserve.

While the ships were fitting out, the King went to see them, first in the Medway, afterwards at Portsmouth. His Majesty was in his element during these visits, and his obvious delight in all he saw pleased everybody. He inspected the fleet, the dockyard, the marines in their barracks, and the victualling yard at Weevil. He even took the Queen—at nine in the morning—' to see the whole process' in the rope and tar houses, which he had already visited in private so that ' my attention might not be taken off by hearing the story of John the Painter' from garrulous workmen. ' I have no object,' he told Lord North, ' but to be of use . . . no one is more hearty in the cause than myself.' Many rewards and promotions were given on this occasion, among them a baronetcy

---

[1] *Seasonable Advice from an Honest Sailor* (1746), p. 73.

to Samuel Hood, the Commissioner at Portsmouth Yard.[1]

In France the Comte d'Orvilliers was fitting out the main fleet at Brest, while the Comte d'Estaing had eleven sail of the line and a 50-gun ship at Toulon. The squadron in the Mediterranean was the more advanced in readiness for sea ; and the most effective way to deal with it was to send an equal force to watch Toulon, or at least to intercept the squadron if it passed through the Straits of Gibraltar. But the state of our preparations did not admit of detaching so large a force from the main fleet until May, which as far as we could judge from intelligence reports was too late.

For many weeks the British Cabinet could not find out whether the ships from Toulon were to join d'Orvilliers or cross the Atlantic. This chapter shows how extremely hard it was to deal with this uncertainty. If d'Estaing went to America we must send ships after him, since Howe's squadron was much weaker than his ; if he joined d'Orvilliers we should need all our strength at home, especially as the attitude of Spain was in doubt. Vice-Admiral the Hon. John Byron was eventually given command of thirteen ships of the line with which to counter the Toulon squadron, but it was decided after long discussion not to send him away from home till it was certain that d'Estaing had left European waters. Keppel said afterwards that five ships might have been sent at once to Howe, though we could not spare a force equal to d'Estaing until we knew his destination ; but this did not take into account the possibility that Howe had already dispatched the expedition to St. Lucia in accordance with his secret orders of March 21 and 22. There seems no doubt that, having failed to stop d'Estaing from sailing, it was right to keep Byron's ships at home, stored for foreign service, until the destination of the French was known for certain. Neither Keppel nor Sandwich could agree to Lord George Germain's proposal to send a squadron to meet d'Estaing

[1] *Corr.*, 2324, 2325. The first paper is the King's diary of his visit to Portsmouth, May 2 to 6.

in the Straits of Gibraltar before the main fleet was ready; nor could they accept without proof his easy confidence that the French were bound for America.[1]

Captain Evelyn Sutton of the frigate Proserpine was sent to Gibraltar to obtain this proof. He carried instructions, dated April 17, to Vice-Admiral Robert Duff, who commanded the small squadron on the Mediterranean station. Duff was to send the Proserpine and one of his own ships to wait for d'Estaing, one outside and the other within the Straits; they were to find out his force and destination, and then make the best of their way to England with the news. The French left Toulon on April 13, but did not reach the Straits till a month later. On May 16 d'Estaing was sighted by the Proserpine, which was cruising inside; as soon as she had made out his force, she bore away for Gibraltar to send in a boat to Duff with her news; then she followed the enemy to the westward. Though she lost them in the night, she heard of them next morning from a Dutch man-of-war, and in the afternoon she met the cruiser that was watching outside the Straits. This was the Enterprise, commanded by Sir Thomas Rich. She had sighted the French off Cape Spartel at midnight, but had just lost them when the Proserpine joined her. The two ships set off in pursuit together, and found the French at dawn next day, May 18. Sutton shaped course for England directly, leaving Rich to follow d'Estaing until there could be no doubt of his destination. On the 21st the cruisers met once more, and stayed in company for two days; the Proserpine arrived at Falmouth on June 2, the Enterprise reached Plymouth on the 3rd.[2]

[1] A summary of Byron's instructions is in App. B below, p. 374. See *Parliamentary History*, xx. 387, 397, for Keppel's wisdom after the event; and for St. Lucia, chap. v below and vol. i, chap. vi. Fortescue, *Corr.*, 2316, gives Germain's view.

[2] Secret Orders and Instructions, Masters' logs, Proserpine and Enterprise.

The Alarm, Captain Robert Man, also saw the French on May 17 while returning to Gibraltar from the Tagus (Captain's journal, Alarm).

The destination of the French was now known for certain, so Byron was told to sail for Sandy Hook at once. A foul wind kept him at anchor for two days, but he left Cawsand Bay on June 9.[1]

Keppel put to sea three days later with twenty ships of the line to cruise in the traditional station between Ushant and Scilly. We were not yet at war with France ; and the difficulty of the situation, so well illustrated in these papers, may be compared with that in 1755 described by Sir Julian Corbett in the third chapter of *England in the Seven Years' War*. As soon as Keppel was fairly at sea, he was surrounded by French frigates— or so it seemed, since he had so few of his own. The only way to be rid of the nuisance was to seize them, which his instructions of April 25 allowed him to do : ' In case any French frigates of war should attend upon the fleet, or appear to be watching your motions, you are to oblige them to desist, and on their refusal to seize them and send them to England.' On June 17, the Alert sloop brought the Coureur lugger into the fleet, but the Belle Poule escaped from the Arethusa after a running fight that lasted from seven in the evening till nearly midnight ; the Licorne and the Pallas were taken on the 18th and 19th respectively. Papers found on board these ships told Keppel that the force assembled at Brest was much superior to his own, so he returned to St. Helen's on the 27th : a movement fully in accord with his instructions, but very unwelcome to the populace and the King.[2] This hasty decision to return created an atmosphere of distrust between Keppel and Lord Sandwich, an atmosphere which was intensified by the violence of the newspapers. Ironically enough it was Palliser's rôle to reassure both parties (see below, p. 110).

[1] His orders were dated June 5. He received them on the 7th.

[2] Appendix A contains a summary of the secret instructions given to Keppel during the campaign. See below, p. 98, for the King's remarks.

The two French frigates were bought into our service, the Pallas being renamed Convert. The Belle Poule was captured two years later.

Lacour-Gayet, 111–18, gives the French story of the encounter.

In spite of the theoretical advantage of the French system of manning, and their freedom from the wear and tear our ships had suffered during their cruises against American privateers in 1777, the main fleet of France was not fully prepared for service until late in June. They sailed from Brest on July 8 ; and two days afterwards Louis XVI declared war in form, giving the detention of his frigates as one of his reasons, though d'Orvilliers had in fact already retaliated by capturing the Lively on the 9th.   The British fleet put to sea once more the day after the French, with orders of July 3 to ' commit all acts of hostility ' against the French if they should begin first.   On the 19th, this order was repeated without the restriction, the French declaration being by then known to our government.[1]

When Keppel sailed he had only twenty-four ships of the line against the thirty-two with d'Orvilliers, but six more joined him before he met the enemy ; moreover, he had some advantage in weight of metal, a blessing seldom granted to British admirals ; and as two of the French ships parted from their fleet, when the day came the numbers were exactly equal.   The fleets came in sight, some 20–25 leagues west of Ushant, on July 23. After four days' manœuvring they fought a sharp inconclusive action on opposite tacks, with the French to windward.   The lines of battle are given below, with the ships newly commissioned in 1778 marked with a star :

Sir Robert Harland		*The Comte Du Chaffault*	
Monarch	74	Dauphin royal	70
Hector	74	*Duc de Bourgogne	80
Centaur	74	*Alexandre	64
Exeter	64	Bien-Aimé	74
*Duke	90	*Couronne [flag]	80
Queen [flag]	90	*Palmier	74
Shrewsbury	74	*Saint-Michel	64
*Cumberland	74	*Indien	64
*Berwick	74	*Glorieux	74
Stirling Castle	64	*Amphion	50
		*Vengeur	64

[1] Cp. Lacour-Gayet, 118–28.   The declaration of war is on pp. 118–20, a letter from the King to the Admiral of France.

Admiral Keppel		*The Comte d'Orvilliers*	
Courageux	74	Réfléchi	64
*Thunderer	74	*Ville de Paris	90
*Vigilant	64	Actif	74
Sandwich	90	Magnifique	74
Valiant	74	*Bretagne [flag]	110
*Victory [flag]	100	Fendant	74
Foudroyant	80	Eveillé	64
Prince George	90	*Actionnaire	64
Bienfaisant	64	*Orient	74
*Vengeance	74	*Artésien	64

Sir Hugh Palliser		*The Duc de Chartres*	
Worcester	64	*Sphinx	64
*Elizabeth	74	Robuste	74
*Defiance	64	Roland	64
*Robust	74	*Fier	50
*Formidable [flag]	90	*Zodiaque	74
Ocean	90	*Saint-Esprit [flag]	84
*America	64	Intrépide	74
Terrible	74	Triton	64
Egmont	74	*Solitaire	64
Ramillies	74	*Conquérant	74
		*Diadème	74

The French order was reversed during the action, with the Duc de Chartres in the van ; the ships that missed the action were the Duc de Bourgogne and the Alexandre, both belonging to Du Chaffault's squadron. The frigates and smaller vessels attached to the fleets were the following :—

BRITISH : Arethusa, Fox, Milford, Proserpine ; Pluto fireship, and Vulcan fireship.

FRENCH : Junon, Sibylle, Fortunée, Résolue, Sensible, Nymphe, Surveillante, Danaé, Iphigénie ; corvettes Sylphide Hirondelle, Lunette, Curieuse, Favorite ; luggers Espiègle, and Chasseur.[1]

This is not the place for details of the battle, nor can anything be gained by discussing what might have happened ; but it may be worth while to mark some possible reasons for the lame result. There is Jervis's well-known theory, propounded when he saw the indignation of the people at Plymouth : that equal fleets cannot produce decisive actions unless they are both determined

[1] The British line of battle is taken from *Minutes of the Trial of Admiral Keppel* (Official Edition), and the French from Lacour-Gayet, 91, and App. III, IV.

to fight it out, or one of the commanders misconducts his line—a theory similar to Shovell's in 1702.[1]

A more fundamental reason for the want of decision lies in the fact that both officers and men were out of practice at the beginning of the war. None of the officers had manœuvred in large fleets for many years, nor had the men in the newly-commissioned ships had time to settle down. Professional rustiness showed itself in several ways : Keppel did not appreciate how much Palliser's ships must have suffered—his division lost as many men as Keppel's and Harland's put together— while Palliser did not make sure that the Admiral was fully informed of the fact. Sir Hugh was blamed for not shifting his flag when he found the Formidable could not make sail. This too, no doubt, was partly the effect of rustiness of mind, though in those days the close personal association between an admiral and the officers and the pick of the men in his flagship made him hesitate to leave them. The comments of John Inglefield, who was then a lieutenant in Alexander Hood's ship, the Robust, seem much to the point. He called the action ' disgraceful to both nations, though more so to the French.' [2]

D'Orvilliers was the first at sea again after the action, though he did not stay out long. He sailed on August 17, protected the coasting trade of St. Malo, tried without success to attack a convoy in the mouth of the Channel, and ranged as far south as Cape Finisterre. On September 18 he returned to Brest with three prizes, one of them the frigate Fox, Captain Windsor, which was taken by the Junon off Ushant a week before the fleet entered harbour.[3] Keppel's third cruise, which

---

[1] Jervis to Jackson, July 31, quoted in *Life of Keppel*, ii. 51. Shovell to Nottingham, July 18, 1702 (S.P. Dom. naval 67). Cp. Lord Robert Manners to the Marquis of Granby (Aug. 9) : ' It was more a skirmish than an action. . . . We find the people at this place highly exasperated against us for not doing more ' (Rutland MSS. iii.).

[2] *A Short Account of the Naval Actions of the Last War*, 1788.

[3] Cp. Lacour-Gayet, 135–7, for the second cruise of the French fleet.

lasted from August 23 until the end of October, was not more eventful, but he did what was required of him and saw the trade home in safety. So long a cruise undertaken at this season of the year with a large number of ships, not yet sufficiently trained to be called a fleet, was physically exhausting. Moreover he was desperately anxious to retrieve the failure at Ushant, and his fruitless search for the French fleet tried his patience and his temper to the utmost.

Note : Keppel, perhaps because he was an ' opposition admiral,' wrote very frequent private letters to the First Lord. Most of them are printed here ; those only are omitted which deal with small details or are superseded by later letters.

TO ADMIRAL KEPPEL

Admiralty, 15 November 1776.

Sir—I am commanded by his Majesty to signify to you that he thinks there is a probability of his having shortly an occasion for your service to command the fleet that is now equipping for sea.

After so distinguished a mark of your Royal Master's approbation in selecting you from the whole list for so important a trust, it would be presumption in me to add anything upon the occasion except to say that I never executed any orders from my sovereign with more real satisfaction than I do the present.   I am [etc.].

FROM KEPPEL

Audley Square, 15 November 1776.

My Lord—This afternoon brought me the honour of your Lordship's letter informing me of the commands you had received from his Majesty to signify to me the probability of shortly having an occasion for my service to command the fleet that is now equipping for sea.

I beg his Majesty may be assured of my zeal and readiness to obey his orders when it becomes his pleasure to direct me to that command.

I must return your Lordship thanks for the very polite and obliging manner in which you have been pleased to convey to me his Majesty's intentions and distinguished mark of opinion and approbation ; and I have the honour to be with much respect [etc.].

FROM THE KING

Kew, 18 November 1776, 52 m. past 6 p.m.

Lord Sandwich—I have this day seen Vice-Admiral Keppel, who very clearly expressed his readiness of accepting the command of a fleet should the present preparations come to anything serious. I have therefore his consent to appoint him to such command whenever I may judge it expedient.

FROM KEPPEL

Audley Square, 23 May 1777.

I have little to trouble your Lordship upon, but cannot longer refuse myself asking you how far I may reckon upon being my own master. I really do not mean to draw from you any explanation that may be improper, nor do I feel inclination to attend my amusements in preference to service of *importance* that his Majesty may call upon me to execute, though believe me, my Lord, it is pleasing to me not to be wanted. The friendly disposition that France is said to be in towards this country allows my having thoughts of going abroad, first to Aix-la-Chapelle, and passing the next winter in some warmer climate than England. I am [etc.].

TO KEPPEL

Admiralty, 24 May 1777.

The language of the Court of France is undoubtedly very pacific, and appearances in general

PLATE II.

ADMIRAL THE HON. AUGUSTUS KEPPEL
from the portrait by
SIR JOSHUA REYNOLDS, painted in 1779 for JOHN LEE, and now in the
possession of F. S. HAMILTON, ESQ.

lead me to hope that there is no immediate probability of a rupture : more I cannot say, as
many unexpected events may alter the face of
things and darken the present pleasing prospect.
However, I think nothing can happen so suddenly
as to make it necessary for you to break in upon
your plan of amusement for the summer. I will
only beg that, some time before you leave Aix-la-
Chapelle, you would trouble yourself to let me
know that you are preparing for your journey
in search of a warmer climate. By that time,
possibly, I may be able to speak with more
certainty with regard to peace or war. And
while you remain at Aix-la-Chapelle you will be
so near at hand that, if any farther equipments
should take place, no time would be lost, as I will
take care that the Victory shall be commissioned
and be getting ready while you are in your return
to England. I am [etc.].

FROM KEPPEL

Audley Square, Sunday, 15 March 1778.

I have reflected on the information your Lordship communicated to me yesterday, that I might
probably in a few days be ordered to take the
command of the fleet now fitting out.

Your Lordship will not wonder that, if this
fleet is soon to be brought to action against those
of France and Spain, I should feel some anxiety
concerning a situation in which the security of my
country and my own reputation are at stake ;
under these circumstances I trust your Lordship
will forgive my troubling you with this letter. I
have already informed your Lordship that previous to my receiving orders to hoist my flag I
must desire an audience of the King, and submit

II.   C to his Majesty my respectful thoughts on this occasion. Besides which, I think it necessary to lay some matters before your Lordship for your consideration.[1]

It is undoubtedly the King's ministers who are to judge of the degree of force proper to be sent in quest of the enemy. Their situation enables them to know the strength of that enemy, what other services are required, and what force can be spared for this; they are responsible for the degree of force's being adequate to the service. The commander is only answerable for making proper use of such as is entrusted to his care.

I need not inform your Lordship that the strength of a fleet consists more in the goodness of the officers, in the manning of the ships and in their condition, than in their number. As I must be ignorant at present of the true and exact state and condition of the fleet, I cannot comment upon it; but it may be highly necessary that many flags should be hoisted some time before the sailing of it upon service; and directions should be given to assemble the ships as soon as possible, that if my service is required I may be able myself to inspect them and report to the Admiralty those which I think are properly manned and fit to go to sea. Of the ships I shall so report, I shall be ready to sail with, whatever number I shall receive orders to proceed to sea with. My strength will then be what it really appears to be; but if I have a greater number of ships ill manned and unfit for sea, I may be to answer for operations proportionate to my apparent, not my real, force.

If, therefore, his Majesty should be advised to order me to take such ships as I have not reported fit for sea, I must beg to have it expressed in my

[1] The Admiral saw his Majesty next day. *Corr.*, 2227.

orders that I am to take with me such ships, notwithstanding their names are not in the list of ships I have reported fit for sea. I must also desire that my orders and instructions may on all points be explicit and clear.

Your Lordship will, I am sure, excuse my entering into this explanation when you consider the very delicate situation in which I stand, called upon to take upon me the defence of the kingdom at sea under an administration upon which I have not any claim for the indulgence of friendship. I am [etc.].

STATE OF THE FORCE AT HOME [1]

[Draft, corrected by Lord Sandwich and endorsed by him : ' List of ships of the line at home March 1778 and reasoning upon the strength necessary for home defence.']

The following is the list of ships intended to be immediately put under the command of Admiral Keppel for the protection of the home seas, which fleet must be augmented from time to time according as we receive information of the strength and motions of the enemy, viz. :

	Guns		*Guns*
Prince George	90	Courageux	74
Queen	90	Grafton	74
Princess Royal	90	Ramillies	74
Ocean	90	Hector	74
Sandwich	90	Monarch	74
Foudroyant	80	Shrewsbury	74
Valiant	74	Culloden	74
Royal Oak	74	Bienfaisant	64
Terrible	74	Conqueror	74
Bedford	74	Asia	64

[1] The tables on pp. 270–274 show how the ships named were eventually disposed.

There then will be left at home in condition for service : [1]

	Guns		Guns
Invincible	74	Russell	74
Resolution	74	Boyne	70
Centaur	74	Burford	70
Fame	74	Belleisle	64
Egmont	74	Exeter	64
Albion	74	Europe	64
Sultan	74	Monmouth	64
Torbay	74	Trident	64
Prince of Wales	74	Stirling Castle	64
Cornwall	74	Medway	60

All services for the immediate protection of our distant possessions must be taken out of these ships. These services it is to be supposed are a Mediterranean squadron, a reinforcement to the Leeward Islands and Jamaica, one line of battle ship at least to Newfoundland, two or three to the East Indies, and a ship to carry out the [Peace] Commissioners [to North America].

There are besides these ships the following in commission, several of which are in great forwardness especially those marked * ; and if men came in fast they will soon be ready for sea. The question, therefore, seems to be whether our coast is safe if we wait for the coming in of these ships to be added to Admiral Keppel's fleet, for I must say that his 20 ships are not sufficient for that purpose.

	Guns		Guns
Victory	100	Thunderer	74
Formidable	90	Vengeance	74
Duke	90	Defiance	64
*Robust	74	Vigilant	64
*Berwick	74	*Ruby	64
*Cumberland	74	*America	64
*Elizabeth	74		

[1] See next page, the state on March 28.

Our deficiency of frigates is an irretrievable misfortune, as our trade must be exceedingly exposed for want of convoys and cruisers. Therefore, everything that can be purchased or hired that will bear arming should be taken up without a moment's delay ; and particular attention should be had to the guarding our coast by land forces and batteries, as alarm must be expected from privateers, which we shall not be able to keep at a distance as formerly for want of frigates.

N.B.—Eight of the 20 ships belonging to Admiral Keppel's squadron are now at sea but expected home with the first westerly wind.[1]

STATE OF LINE OF BATTLE SHIPS AT HOME, 28 *MARCH* 1778[2]

[In Lord Sandwich's writing.]

Invincible	.
Resolution	. at sea with Captain Digby.
Centaur .	. in dock, and cannot be ready in less than three weeks or a month, though fully manned.
Fame .	.
Egmont .	. run ashore at Lisbon and doubtful whether she must not be docked.

[1] Valiant, Bedford, Grafton, Ramillies, Monarch, Culloden, Bienfaisant, Asia (List Book).

[2] In a similar list, dated April 7, the Fame is earmarked for the East Indies and the Ruby for the West Indies ; the ships not marked for foreign service are shown as 'disposable and will probably be ready all in six weeks' ; and the Robust, Berwick, Cumberland, Elizabeth, and America are added.

Captain Digby's squadron of five of the line and a frigate, cruising in the Bay of Biscay since early in February, returned on April 2 (Master's log, Ramillies).

Albion .   . fitting for the East Indies.
Sultan .   .
Torbay .   . ordered to be docked and re-
                     fitted at Plymouth.
Prince of Wales Admiral Barrington's ship.
Cornwall   . at sea with Captain Digby.
Russell .   .
Boyne   .   . intended for the West Indies.
Burford .   . intended for the East Indies.
Belleisle .   . intended for the East Indies, but
                     still at sea.
Exeter .   . at sea, but expected home very
                     soon.
Europe .   . intended for Newfoundland.
Monmouth   . intended for the West Indies.
Trident .   . to carry out the Commissioners.
Stirling Castle . wants to be cleaned.
Medway .   . just returned from the Mediter-
                     ranean and must be docked.
Ruby   .   .

LORD SANDWICH'S OPINION, 4 APRIL
1778

[In his own writing and endorsed by him : ' written
    at the Cabinet Council.']

My opinion is that it will be very unsafe to
leave England and Ireland without a much larger
force than Admiral Keppel's 20 ships of the line
for their defence. The additional force that I
think necessary must be determined by the force
that France and Spain have ready for sea, as our
principal object must be our defence at home ;
when that is secured detachments may be made
as exigencies require. I think that it will be very

dangerous to divide our naval force till we have more ships of the line ready for sea.

LORD SANDWICH'S OPINION, 6 APRIL 1778

[In his own writing and endorsed by him : ' laid before Council and given to the King the same day.']

It is my opinion that there are not ships enough as yet in readiness to form a squadron fit to meet the Toulon fleet under Monsieur d'Estaing unless we were to sacrifice every other intended service to this object, or to send out Admiral Keppel with a proper force to meet Monsieur d'Estaing, which however seems to me a very dangerous measure, as our own coast and Ireland would then be subject to alarm as the Brest fleet would be superior to anything that we shall have ready for sea till Admiral Keppel's return.

MINUTE OF CABINET, 11 APRIL 1778

Present :

Lord Privy Seal	Lord North
Lord George Germain	Lord Amherst
Lord Sandwich	Lord Weymouth

That the First Lord of the Admiralty do report to this meeting whether a fleet equal to the Brest fleet can be ready within a fortnight to convoy the relief intended for Gibraltar as far as Brest, and then to detach two or three ships to convoy that relief to Gibraltar.

FROM THE KING

Queen's House, 14 April 1778, 50 m. past 4 P.M.

Lord Sandwich's account of the Victory's having got down to Blackstakes yesterday has given infinite satisfaction unto me, and I trust the Formidable will be as fortunate to-morrow.[1]

I have received a message from Lord Hawke to express his sorrow that his health disables him from offering his service, or from coming at this time to Court and of attending in Parliament ; but that he thought it his duty to assure me that, whatever others might from private views declare, that he is convinced a finer or better officered and equipped fleet never was seen in this kingdom than the present. I thought the testimony of so brilliant an officer must afford pleasure unto Lord Sandwich, and therefore have sent him this account.

THOUGHTS SUGGESTED BY THE HON. ADMIRAL KEPPEL

[Endorsed as above by Mr Stephens. The paper is in the writing of Keppel's secretary, George Rogers, with marginal notes by Lord Sandwich.]

15 April 1778.

The admiral in command of the fleet must hope for and expect distinct, clear, and positive instructions.

[Ld. S.]—Such instructions will be given.

---

[1] This is an answer to a letter printed by Fortescue, *Corr.*, 2297.

The number of the French fleet, if joined at Brest by the Toulon squadron, may be computed near upon forty ships of the line.

Suppose the two fleets actually joined : how far and in what degree is battle to be offered them, the English fleet considered at twenty-five or nearly thirty sail of the line ?

[Ld. S.]—If the superiority of the French fleet is not very apparent, he should be ordered to give them battle.

It is supposed the Toulon fleet may escape the vigilance of the British and get into Brest Water. The junction of the fleets effected, it becomes necessary at this moment to consider and determine whether the King's fleet is to continue at sea or go into port for reinforcement. If the latter is determined, what port ?

[Ld. S.]—If the two fleets are joined and are superior, which will then most likely be the case, Admiral Keppel to return to St. Helen's for reinforcement, which from time to time will be ordered to assemble at that place.

It must be an object to collect at Spithead a second fleet as fast and with every exertion possible ; events that are probable and possible show the necessity.

[Ld. S.]—This will be done as much as possible.

The Toulon fleet escaping the King's fleet, which has a probability in it even allowing them to get sight of each other, the nearness of their port, perhaps good sailing in their ships and unwillingness to risk a battle, may determine them to run for it ; the English fleet in course will pursue with the hopes of bringing their rear and worst sailing ships to action. I imagine this to happen near the port of Brest and that the French fleet are able to lead out of that harbour and unite with the flying Toulon ships. It should at this time be determined how far the King's Councils would have their admiral risk an unequal fight.

What is above stated may never happen, yet it appears wisdom to suggest probabilities and possibilities for the King's ministers to be aware of and give direct instructions upon.

[Ld. S.]—This is answered in a foregoing article.

If the King's fleet, upon the possible event as stated, should be ordered to Spithead and there be joined by a sufficient force, they will be immediately ready to meet the enemy and certainly with greater probability of success. Under every consideration, taking the safety of his Majesty's home dominions as the principal object, a fleet must be assembled hastily at Spithead to be ready for junction with the other great fleet ; for even under the good fortune of bringing the Toulon fleet to battle the King's fleet must be considerably disabled, the French fleet in Brest Water ready, and perhaps the Councils of France bold enough to risk pushing their fleet up the British Channel.

Every thought should be given to the defence of the coast in opposition to the armaments of France on the opposite shore. It is certain the alarms in England the moment the great fleet is sailed will be augmented, and there will be many imaginary apprehensions ; but it is to be hoped, though all may not be true, the Councils of England will not encourage themselves with the belief of security. Surely and beyond doubt the French will make some attempt, most probably in more places than one. Frigates, armed ships, cutters, and such craft, must be brought in view.

Several frigates will be wanted to sail with the cruising fleet, also cutters, a constant communication with Plymouth for the information of Government.

If in cruising the chasing ships fall in with French frigates or one or two ships of the line upon their own coast, mid-channel, or near the coast of England, what conduct is to be observed towards them ?

[Ld. S.]—If any line of battle ships fall in our way, to attack and take them.

If line of battle ships, one or two or more, should be ordered as convoys to the Gibraltar succours, I think the senior captain of the ships at Spithead, if a proper person, should be entrusted with the charge and appointed with a distinguishing pendant ; and his orders should be given by the Admiralty distinct from the orders of the admiral. If any detachment is made from the cruising fleet to reinforce the convoy a part of the way and to return to the rendezvous, such force the admiral may direct in consequence of instructions to be given to him for that purpose.

[Ld. S.]—This commodore to accompany the fleet as far as Ushant, and to part company when the admiral thinks proper.

MEMORANDUM BY KEPPEL

[No date, but the subject matter is the same as that in a letter
. from him of April 16.]

The number of flag officers being put immediately into commission seems a measure both prudent and necessary, and must with foreign powers have its effect. The particular number or the gentlemen named, his Majesty will be properly advised upon.

In forming a line of battle, the chief admiral's placing himself in the centre of the fleet seems to point itself as a most necessary disposition of himself ; and yet it was otherwise when Admiral Byng commanded in the Mahon naval action, by which the Admiral, in the greatest ship, did not get to oppose in battle the French admiral, who was in the centre of his fleet. If Admiral Byng had any reason for the mode of the line of battle he formed, it was the want of a third officer in command to form the fleet in three divisions, which has been urged by his friends as his defence upon that part of his conduct. For which reason, I do conclude that no fleet of twelve or thirteen ships of the line of battle will in future be appointed without three flag officers when that fleet's service promises the *probability* of battle with that of the enemy.

For home service with the great fleet I should propose the number of flag officers to be proportionate to the number of ships ; and I think there should be a flag officer to every five or six ships, which calls for five flags to thirty line of battle ships, one admiral, two vice, and two rear admirals, the rear admirals placed in 74-gun ships to be always ready for detachment. Two or three admirals should be held ready to relieve any of the first set that may from infirmities be obliged to recruit themselves on shore.

It is understood Sir Hugh Palliser is to hoist his flag directly. I should hope Sir Robert Harland will also do so. Admiral Barrington, if he should not be sailed upon other service, will be a very proper officer as a rear admiral, and likewise Admiral Hyde Parker.[1]

In completing the fleet for the sea there promises the greatest want of midshipmen that can be imagined, for which reason it will be found expedient to re-establish the service in trading ships to go into part of the six years directed as the period of time that admits of a young person's receiving a commission.[2]

I must beg Captain Jackman may be embarked on board the Victory, and that he may discipline such a proportion of marines as the Admiralty shall judge proper can be spared.

It seems absolutely necessary that the marines serving as part of the army in North America should be directly sent home; in the meantime soldiers will be wanted in their place for the ships.[3]

---

[1] The main fleet consisted of 30 ships of the line in the action of 27 July 1778, and had three flag officers: Admiral Keppel, Vice-Admiral Harland, Vice-Admiral Palliser. Byron had two subordinate flag officers for his thirteen ships: Rear-Admiral Hyde Parker and Commodore Evans.

Admiral Barrington sailed for the Leeward Islands in May.

[2] See below, p. 61, for Palliser's recommendation of this when writing about Lord Sandwich's son Robert.

[3] The Cabinet had resolved on March 18 that the marines in America should be brought home.

FROM KEPPEL

Audley Square, [Thursday] 16 April 1778.

By your Lordship's conversation this morning I could collect that the wish on your part was that no delay in the movement of the succours for Gibraltar should be laid to the fleet's not being ready. I should hope there will be no danger of that; and as to my own movement, however inconvenient it may be, it must give way to the public service. I will hurry all that I can in my private business, and will be ready to leave London on Monday or Tuesday next in the afternoon. I had proposed to myself taking up a few minutes of the King's time before taking my final leave, and shall feel some disappointment if I don't contrive it. I will endeavour to see your Lordship to-morrow if I possibly can and know your commands.[1]

I enclose you a most sanguine letter from [Captain] Sir John Lindsay. However he may be mistaken, the quick movement of this important ship, the Victory, is really flattering; and if we can get near the time that over-zeal hopes for, it will be a great event and exertion. The one hundred men I proposed plundering from the Medway, and the soon arrival of the Antelope, would complete every wish; if she is ordered to supply the Victory, the Salisbury's crew will give

---

[1] Next day, in the evening, the King wrote to Sandwich: ' I certainly at this time should not like to disoblige Admiral Keppel. I therefore desire you will appoint him to be punctually at St. James's next Sunday at eleven.'

A memorandum by Keppel, apparently given to His Majesty at this time, is printed in *Corr.*, 2312.

life to the Formidable. Your Lordship sees my readiness to dispose of what more properly belongs to yourself : I have no doubt of your exertion and goodwill in the Victory's concerns, and will therefore at present give you no more trouble about her.[1]

But I cannot refuse myself writing a few lines in this letter for your consideration upon the critical situation of this country regarding its fleet. One mistake or accident ruins all. It therefore should be considered well, and the force detached and separated as little as possible. Five ships in the East or West Indies are in my poor opinion at present either too few or too many ; they may be demolished in detail. If the enemy send a very large squadron you must have one ready to follow them ; keep them named and collected at Spithead for the East or the West, or to join first the grand fleet. If necessary the trade must sail, a ship of the line to each convoy might be appointed ; the chief commanders may go themselves, a ship of the line more or less will aid little in the safety of our foreign dominions. Four or five ships will be unequal to face bold and large undertakings of the enemy, equal force if it can be ready must follow from hence.

I am afraid I may have completely tired you. Be assured my Lord what I have written is from a conviction in my own mind upon the propriety of it. England and Ireland must be the first object, and I dare hope will be considered as such. I am [etc.].

[1] The Medway, Antelope, and Salisbury were the lately-relieved flagships on the Mediterranean, Jamaica, and East Indies stations respectively. They had all been four years away from home.

FROM KEPPEL

[In his writing : not signed.]

April 17.

The following the French fleet, if it should slip and sail out of Brest unobserved, except up the Channel or to Ireland, seems to be too important for your admiral to decide upon. The leaving the English Channel but for one day, except upon the moral certainty of regaining it in time, appears full of danger to the safety of the Kingdom.

Your admiral has some wish that the Gibraltar succours should be directed as much void of contingent as possible, as he foresees the certain loss of one easterly wind if it is delayed, which may be of very great consequence, the loss of time in getting the ships back from Gibraltar, the encumbrance this convoy must be even for two days to a cruising fleet, and the dangers accidental that may happen in the night ; cruising to preserve a station and making a voyage is very different in the hazard of navigation. If two ships are too weak for the convoy across the Bay make it four, and direct the two back from Cape Finisterre to the rendezvous. The above is stated from the apprehensions attending the contingencies of the French being more or less at Brest ; if they are there in number you would not allow of much increase to the force of the convoy. If there should be some appearance that the French have detached, it must be too uncertain where they are gone for the admiral to decide to part with more force than one, two, or three ships at most ; but, to determine that, much loss of time will elapse as well as common accidents to the convoy. If they can't be escorted by nine or ten ships of the line, risk they must and will run, but to do better under every circumstance of the moment I am unable to advise upon.

The seizing of frigates as well as ships of the line is for consideration. The moment of such an event, would you be immediately informed of it? Would the measure of seizing every French tender be proper? The great question of war will be brought to the moment of certainty. The length of time for keeping the sea must be considered. Great attention must be had to avoid disabling the fleet either in stores, provisions, or sickness among the crews.

FROM LORD NORTH

Bushey Park, 23 April 1778.

My dear Lord—There is very good authority to believe that the Comte d'Estaing will sail with six ships of the line from Toulon. It is said that he expects to be joined (but I do not know where) by three more ships of the line from the West Indies, and by three more ships of force which have been for some time building in North America. He hopes likewise to be assisted by several frigates and smaller vessels belonging to the Americans.

What I have mentioned depends upon good authority, but I think that it is almost certain that the destination of the Comte d'Estaing is North America. Every circumstance that I can learn seems to confirm it. If he arrives there unmolested, he will do a great deal of mischief even with six ships. He expected to sail either on the 20th or 21st of this month. If he is sailed, it is only with six ships of the line: if he is determined not to leave Toulon with a smaller number of ships of the line than ten, he has not yet been able to set out. I am [etc.].

P.S.—There has been such pains taken to conceal M. d'Estaing's destination, and the success of his expedition is apparently so much at heart, that I do not think it probable he will be inclined to strike any stroke in the European seas unless attacked. It may therefore be less dangerous to send out a squadron of seven or eight ships of the line to watch his motions, and to attack him only in case they shall think themselves superior or equal. This is a nice point. I am rather inclined to run the risk, and wish you would consider it. I send this letter to Mr Stephens, who will send it after you.

SIR STANIER PORTEN TO MR. STEPHENS[1]

St. James's, 25 April 1778.

Sir—I have Lord Weymouth's directions to send you, for the information of Lord Sandwich, the enclosed copy of a letter received this day from Mr Poyntz, charged with his Majesty's affairs at the Court of Turin. I am [etc.].

[Enclosure]

A CYPHER LETTER FROM MR POYNTZ TO MR CHAMIER, DATED TURIN, 12 APRIL 1778, 8 O'CLOCK AT NIGHT.

Sir—The different and repeated advices sent to me of the state of the armament at Toulon have

[1] Viscount Weymouth was the Secretary of State for the Southern Department. Mr. Anthony Chamier and Sir Stanier Porten were his under secretaries.

made me rather too confident in my two last letters about the time which was thought requisite for its thorough completion. I have this moment received information, and have but just time to acquaint you, that there are actually in the road six frigates and nine ships of the line, which are to be joined by three others who are taking in their provision of water. M. d'Estaing arrived at that port a few days ago and is to hoist his flag on board the Languedoc. Reports are more numerous than ever. Among others it is said that twenty thousand men are ordered to march into Provence. The squadron in the road is expected to sail about the 20th instant.

I have but just time to save the post, must therefore abruptly break off. With [etc.].

FROM NORTH

Bushey Park, 27 April 1778.

I send you a list of the Toulon squadron which I received yesterday, and which is nearly the same as that brought by Mr Swinton. I apprehend that the two ships whose names are not known are the two ships that have been long building in North America, for the fitting out of which the Comte d'Estaing carries the necessary cordage, sails, etc.

There can now be no doubt of his destination. He is certainly bound to North America, and will probably begin his operations either upon the fleet in the harbour of New York or against the army at Philadelphia.

The enclosed paper contains also a list of ten frigates which sailed from Brest on the 17th of this month.

I have in consequence of your Lordship's letter desired Lord Weymouth to call a Cabinet on Wednesday morning . . . I am [etc.].[1]

TO KEPPEL

Admiralty, 28 April 1778.

Sir—Though I have nothing very particular to trouble you with I cannot refrain from writing to you, lest you should imagine I had forgot my promise of giving you every information that is any way connected with the important business in which you are concerned.

It now seems to be without a doubt that Monsieur d'Estaing sailed with 12 ships of the line and many frigates, together with some troops and all warlike implements for a siege, on the 13th of this month ; and it is said that he is to be joined by several frigates from Brest ; it is also said that La Chimère, one of d'Estaing's frigates, sailed before him for Cadiz. There is every reason in the world to believe that he is bound to Boston, probably with an intention to attack Nova Scotia and Canada, or perhaps to fall upon Lord Howe's fleet and to cut off our army upon the American continent. However, we cannot for certain say where he is going, and therefore our dilemma is

[1] Lord North's list of d'Estaing's squadron agrees almost exactly with that given by Lacour-Gayet, 629–30, except for two extra and nameless 50-gun ships.

On April 24 Mr. Stephens wrote as follows : ' The paper received from Lieutenant Swinton may be depended upon ; he left Paris on Friday last and obtained it a few days before from one of M. de Sartine's private secretaries. Swinton says that d'Estaing is not to come to Brest. He is going on a secret expedition, but nobody at Paris will venture to declare even what their conjectures are upon that subject.'

very great, particularly as we are not able to make any detachments from home consistent with the security of this island. Whether this situation of affairs will occasion any alteration in your instructions I cannot yet say; but you may be assured that you shall have the earliest information from me of everything in which I think you are in the least degree interested.

I have had the honour of attending his Majesty on a very pleasant, and I hope not useless, expedition up and down the Medway. We passed much time on board the Victory, and I cannot express to you how much the King was pleased with her appearance. As I find that the Antelope is sailed, I hope in the course of a week she [the Victory] will have strength enough to proceed to the Downs. Their Majesties will certainly be in Portsmouth on Saturday at two o'clock, and we depend upon you and the rest of our friends of the Navy to suggest and prepare whatever may be necessary for their proper reception and amusement. If you should be ready to sail while they are on the spot, it would naturally be the highest entertainment they could receive; but serious business must always have the preference over the amusement even of crowned heads, therefore the time of your sailing will, I am persuaded, in no degree be influenced by this consideration. The yachts for the King's accommodation sailed from Greenwich this morning at four o'clock.

Admiral Campbell has orders to strike his flag and to repair immediately to Portsmouth to act as your captain.

I flatter myself that the measures we have taken will prevent any farther scarcity of beer at Portsmouth, any directions to restrain unnecessary saluting [*sic*]. Lord Amherst has engaged that the marines shall on Saturday next be relieved from doing duty at Haslar Hospital and Forton Prison, which I understand will give us 150 disposable men for the ships of your squadron, or those that may be left at Portsmouth.

I am sorry to hear that the three ships in the harbour are not likely to be ready in time, but I own I was always of opinion they would not.

I hope to have the pleasure of seeing you on Friday next, and am with great regard [etc.].

FROM THE KING

Queen's House, 29 April 1778, 5 m. past 9 A.M.

Lord Sandwich—By some intercepted letters which have just been communicated unto me by the secretaries' office, I have not the smallest doubt that d'Estaing's fleet is gone with Deane and Gérard [de Rayneval] to attack either Philadelphia or New York. I think this so very material that without loss of time I transmit this intelligence unto you. Keppel, in his own paper, mentions that if certain intelligence arrives he must be authorized to detach. I think, by the day I arrive at Portsmouth, we must receive some information of this ; and if that is the case we must strengthen Lord Howe, for should his fleet and the army under his brother be destroyed, no one can answer what confusion it may not occasion at home.

I know very well, and I have with pleasure seen, every effort is used to fit out the fleet. I trust every vessel that can be hired or bought will be collected, to be fitted as frigates and small craft, which, from having been obliged to send of that kind everything we had to America, has crippled us in a most essential article.

FROM THE KING

Queen's House, 30 April 1778, 27 m. P.M.

I am thoroughly convinced that Rear-Admiral Parker is well qualified to execute the commission ; and as he can be sooner ready to sail than Vice-Admiral Byron I approve of the alteration, provided his being a junior admiral to Gambier does not occasion that gentleman's interfering, and I should not think that either more likely to have the most prudent or most skilful conduct pursued. I do not mean by this to hint any doubt of Gambier's parts, but of his prudence.[1]

FROM NORTH

[30 April 1778.]

When Admiral Parker arrives at Halifax he will find there Admiral Gambier, and must, I suppose, put himself and his fleet under his command. Would that be right ? Or is it desirable ?

To say the plain truth I have seldom heard any seaman speak of Gambier as a good naval officer or as one who deserved to be trusted with any important command. Is not this circumstance an objection to Admiral Parker ? He must either put himself under Gambier's command or

[1] Cf. *Corr.*, 2320, 2321.

he cannot avail himself of Gambier's ships.[1]   I
am [etc.].

FROM MR. STEPHENS

Admiralty, 30 April 1778.

My Lord—Your Lordship will see by the enclosed billet from my Lord North that it is wished
that Mr Byron should proceed upon the present
service.   I have therefore dispatched a messenger
with a letter to him to desire the favour of seeing
him to-morrow morning by or before ten o'clock.[2]

I have sent orders by express to Lord Shuldham
to use all possible means to get the Albion and
Monmouth into the Sound and to complete their
spirits up to their other species of provisions, which
is all that they want to enable them to proceed to
sea.   And I hope to be able to-morrow to send
Commodore Evans his orders to proceed off
Plymouth Sound with the ships and frigates that
he is to carry from Spithead.   If your Lordship
would not have him sail till the King has visited
the fleet, you will have it in your power, being
upon the spot, to restrain him.[3]

I have seen Lord George Germain.   I mentioned

[1] Cf. *Corr.*, 2320, 2321.

[2] Lord North's note, dated Thursday [30th] ½ pt. 5 P.M., runs
thus : ' His Majesty seems to prefer Admiral Byron to the chance
of having the fleet under Mr Gambier.   I hope, therefore, that
the Albion may be got out of the harbour in time and that the
whole fleet may soon be clear of the land.'
Vice-Admiral Byron had been appointed to succeed Commodore
Sir Edward Vernon in the East Indies, and the Albion 74 was
fitting out to carry his flag.   He shifted to the Princess Royal 90
shortly before sailing to North America.

[3] Vice-Admiral Lord Shuldham was Commander-in-chief at
Plymouth.   Commodore John Evans was the third in command
of the squadron that eventually went to North America with
Byron, Rear-Admiral Hyde Parker being in the second post.

what your Lordship commanded me to say to Mr Knox respecting the squadron's wintering abroad, but I did not leave his Lordship at all disposed to alter the letter which you saw this morning. The motions of this squadron must be so much influenced by the motions of the French that his Lordship does not think himself authorized to fix a time for the return of the former without being even able to guess what may be the intentions of the latter. I found his Lordship not a bit better disposed towards Mr G[ambier] than other great personages.

     . . . I have [etc.].

TO MR. STEPHENS

Portsmouth, 1 May 1778.

Dear Sir—I write this letter with the concurrence and advice of Lord Mulgrave and Sir Hugh Palliser, who are now with me.

We think it absolutely necessary that the fleet now going out in pursuit of Monsieur d'Estaing should not winter abroad, as we have no certainty where their ultimate destination may be and therefore can have no certain means of supplying them with stores and provisions so as to keep them fit for service. The sending so great a part of our fleet to remain abroad under such precarious circumstances, which must render any other detachment utterly impracticable, seems to me to be a very dangerous measure. It may be very advisable to send the squadron in pursuit of Monsieur d'Estaing wherever he may be likely to be found ; the destruction of his armament will be a very important and decisive blow. But the watching that squadron without a certainty of being able to bring them to action, with all the inconveniences that must attend the long absence of so considerable a part of our naval force, must be productive of infinite disadvantages to the public service.

I must desire you to lay the contents of this letter before Lord George Germain, through Mr Knox or otherwise, in hopes that on consideration his Lordship will join with us in opinion that the ships should be ordered home when the winter sets in, or sooner if the service on which they are sent is executed, which is that of preventing M. d'Estaing from attacking us with success either in America or the West Indies.[1]

I shall be obliged if you will send me a copy of this letter as I have no one with me that I choose to employ in such secret business.

The ships at this port will all be ready to sail in two or three days except the Cumberland, which, however, is manned and victualled, and it is hoped will come out of the harbour to-morrow ; but if I find she is not likely to be ready at the same time as the others, we will substitute some other of the ships at Spithead to supply her place. I am [etc.].

[1] On May 2, Germain wrote to Knox, his Under Secretary : ' I have laid before the Cabinet the letter of Lord Sandwich, and their Lordships were unanimously of the opinion that no alteration should be made at present in the instructions to Admiral Byron. You will be so good as to acquaint Mr Stephens with this resolution for the information of Lord Sandwich.'

Byron's instructions, dated May 3, were founded on a letter of April 29 from the Secretary of State to the Admiralty. Neither of these letters contains a time limit for his return, but he was told to come home if he ' shall receive no information that shall give you reason to suppose the destination of the said French squadron is either for North America or the West Indies.' A summary of the instructions, found at Hinchingbrooke, is printed in Appendix B.

[*P.S.*]—Would it not be better that Admiral Byron should come here and sail with the body of his fleet and go on board his own ship as she joins him at Plymouth ? Pray consult Mr Byron upon this point.

FROM STEPHENS

Admiralty, May 1, near 12 at night.

Your Lordship will find by the letter which I send you from Mr Byron that he accepts the command of the squadron intended to be sent after d'Estaing, and that he met with a most gracious reception from his Majesty. He made no kind of difficulty when I broke the matter to him, though to be sure it does put him to very great inconvenience to set out so suddenly and without having made any preparation at Plymouth for such an expedition—not to say a word of abandoning the command in chief in the East Indies to serve perhaps in a subaltern capacity in North America.[1]

---

[1] Byron wrote to Lord Sandwich from London on May 1 as follows : ' By a letter from Mr Stephens late last night I received your Lordship's commands, and as soon as I could procure post horses came immediately to town, but too late for the Levée ; however, I had the honour of a long conference with his Majesty, who was pleased to point out to me the service I am intended for. I find it is expected I should sail directly. As I thought myself certain of going to India many things I sent by Captain Vandeput in the Asia [which sailed on April 27 for the E.I.], and what I have left all here in town, so that I think I have a chance of going to sea with only a purser's kit, though I have hired a waggon to carry them to Plymouth.'

On January 27 he had written from Pirbright : ' 1 . . . am ready to go to any part of the world I may be ordered to . . .'

Lord North wrote thus to Stephens on May 1 : ' I understand that Admiral Byron undertook the command with great alacrity, and set out early this morning for Plymouth ; but I think the addition of Admiral Parker to his squadron is a right measure,

I think it is evident by the advices received by this day's mail that d'Estaing is bound to North America. I am sorry to see by those advices that the Brest squadron is so numerous and so forward in its equipment.

[The Drake sloop is taken, but the Thetis may retake her (see vol. i. p. 273).

The Boyne and Monmouth are wind-bound in the Hamoaze ; the Torbay is in dock at Plymouth, the Milford coppered and undocked.

An Opposition motion ' that the Bill respecting contractors be read a second time,' has passed the House of Commons.]

I am [etc.].

FROM MR. ROBINSON

Downing Street, 5 May 1778.

My Lord—We are extremely impatient here to receive an account that the fleet to follow d'Estaing's is perfectly ready, and that it has seized the first moment and spurt of a fair wind.

We have had a touch on it in the House of Commons to-day, and we shall, I suppose, have it again to-morrow. Mr Pulteney[1] averred that Administration received an account of d'Estaing's having sailed as on Monday was a sevennight, that no Cabinet was held thereon until Wednesday, and that the orders for our fleet to sail after them was

and the orders to be given in case Admiral Byron should not go well calculated to remove the objections made to giving the command of the fleet to Admiral Parker. The great point is to get the fleet out as soon as possible. I dare say Lord George Germain will approve what is proposed, but have sent you back Lord Sandwich's letter that you may communicate it to him if you think it necessary.'

[1] William Pulteney, M.P. for Shrewsbury.

not issued until some days afterwards; that he desired these things might be remarked in the House of Commons for a future day, and that it might also be remembered that the wind was fair till Friday last; that if, after all the declarations made and the vast sums allowed by Parliament, we had not a fleet ready to sail on 24 hours' notice, the ministers ought to answer for it with their heads.

Indeed, my dear Lord, things will soon run very high, and there appeared in the House to-day more real ill humour than I have seen in it. We were hard run yesterday, you will hear, and but barely threw out the Contractors' Bill; the Irish Bills will not, I think, tend to soothe the House, for all parts of the kingdom are petitioning against them, and our friends the country gentlemen, who generally stand by us, are much out of humour about them. To be beat upon them will be bad indeed; but in truth things are so that you must not be surprised if we are, and then I leave your Lordship to judge what may follow.[1]

Captain Deane will be much obliged to your Lordship for the Jamaica station. . . .

Be so good as to excuse the haste in which I scrawl this while Lord North is writing to his Majesty, and believe [etc.].

[1] Lord North wrote to the King in the same strain. The King replied from Portsmouth that the delay was not due to neglect, but to necessary additions of stores for the ships destined for America, and he wrote: 'It is very absurd in gentlemen unacquainted with the immense detail of naval affairs to trouble the House of Commons with matters totally foreign to truth. If I was now writing from my own ideas only, I should be as absurd as them; but Keppel, Palliser, Parker, and Hood, are men whose knowledge in that science may be trusted . . . Byron only left London yesterday; Parker will therefore reach Plymouth before the other is ready to sail [from Plymouth]' (*Corr.*, 2327, 2328).

FROM KEPPEL

Prince George, Spithead, 5 May 1778.

I am afraid what I have heard relative to the accident of fire on board the Torbay [74] is too true. I condole with your Lordship upon it and upon the general disappointment of a promising cruiser of force. I particularly shall feel the loss of her, and my strength more diminished than to be wished.[1]

The pressing and essential service that the detached fleet is going upon must have every well-wisher to his country's assistance in ; and I am sure no man in England will be more anxious for their success than myself. However, their being taken from my command renders my force reduced, and indeed feeble for the numbers left me ; I mean that of having so many raw ships in lieu of ships of old crews and habituated to the sea for these twelve months past.[2]

I don't wish your Lordship when you read this letter to consider it as a complaining one of my situation ; but I cannot refuse myself saying that I don't feel quite so confident of the complete service, from the many untried ships that now compose the fleet, as I promised myself from the ships that the service has required being detached

[1] The Admiral had a special interest in the Torbay, for he commanded her in the previous war, notably at Quiberon Bay. She was a very old ship, built in 1730 as the Neptune 90, and cut down to two decks and re-named in 1749. As the Neptune, she carried Lestock's flag at the battle of Toulon. After her injuries from the fire were repaired, she went to the Leeward Islands ; she was one of the half-dozen ships with Edmund Affleck that continued the chase all night after The Saints.

[2] This second paragraph was used later by Lord Sandwich to show that Keppel's fleet ' was not despicable when he first took the command ' : see below, p. 268. See also p. 122.

upon foreign service. Having said so much I will dwell no longer upon the subject, and only promise to do my best for the King's service.

I have no order to take the Cumberland again under my directions. I wish the Thunderer had a prospect of getting round soon. If all hopes of the Torbay's being quickly repaired is over, her complete ship's company might bring the Duke to sea.

The want of provisions here I fear will retard the fleet's sailing. I should imagine Plymouth is now so free of ships that they might be recruited there, if an express was sent to have the Victualling Office vessels loaded ready for them. I don't apprehend at this season of the year the fleet would hazard any danger lying in the Sound ; but I beg your Lordship will not think my suggesting a word upon this matter is from a wish in me to meddle in any directions you may have already thought proper to give. I am [etc.].

FROM KEPPEL

Prince George, 6 May 1778, evening.

The arrival of a French brig with her colours hoisted I did not expect to have seen happen in the present situation of affairs between the two nations ; but as it has happened I should wish the fleet to avail itself, if it can be done with convenience, of her cargo from Teneriffe of wines. She is consigned to a merchant either at Portsmouth or Gosport ; and if my proposal has not material objection the Agent Victualler, Mr Oakes, might expedite the business without much loss of time and the fleet get a small supply of wine that would be of infinite service, provided the sort of wine is not sour but of a strong cordial description.

This day's wind is favourable for Sir John Lindsay to get the Victory from Blackstakes to the Nore. The Antelope was not arrived there the 3rd at the post's leaving Sheerness, which makes me fear the delay of two or three days.

My letters from different hands seem to believe that Monsieur d'Estaing will certainly rendezvous at Cadiz. If so, will it be certain enough to determine the sailing of Admiral Byron that d'Estaing will go to *America* ? If the giving it to be understood that his fleet is bound *there* should be with the view to deceive, and that it rounds into the Bay of Biscay and joins the French fleet at Brest, and Mr Byron's squadron gone, it will leave this country very inferior indeed to the French when joined. This fancy may be trifling, but as it has occurred I could not refuse myself suggesting it to you what is merely possible upon the matter.

If the Gibraltar reinforcement of troops is to be delayed till the fleet under my command is complete for the sea, I wish they may not be sickly before they sail ; our ships have gone down hill latterly very much upon the necessary preference that has been given to Vice-Admiral Byron's squadron.

The Robust was to sail this morning from the Nore. If so, provided it does not over-blow, she will be in the Downs to-morrow. I am [etc.].

I have remained on board these two days by way of rest and regulating some necessary business. I have been tormented with the spasms, but am now rather easier and at your Lordship's call.

TO NORTH

Portsmouth, 7 May 1778.

My dear Lord—If the report you have sent me concerning Messrs Deane &c. being gone out in the Zélé is true, it is a strong confirmation of what we have lately heard from many quarters, namely that d'Estaing is gone to Cadiz. It is therefore of the last importance that we should have some certainty on this subject before Admiral Byron is sailed ; for a detachment of 13 line of battle ships to America, if the whole fleet of France and Spain remains in Europe, will leave us absolutely at the mercy of the House of Bourbon, whose united force at home, in commission and fit for sea, amounts to upwards of 70 sail.

I have just received what I believe to be an authentic account of the fleet at Cadiz from Admiral Duff, which I enclose, but must beg your Lordship to return it to me. The way I make out the number is :

Spain	28
Brest	25
d'Estaing . . .	12
Left at Toulon . . .	6
	71

I do not say this by way of finding fault with anything that has been done : on the contrary I think that if we are well assured d'Estaing is gone to America, the detaching Admiral Byron's squadron after him is a wise measure. But at the same time it is necessary that your Lordship should be master of the whole, and give it the mature consideration that so momentous an affair demands.[1]   I am [etc.].

FROM NORTH

Downing Street, May 7.

Notwithstanding my letter of yesterday you may be pretty certain that Mr d'Estaing's fleet is going to North America. I have received from good authority the following particulars :

They are to make the first land in America they can.

As soon as they see any English ships acting hostilely against an American, they are to begin their operations against the English.

The fleet was to have sailed from Toulon on the 21st or 22nd, but upon hearing that we could not intercept them in the Straits if they made haste, fresh orders were sent to them to sail on the 13th if the wind permitted. Four American captains, escaped from our prisons, sailed on board the fleet.

The Brest squadron of 25 ships of the line will soon be ready, and is to sail as soon as Keppel sails and give him battle. *N.B.*—I think the latter part of this intelligence doubtful.

If the French fleet succeeds, the Comte de Broglie is to attempt an invasion. *N.B.*—This is not so confidently told as the rest.

The ten frigates which sailed from Brest are

[1] Vice-Admiral Robert Duff was commanding the Mediterranean squadron. His letter was dated Gibraltar, April 10 ; his intelligence report gives a state of the Spanish fleet and says the Toulon squadron was expected to join them at Cadiz.

not gone to foreign service, but are spread round the coast to protect the French and American trade, and to act hostilely against ours upon a declaration of war.

I have sent to the King lists of the French and Spanish navies, and some other material papers of intelligence, which his Majesty will show you. I have not time to copy them a second time. The wind has wavered a little this morning. I hope in God it will change by Friday, when the King tells me that the fleet will be ready to sail.[1]   I am [etc.].

FROM NORTH

Downing Street, 8 May 1778.

Upon farther inquiry I find that the intelligence communicated by me to your Lordship is in some degree different from what I mentioned : it is that the Zélé, having M. Gérard and Mr Deane on board, sailed *before* the rest of the squadron, not that she separated from them after they had sailed. Every other circumstance and every other piece of information confirms the destination to North America, which I believe to be the true one. It is now so long since your frigate sailed for Gibraltar that you must, I think, receive some authentic intelligence of the course held by M. d'Estaing's fleet, upon his passing the Straits, before Admiral Byron sails from Plymouth.[2]

[1] The King and Lord Sandwich were at Portsmouth. His Majesty sent off these papers to Sandwich at 4.40 next morning.

Gentlemen in London sometimes forget that the wind does not blow from the same quarter everywhere. Cp. Fortescue, *Corr.*, 2329, 2330.

[2] The Proserpine left England on April 20 and reached Gibraltar on the 27th (Master's log, Proserpine).

I think if Spain meant to strike a blow *immediately*, it is hardly possible to conceive they would hold the language they do. I do not believe the whole of their professions, but think that their declarations are not consistent with an immediate rupture. I own my incapacity to decide between the opinions of men of better discernment than myself, but will send your Lordship's letter without delay to the other lords of the Cabinet, and learn if any of them think there is any ground for altering their opinions. In the meanwhile every preparation and dispatch must go on for sending Admiral Byron to North America according to our last resolution, which must not be retarded a moment unless prevented by a counter order from the Secretary of State. I have [etc.].

P.S.—As soon as I have seen the other Cabinet ministers I will send another messenger to your Lordship ; but I hope that there will be no delay of any kind on account of the intelligence already received, as the reasons which lead us to suppose the destination of Monsieur d'Estaing being to North America greatly outweigh everything that we have heard to the contrary.

I will return the enclosures when the Cabinet has seen them.

FROM NORTH

Downing Street, 8 May 1778.

I have shown your Lordship's letter, the letter you received from Admiral Duff, and the list of the Spanish fleet, together with the enclosed extract of the advices from Paris, to Lord Weymouth, Lord George Germain, Lord Dartmouth, and Lord Gower. They are all of opinion that nothing contained in those papers will justify a change in the destination of Admiral Byron's fleet. They continue to think that every dispatch should be used to send it off to North America, unless you should, before its departure, receive certain accounts that the Toulon fleet is arrived at Cadiz, and either continues there or has sailed in a route which clearly indicates that its destination is towards a different quarter of the globe. I think it highly probable that you may already have received by the Proserpine such intelligence as must put out of doubt the proper line to be followed. In the meanwhile, the sentiments of all the Cabinet ministers in town are unanimous for sending the fleet to North America as soon as it can sail.

It may be the intention of Spain to assist M. d'Estaing with a squadron in his expedition to North America; in that case it is to be wished that our fleet should be stronger, and this contrary wind, if it continues, will afford an opportunity of adding some ships to Mr Byron's squadron.

Although I am not one of those who think an invasion of these islands impracticable, nor am convinced that France and Spain will attempt it, yet I think the enterprise so arduous that they will not for some time be in a condition to carry such a project into execution. The danger of our army and fleet in North America appears to me more probable and more immediate; besides, although I pay little credit to the sincerity of the Court of Spain, and believe that they harbour very hostile designs against us, I cannot conceive it possible that they would hold such a pacific language just at the very moment that they intend to unite in an attack upon our possessions in Europe. I have [etc.].

P.S.—If you can contrive to send a shipload of prisoners to be exchanged in America, I should think it advisable to do it without delay.

FROM KEPPEL

Prince George, Spithead, 9 May 1778.

When I arrived at Portsmouth the 23rd of April the list of the ships I was honoured with the command of, and their increasing good condition, I must own afforded me rather sanguine hopes, in case the French fleet had made its appearance from Brest, that I was likely to be in a situation of rendering service to my country; and with that hope I was very anxious for its hasty completing with provisions and stores. My flattering hopes have been very much altered since the determination of taking eleven of the finest ships from under my command for foreign service, as it leaves me in a situation I must think alarming for the safety of the King's home dominions. The number of the ships named and put under my command now is twenty-two; one of 74 guns in that list [the Torbay] is unfortunately so burnt as to be unfit for service, which reduces the list to twenty-one. Of that number, four are in Portsmouth Harbour, and only one of that four can be called fit for action, the other three wanting men; two ships of the list not arrived from the eastward, and will be in want of men to complete when they do. This account makes, of the twenty-one ships, five not at Spithead, though hourly expected, that will be in want of men ; the Bienfaisant at Plymouth, but when she arrives a conditioned ship. I believe your Lordship will allow this state of the fleet to be fairly painted.

And now let me suppose the Brest fleet to be of the force some intelligence makes it, and that it is to be ready for sea the 10th composed of twenty-five ships of the line of battle. What is to prevent its being in the opening of the Channel for the chance of intercepting Vice-Admiral Byron's squadron ? Or suppose the French enterprising, and that they find that squadron in Plymouth Sound, attempt to destroy it, and for a *coup de main* land and destroy the docks there : I fear there is not a troop there to resist them for a day. But I will imagine they do nothing till Vice-Admiral Byron's squadron is gone and no more protection to this country can be expected from them. The French fleet come up Channel, and it is known they are off the Isle of Wight with a fleet, call it twenty-five, call it twenty-one, and with a numerous attendance of frigates : may I ask what the King's ministers expect I am to do, with my force as I have described it ? I would not put such a question if I could say I had a collected force with me (manned and in condition) of twenty-one ships of the line. I certainly have no such force at present, and it is the danger that is drawing, perhaps, so near as a week hence that obliges me to trouble your Lordship with my thoughts before the detached fleet is out of reach. Every hour of the day calls upon me for the most serious reflection how I am to defend this country with success and glory to the King's flag and my own honour.

I trust your Lordship will not read this letter without giving it the attention that so serious a subject requires. Before I close it, I venture to state a hope I have, should Mr Byron's squadron proceed, that he may be directed very pointedly to have his thoughts towards England again, so as to be able to make part of its force as soon at least as M. d'Estaing can be supposed to join the fleet of Brest.

In what I have troubled your Lordship with, I feel that I have done my duty to my king, to my country, and to myself, and am [etc.].

FROM NORTH

Downing Street, Tuesday morn., 12 May 1778.

The best intelligence I have received leads me to think that M. d'Estaing will go directly to New York. If it is the opinion of the best seamen that if his destination were uncertain New York would be the best point for Mr Byron to make, should not this circumstance be suggested to him, and should not it be recommended to him to direct his course that way rather than to Halifax ?

I rather choose to ask this question of your Lordship than to decide, as I am very diffident of my judgement on any point of this nature.[1] I am [etc.].

FROM SIR HUGH PALLISER

Ocean, Spithead, 12 May 1778.

My Lord—The Boyne arrived yesterday, as did the Robust and Ruby this morning ; and

[1] On May 9 Commissioner Hood, writing with great knowledge of the station, suggested to the King and to Sandwich that Byron should go to New York instead of Halifax. Byron's instructions were altered in that sense on May 18. (*Corr.*, 2332, and Secret Orders and Instructions.)

from Captain [Alexander] Hood's account we may expect to see the Victory to-day.

Now that the Formidable is in regular turn to be next manned your Lordship will expect I should form plans for it, especially as the getting her round immediately is a very desirable object. Captain Bazely writes that her guns and provisions are on board; but the Greenwich men being taken from him, he has not strength to put his rigging in order for sea.

I reckon upon 50 men from the Diligence; and if your Lordship approves of the Greenwich and dock men carrying the Medway to Woolwich, 100 I think with her petty officers may be taken from her; and 50 may be taken of the Conquestadore's complement, she having now no men to guard. These, together with chance men by tenders and other ships' men, with the few she has will, I hope, carry her to the Downs, where 50 of the last entered may be taken from the Buffalo which will be soon replaced, the India ships being daily expected. With these supplies I hope on her arrival here a hundred men may be taken from the [Princess] Amelia, she having few to guard. If your Lordship approves of this plan I think Admiral Keppel's squadron may soon be reinforced with a 90-gun ship.[1]

The Bienfaisant and Arethusa are just come in. The ships in the harbour have made the signal for sailing, but I fear the wind is too far to the southward for them to get out.

Rear-Admiral Parker remains at St Helen's with the wind fresh at W.S.W. I confess I shall not be sorry to see him remain there until you are certain whether Monsieur d'Estaing proceeds to

[1] The Conquestadore and Princess Amelia were receiving ships for newly-raised men at the Nore and Spithead respectively.

America or Brest, and what use the Spaniards mean to make of the very formidable fleet they have ready. No doubt France has been early informed of the squadron we have ordered for America : may they not thereupon order d'Estaing from Cadiz to Brest, although he was originally intended for America ?   I have [etc.].

TO LORD WEYMOUTH

Admiralty, 13 May 1778.

My Lord—I received his Majesty's commands to-day to send an express to Plymouth to stop the sailing of Admiral Byron's fleet till further orders, upon an idea that we must very soon receive certain intelligence whether M. d'Estaing is gone to Cadiz or not.[1]

His Majesty also directed me to desire your Lordship to call a meeting of his servants to-morrow to consider whether Admiral Byron should (in case of M. d'Estaing's being gone out of Europe) be directed to sail for Halifax or New York, and also whether the squadron under the command of Admiral Byron should not be ordered to return to England as soon as the winter sets in. I am [etc.].

FROM PALLISER

Ocean, Spithead, 14 May 1778.

Many thanks to your Lordship for your ready attention to what I took the liberty of writing

[1] This order was formally approved next day at a Cabinet meeting by the following ministers : Lord President, Lord Privy Seal, Lords North, Sandwich, Amherst, Weymouth, and George Germain (Cabinet Minute).

about the Formidable's men. . . . I am at present better situated in a well-manned and a well-disciplined ship. The Victory and the Formidable will both be some time before they are in those respects equal to the Prince George and Ocean. The sooner they have fixed companies the better.

I am quite uninformed of what passes here, therefore can give your Lordship little or no account of the progress. Mr Keppel's line of battle is composed of 21 fine ships, if they were all manned ; but I fear the America, Robust, Cumberland, Elizabeth, Berwick, and Victory want many, and the Terrible sickly.

By a man from the Gumpus [? Grampus, armed storeship], I am told Lord Howe sailed from Rhode Island the beginning of March.

I find the language here begins to prevail that we are in want of ships for the present occasions. I take all opportunities to contradict it, and insist that we want only men, having many ships ready to receive them and more preparing for it. I wish you would be so good as direct Mr Stephens to send me one of the weekly progresses, the one before the latest received will serve my purpose.

When once Admiral Byron's squadron is gone I shall consider it as very uncertain when they will return or where they will pass the next winter ; and as I know no dependence can be had on contractors for large supplies of provisions on the foreign stations in case of a war, so I think your Lordship will judge it right to order the Victualling Board to have sufficient supplies provided for those in America to carry them up to the middle of next summer—to be there before the winter sets in, also to have a quantity more shipped in readiness to be sent wherever Admiral

Byron's squadron or parts of it may be detained longer then we at present foresee. These timely precautions are necessary to prevent disappointments to the service.

The Navy Board should be equally provided respecting stores. I should hope the East India storeships will answer all our purposes for foreign supplies ; in that case the Buffalo, Grampus, and Leviathan, with 50 or 60 guns and 350 or 400 men, will prove complete ships for the Baltic and Channel convoys, and will do for that service many years.[1]

I am of opinion that some of the unnecessary niceties observed on many occasions on inspecting into ships' defects might be safely avoided ; and although nothing is so difficult as to get the better of old customs and prejudices, yet I think much may be done in this way by your Lordship's language on the subject with Mr Hunt, in the beginning of his office, which may be a counterpoise to Sir John's over care and timorousness.[2]

Your Lordship sees I freely use the liberty which your Lordship indulges me in of suggesting whatever occurs to me respecting the service : your Lordship always has it in your power to check and correct me therein, always submitting

[1] These were old ships of war, originally the Captain 64, Buckingham 70, and Northumberland 70 respectively. In 1777 they were turned into storeships and given thirty small guns each, roughly the armament of a 32-gun frigate, but rather weaker. The Buffalo had already been restored as a fourth-rate of 50 guns when Palliser wrote ; she was afterwards increased to a 60, and played her part in Howe's relief of Gibraltar in 1782. The Leviathan became a 50-gun ship in 1779 ; she and the Grampus foundered at sea in the course of the next two years. See below, pp. 304, 307.

[2] Edward Hunt had lately joined Sir John Williams as Surveyor of the Navy. Sir John had held the office since 22 June 1765 ; and since the death of Sir Thomas Slade in 1771 he had been alone.

whatever I may offer to your better judgment. I have [etc.].

P.S.—Lord Rockingham is at Portsmouth on a visit to Admiral Keppel.

May 15th. I have just seen Mr Montagu, who is very well, grown a good deal, and is very well spoken of and without flattering. I don't know how he stands as to time, but I conclude he does not want much ; he has been 4 years 8 months in the Salisbury, and I suppose he had some time in the yacht. Your Lordship remembers that in the last war two years of the six at sea was admitted in the merchants' service : may it not be equally proper now—by this means he may be passed ? I don't find amongst the commissions come down one for Mr [Lord Robert] Manners for the Ocean ; if he is otherwise disposed of, I shall be glad to have Mr Montagu either in the Ocean or Formidable till he can be disposed of more to your Lordship's mind.[1]

I understand the Salisbury has a tolerable company. It is a pity they can't have some pay and some leave of absence on being turned over. Upon her arrival at the Nore Captain Walters [Salisbury] and Bazely [Formidable] must join their address in reconciling them to it on promises of all possible indulgence hereafter.

The wind is still at W.S.W., more moderate but still keeps the ships in the harbour, and Admirals Montagu[2] and Parker at St Helen's.

[1] Lord Sandwich's son Robert is shown as a midshipman in the muster book of the Formidable. He became a lieutenant on 5 April 1779.
[2] Vice-Admiral John Montagu was about to resume the command in Newfoundland.

I understand by Admiral Keppel that Lord
Rockingham says there is no positive accounts of
Monsieur d'Estaing's having passed the straits or
of his being at Cadiz. During this interval of
tranquillity and peaceable professions of Spain,
why may not messengers pass and repass between
England and Gibraltar with dispatches in cypher ?
I think this was practised till the declaration of
the last war.

By the late arrival of the German and American
transports and a number of merchant ships, the
appearance of ships at Spithead, in Stokes Bay,
on the Motherbank, and St Helen's would
countenance any reports that might be propa-
gated, if it was thought advisable to divert the
French and Spaniards with an alarm of expeditions intended—suppose to Buenos Aires, to
assist the Portuguese in that quarter and to
favour insurrection in the Spanish settlements in
the South Sea. Indeed I think such measures
would be justifiable after the part France and
Spain have acted respecting our colonies. Independent states and a free trade in the South Sea
would affect the Spaniards as much as the loss of
America will affect Britain.

FROM SIR THOMAS PYE [1]

Portsmouth, 17 May 1778.

My Lord—Yesterday came in here a smuggling
vessel, I believe from Havre-de-Grace, a passenger
in which tells me that 'tis reported there that the
fleet from Toulon is destined for the destruction
first of Lord Howe and his squadron then to go

[1] Admiral and Commander-in-chief at Portsmouth.

up the River St Lawrence ; that the coast opposite the English coast is full of troops, who give out are meant to invade England so soon as the fleet is gone in pursuit of the French fleet, but he says he could not learn of any kind of boats or vessels that are preparing for an expedition of that sort, and in his own opinion says he thinks they fear a visit from us ; that the King of France is going to follow the King of England's example to animate the fleet of France by his presence. Though there is nothing of any great importance, I thought it proper to communicate what transpired here from Havre-de-Grace. I have [etc.].

P.S.—He further says a report likewise prevails that the Toulon fleet is put into Cadiz.

FROM KEPPEL

Portsmouth, 17 May 1778.

I am obliged to be on shore, though much against my inclinations ; but the unavoidable hurry and confusion attending a change of ships and its crew makes such a situation impossible for me to remain in. I however hope it will soon be over, though there are material matters to be done to the Victory before it can be said that she is fit for sea service. Commissioner Hood ordered the builder to lose no time in getting what is wanted expedited without waiting the delay of the post's bringing the Navy Board's directions. The very stormy weather prevents my knowing exactly the progress of the Victory since I left Spithead, but your Lordship may rest assured that there is no inclination to idleness among us here.

My letters of information relative to d'Estaing's fleet seem to differ very materially : in some he is supposed to have been seen the 28th of April off the island of Majorca, and on the 29th off the coast of Barbary near Algiers ; another account says the Toulon fleet anchored off Cadiz, sent a frigate into the harbour, they remained there some days then sailed with a fair wind steering S.W., they consisted of 12 ships of the line and 10 frigates— this description of that fleet has no dates belonging to it. If d'Estaing's squadron is as crowded with men &c. as several accounts make them to be, there is great probability of their being soon very sickly. I wish, however that is, that Lord Howe may have got the whole of the King's force in America nearly to New York, and that he may have timely information to make the best of his situation. As Monsieur d'Estaing has American pilots on board for the Chesapeake and the Delaware, his destination is most likely to be one of those two parts. The squadron under Lord Howe and the army under his brother are objects for the French force more tempting than any other. They destroyed, France and America may be sure that every other post must fall ; on the contrary, while that force can be called upon entire and joined by a respectable detachment of ships from this country, the picture may change more favourably.

Whatever becomes the determination of the King's councils in this important crisis for decision, the extraordinary bad weather must prevent any of the outward-bound fleets from stirring. I hope before the wind changes that good intelligence will permit all the foreign force and convoys to be in motion when the wind gets easterly. I fear the Gibraltar embarkation may suffer in sickness by their being delayed ; they must run some risk, and that is increasing every day unless a fleet of force could see them into the Straits of Gibraltar, and I am to suppose that impossible while the French have a fleet at Brest of twenty-five ships of the line. If they had sailed as soon as they embarked they would now have been well forward on their voyage. The getting the Exeter and transports back to England I shall wish much for, and I hope your Lordship has thought it advisable to have the transports filled with stores of wine from Gibraltar for your victualling stores here. It may be advisable to write overland to have the wines ready. I think I understood you that you meant to order the Worcester home directly.

I am sure you keep in your thoughts the appearing necessity of exerting every nerve for completing the King's ships with men : the wants are great. I troubled you in my last letter about the Prince George, as among the finest ships here, being put in a respectable state ; five such ships as the *Victory, Queen, Ocean, Sandwich, and Prince George* in good condition, well manned, and well commanded, makes a line of battle very formidable.

Your Lordship has not sent a commission for Mr Manners to the Ocean, and by what I have learnt since I wrote last to you I cannot help wishing very particularly that Lord Charles Fitzgerald may be appointed to the Arethusa, and that the young man now in the Arethusa may be sent round to the Milford.

I wish I could form to myself a hope that this country would very soon have a force of frigates, and that many would be in a little time with us from Lord Howe. The French are most assuredly intent upon invading England or Ireland ; if they do attempt it I am certain, without frigates to oppose their embarkations, they will make their

II.   F

landing. If General Howe's army was at home the French might repent of their alertness ; but the little army that appears to be in readiness, I own I am not brave enough to go to my bed with the confidence of the country's being in security. I have no apology to make for the various matters I have wrote to your Lordship upon, I conceive myself in the present state of the country very much concerned, and I am [etc.].

FROM KEPPEL

Portsmouth, 18 May 1778.

Your Lordship is very obliging in answering my letters to you so punctually and complying so readily upon the little matters I trouble you with. I have no inclination to be unreasonable in my requests, and therefore you may rest assured that I shall give you as little trouble as possible upon anything that does not relate to the immediate public concern ; and when that is the occasion I trust your Lordship will give the attention the matters may require.

Sir Hugh Palliser will inform you how very much the bad weather interrupts dispatch, and also the wants of Admiral Parker's fleet will be in to keep complete. I have but little to do with that squadron, though I feel so interested for the whole that I am anxious if that detachment does sail it may go complete and in good condition.

Your Lordship's letter tells me the accounts of Monsieur d'Estaing's being seen off Algiers the 29th of April : how that was known in France is not said by you, or other accounts sent to me that corroborates with that information. Exact intelligence at this moment would be worth a treasure.

To be in time to succour Lord Howe, and not expose this country too much to danger, would be such an event as would change the face of things that at present have but too truly a black appearance.

Sir Thomas Pye has given the Prince George 100 of the Torbay's men, which is 15 more than I kept of the Chatham's in the Victory, which pays my debt upon the score of men to Sir John Lindsay [1] ; but I cannot be enough thankful to him for his zeal and activity in getting the Victory so soon to Spithead.

I find some people conjecture that d'Estaing will still stop at Cadiz, that he will refresh, and then see the convoy fair and safe on their voyage with the smaller of his line of battle ships and repair with the larger part to Brest ; but as this stands upon no sort of real ground to determine upon I only give it to your Lordship as it came to me. I am [etc.].

FROM PALLISER

Portsmouth, 18 May 1778.

If d'Estaing's squadron was no further than the length of Algiers on the 29th past, we have good reason to hope the Proserpine would get the length of Gibraltar as soon as him ; she left this place the 21st [2] with an easterly wind. I think our orders to her captain and to Admiral Duff are as full as possible, and if carefully executed will furnish us with early notice of d'Estaing's route. If his ships

[1] Originally captain of the Victory, now in the Prince George since the change of flagships.

[2] P.M. 20th (Master's log, Proserpine).

are as much crowded with men as we are told they are, I think they will be very sickly before they get the length of Cadiz and be disabled before they get to America, if bound thither, or to any other distant place.

The ships detained at St Helen's will want fresh supplies of beer, water, and provisions. It may not be amiss to order a quantity of each to be ready shipped at Plymouth for them on their arrival, for they ought to carry as much as possible.

Whenever it is certainly known that the Toulon squadron (or the best part of it, which I am inclined to think will be the case) have shaped their course towards Brest, Admiral Byron's squadron (if then at Plymouth) should immediately repair to St Helen's to prevent our force being cut in two ; this has ever been a favourite object of France, and always attempted in the beginning of a war with England.

I am much pleased at the measures which your Lordship says will be taken for manning the fleet. I am satisfied none other will prove effectual. Had your Lordship's sentiments on this head been more attended to, this measure would have been sooner pursued, but it is better late than never.

The apprehensions of an invasion should not be despised, nor the measures against it neglected. I wish every measure that has been taken on the like former occasions to be referred to, and such as are thought best to be prepared for.

I think it very material to be prepared to fit out suddenly the greatest number possible of armed craft fit to attack and destroy such craft as may bring over troops. This is more necessary now than formerly because of our want of frigates. Amongst other things I wish a great number of swivel stocks, I mean some hundreds, to be ready in all our yards or to be made by contract to be ready to be fixed in small vessels when wanted ; and the Ordnance may be given to expect large demand upon them for swivels and small carriage guns. But these hints are all humbly submitted to your Lordship's better judgement. I have [etc.].

FROM KEPPEL

Portsmouth, 11 A.M. 20 May 1778.

I have your Lordship's two letters of the 18th. My letter to you of yesterday will inform you of the Victory's state and the hurry and exertion using to get her wants completed.

The opinion your Lordship seems to entertain, that the Brest fleet ready for sea consists of twenty-five ships of the line and a large number of frigates, is so formidable in its description, under the present state of the fleet of England for home service, that it will require the most serious consideration for those entrusted with the government of this country how far the fate of England will be risked, if in a naval battle near the coast the English fleet should not be conqueror. I am not the person that will offer an opinion upon a matter of such nice importance. I hope I shall do my duty becoming an officer in every situation ; and I might perhaps not be sorry, if I considered myself *only,* to give battle to the French fleet when I might not dare as a councillor to my King to advise it. I enclose to your Lordship the correct description of the fleet under my command at Spithead, with only two frigates ; and I must say that was this fleet even a ship or two superior in line of battle, the want of frigates and the numbers on the side of the French will, although a superiority gained in fight, render the retreat of their fleet too secure under the assistance of their frigates.[1]

What your Lordship mentions relative to the equipping the Blenheim and Princess Amelia is to me the very opposite of my wishes. I am for complete effective ships, which they cannot be ; their men to the ships ready in other respects will be more for the public service. I am in hopes that Lord Shuldham may be able with the Blenheim's men to complete the Duke, and send her to join the fleet in a very few days with extraordinary exertion.[2]

How far Admiral Sir Thomas Pye will be able to complete the ships here I don't clearly make out. The Formidable and the Duke added to the twenty-one ships now under my command would be a great additional strength ; and after that to get forward the Thunderer, Vengeance, Defiance, Vigilant, Centaur, and Resolution will be a considerable increase of force. But where are the men for these ships to be found, and when may I expect more frigates ? I am really uneasy upon the want of such most necessary craft.

[1] Palliser wrote from Portsmouth the same day : ' It would be a comfortable reflection, after the American squadron and the convoys are gone, to have a collected force left at home equal to what France only can immediately bring upon our coast, and which I am satisfied they will do ; but I do not yet see when we shall have a line of battle equal to theirs. As to their great number of frigates, I see no chance for us to equal them. Without a great and speedy increase of men, we shall at home be exposed to insults.'

[2] The Blenheim was a 90-gun ship built in 1761, and the Princess Amelia an old-fashioned three-decked ship of 80 guns ; both had been serving as receiving ships with half crews for some time past. In the August List Book they are shown for the first time under Keppel's command ; but they did not actually join the line of battle until more than a year later, after Hardy's retreat before the combined fleets. See below, pp. 121–2, 133, 136. The Duke was a new 90-gun ship, built at Plymouth and now fitting out there.

If your councils still determine to keep the Gibraltar reinforcement to sail with the home fleet, I don't guess when it is likely to get there. If I am to sail in complete force, I mean with that strength that the King's ministers determine to advise his Majesty to risk a battle with, I will send a cutter to cruise off Ushant ; but as a vessel belonging to the fleet it will be impossible, unsupported, for her to look into Brest and gain intelligence of the French fleet there. If a smuggler of this sort of vessel could be employed, and such a fellow in her tempted to be true, it appears to me the only method to be used, unless we were in force to keep a strong detachment before that port to support a vessel of observation.

I must beg your Lordship to send orders to Plymouth for the Milford's immediately joining the fleet at Spithead, and to Lord Shuldham to complete her men up that she may not demand any here. If there are any Torbay's men left exclusive of the hundred to the Duke, I must beg they may be ordered round.

If Sir Richard Bickerton was ordered to his ship [the Terrible] it would give me more hopes of her getting ready than I can entertain in his absence. I have [etc.].

FROM KEPPEL

Victory, Spithead, 24 May 1778.[1]

I have your Lordship's very obliging letter of the 21st ; and since receiving it have seen Sir Richard Bickerton, who poor fellow is fretting himself I fear to sickness. The recovery of the

[1] The Admiral hoisted his flag in the Victory on May 15 and began to live on board her on the 21st.

Terrible's people keeps no pace with the zeal and desires of the officers of that ship, and I am sorry to say the men that have been returned from the hospital have many of them relapsed and gone again to the hospital more complaining than at first. The insufficiency of the invalid guard at the hospital has allowed of more desertion from it than before ; the old fellows are old sinners themselves, which makes me fear they don't exert themselves so materially as younger soldiers would. In this most unfavourable and indeed unfortunate condition of the Terrible's people, I do not know how to advise better than to propose to your Lordship her being ordered into the harbour to dock and refit ; she will be able to clear herself of everything and get better fumigated, she will get a clean bottom, and probably these useful works will go hand in hand with the re-establishment of the people's health. I have in my public letter to Mr Stephens begged the Terrible may be ordered to dock ; and that no time may be lost, I have applied to Sir Thomas Pye to order her in directly that she may profit by the favourable wind that now blows. I don't yet know whether he will venture to take it upon him ; some *guarded* discretionary power for services of this sort perhaps your Lordship may think necessary to lodge with the admiral here, but it may not be immediately determined upon till you have considered it.[1]

Your Lordship's ideas for the raising of men, an article so much wanted, cannot be managed with too much secrecy and precaution : I heartily wish you good success in your plan.

I have no doubt of Lord Shuldham's using every exertion to dispatch in equipping the Duke ;

[1] Keppel first mentioned the sickly state of the Terrible on April 18.

and as that ship has no other to take the attention of the port, I cannot help thinking she will or may be here in a very short time. The Blenheim, if my information is good, has a large number of good men on board of her.

I find landmen are nearly as much wanted as seamen to make up the regulated proportions ; the weekly account I send Mr Stephens this day will show your Lordship the deficiency of seamen and marines. It falls heavy upon your department to have so large a part of your marines employed upon foreign service as troops in garrison, and that you should have no help of soldiers at home to assist in manning the great ships ; such assistance has ever been given from the Army at the commencement of a war.

The Victory gets forward apace, and I hope I may say is well manned—wants regularity and discipline, which they will get soon after leaving Spithead. The Prince George still wants numbers to complete ; I think Sir John Lindsay will not complain that he has been neglected, that ship as far as she musters is well manned. The Elizabeth and Berwick expect some men from Scotland, though not so many as to make up their full numbers. I wish your Lordship may be able to dispatch the Thunderer and the frigates you have in readiness (men excepted). The ships here will begin to-morrow to take their proportions of wine from the Teneriffe, French vessel, and small as the quantity is, I feel sensible of your attention in getting it for the fleet ; it may be of much service should the ships be unfortunately sickly while at sea.

My letter to Mr Stephens will inform you that I have sent the Stirling Castle, Arethusa, and two cutters to St Helen's ; the Hector joins them this afternoon. Sir Charles Douglas [Stirling Castle] is directed to examine all vessels passing, and to keep the frigate at single anchor ready to push out to sea if any strange cruiser should be looking in ; suppose a French frigate should be upon that errand, would it be proper at all events to bring her in ? She certainly must be sent away if not brought in.

The Rattlesnake [cutter] is to cruise off Ushant north and south for the space of fourteen days, with the view of giving early information if ships of force are seen standing towards the English coast. The Alert cutter goes off the Start for the same purpose, should her captain discover any fleet of force in the Channel.

I grow impatient to learn with certainty something about Monsieur d'Estaing. There are those that say the Toulon fleet are put back to that place. I don't know how to credit that, or whether to wish it, as I do believe a long westerly wind obstructing his passage through the Gut of Gibraltar will most probably make his ships sickly, which may answer a better purpose to this country than that fleet's returning suddenly to Toulon before the sickness has rooted itself. Should you be certain that the French are put back, how will that operate upon Admiral Byron's motions ? Will he have time to get to Gibraltar ? Or will it be more advisable to look with the whole joined at the Brest fleet, and detach, if detachment is necessary, from the fleet at sea ? This idea may be worth your Lordship's consideration ; it is not quite in ripeness with me to give a decided opinion upon.[1] I have [etc.].

[1] An undated note from the King runs as follows : ' I am very clearly of opinion that the moment we hear d'Estaing has passed the Gulf of Gibraltar and gone forward towards America, that

FROM KEPPEL

Victory, Spithead, 25 May 1778.

I have the honour of your letter of the 23rd, and am obliged to your lordship for the appointment of Mr Hughes to the 4th lieutenancy of the Lion.

I shall have attention to the hint in your letter relative to the fleet's going to sea. You may be sure that in everything that concerns myself, or convenience towards making a sea life passable, shall not detain me one hour from the execution of public instructions; the moment the Victory can be said to be in condition for sea service and action, that moment I will take to get away. Every man in the ship is employed in labour, which obliges us to neglect the great guns and small arms. I conclude Admiral Sir Thomas Pye will be directed to complete as many of the ships as he possibly can : the Prince George, the Cumberland, Berwick, Elizabeth, and America call for their greater numbers, the other sixteen ships will want but few, the Victory is well completed. I will flatter myself that I may sail with eighteen or nineteen ships; and if the Admiral has any hidden numbers of men, in that case I may hope for to sail with the whole line, the Terrible excepted. She went into the harbour this morning—I think the most advisable and humane measure towards the saving of her ship's company; and by Sir

Byron must follow him. Should he be returned to Toulon, then Keppel must instantly sail off Brest with such ships as he has in condition, and be joined by Byron and his squadron; and as soon as Keppel can have a reinforcement to render him equal to the Brest fleet, then Byron must be detached with a sufficient force to the Gulf of Gibraltar.' See Appendix B for Byron's instructions.

Richard Bickerton's constant personal attendance I shall expect the best effects from [it] both as to the getting rid of the complaint and recovering the men at the hospital ; and from some regular method he will adopt desertion may be checked, at least I hope it will.

I will not risk naming an exact day for moving, though I may say that I wish the easterly wind had held back for four or five days. I fear we shall not be quite in condition sooner than Friday, it may be Sunday. I wish it may be the first day. I am sure it shall not be deferred beyond the later day.

The numerous convoys, the men that have been given to the armed ships and frigates that command the different convoys, has stripped Admiral Pye very bare, but it cannot be helped. I wish you success in what you are about to answer the calls. Captain Maitland's tender arrived yesterday with upwards of one hundred volunteers from Scotland ; that gentleman has from his interest in his own country supplied his ship with full two hundred men.

If the King's ministers continue determined to delay the fleet under Admiral Byron's command from proceeding to North America till the certainty of d'Estaing's destination, and that it is expedient that his squadron goes off the port of Brest with the King's fleet now under my command and the view of detaching it kept in sight, your Lordship I daresay has it in consideration that the remaining ships must give them some aids of provisions and water before the separation, which must necessarily make my return into port sooner than it would otherwise be, and perhaps it would be thought advisable to strengthen the line of battle with the Formidable and Duke if that can possibly be done.

I had near forgot observing that if the wind should be easterly at the moment of Admiral Byron's receiving his final parting orders, it may be preferable for his proceeding rather deficient in provisions than the chance of losing a favourable wind.   The real zeal I have for the King's service in the station and trust reposed in me must apologise for the liberty I take in suggesting my ideas for the public welfare of his Majesty's forces by sea, and I trust your Lordship will be convinced that I have no other motive for troubling you so frequently.   I have [etc.].

FROM KEPPEL

Victory, Spithead, 26 May 1778.

The Admiralty messenger brought instructions this day for my proceedings, and I will move as soon as I possibly can. I do not guess what success Admiral Pye will have in his press, but I am sure under my present orders I can neither employ the ships' boats upon that service nor permit the operation of it at Spithead, with such delay following of it as must create confusion without end among the outward-bound transports.

I cannot say that your instructions are such as I feel much satisfaction upon when I consider them over.   It is impossible to avoid seeing that, both in case of detaching Vice-Admiral Byron's squadron or detaining him a time that may be thought too long in the event, the blame must fall upon myself.   Indeed there does appear *a positive period* for my sending him away where *the intelligence is certain*, and at which time my instructions decide positively ; but suppose I have information at the time that the Brest fleet is ready to come out to sea, nearly three ships to two in force compared with the King's that will remain under my command, is it meant that I should with seventeen or eighteen ships of the line leave it to the choice of the French to come out or not, to give battle to the fleet under my command after it is reduced by detaching Vice-Admiral Byron's squadron ? I do assure your Lordship that no consideration to myself prompts me to ask you this question, it is the consideration that the fate and safety of the King's dominions most essentially depend upon the issue of a sea battle fought in the home seas. My situation and duty is to obey my orders : be assured I shall, and the question I now put to your Lordship is without wishing to start difficulties but for a clear explanation and direction wherein your officer cannot fail if he is obedient. I am [etc.].

P.S.—As it is most probable that you will have more certain intelligence in town than I may get, I make no doubt but that your Lordship will dispatch it constantly to me for my guidance from Plymouth.

FROM KEPPEL

Victory, Spithead, 27 May 1778.

I wrote yesterday to your Lordship by the return of your messenger. I was rather hurried with the wish I had to dispatch him, which may have occasioned my letter to have some errors in it, though upon the whole I hope it conveyed my thoughts intelligibly. I don't think I can add any further matter upon the subject of the fleet's proceeding. It is not fresh information to your Lordship to say that I don't like thinking that the fleet with me may be reduced to seventeen ships of the line ; it is in reality too few in number to dispute the seas against twenty-six, but I will say no more upon this subject at present.

Sir Robert Harland has my orders to get to St Helen's with such ships of his division as are ready and manned. I shall give Sir Hugh Palliser orders this evening to do the same, and also the Exeter with the Gibraltar convoy. There are so many matters to complete, that even leaving four ships behind me I despair of getting away myself with my own division till Saturday or Sunday. I am this moment going on shore to Sir Thomas Pye to talk upon the subject of manning the Prince George, Elizabeth, Berwick, Cumberland, and America ; the last ship is in hourly expectation of her tender from Ireland with more than she will want.[1] The wind, now at N.N.W., will probably bring her round the land this day. If I must leave these ships I can only say I am truly sorry for it. I am [etc.].

FROM PALLISER

Ocean, Spithead, 27 May 1778.

I did not know of our sailing orders till late yesterday, or I should sooner have taken this liberty of telling your Lordship the satisfaction I feel in the expectation of meeting the Duc de Chartres before our force is divided.

It is not to be described the works necessarily

---

[1] The America's captain, Lord Longford, was raising men from his own countryside.

done to the Victory since her arrival here, but I hope all will be finished to-morrow and (except her foulness) be in all respects fit for service. The Admiral told me last night that Admiral Harland's division should go to St Helen's to-day, as I hope we shall do to-morrow. The Elizabeth, Berwick, and Cumberland are yet many men short. I very much doubt if more than one of them can be completed, for I reckon very little upon this night's expedition, here being very few or no ships except transports.

Your Lordship has been deceived in the promise made of a regiment to supply the want of marines.

When once the embargo is laid I hope it will not be taken off till the fleet is manned ; till that is accomplished we can't pretend to be masters even in the home seas, not to defend our coasts, protect our trade, or annoy our enemies. In the meantime all is exposed, but when once the fleet is manned all will be safe, and the King and his ministers may be easy and adopt what measures they please. It must be a pleasing reflection to remember that your Lordship's counsels to these ends were perfectly right ; and had they been followed in time our present difficulties might have been in great part prevented, as we should have been ahead of our enemies in preparation for war and thereby might possibly have prevented it. I hope I may be excused mentioning this, and for indulging a vanity I have in reflecting that I perfectly agreed with your Lordship's sentiments and disposition.

By a letter from Admiral Roddam of the 22nd I find no orders were then received respecting the Salisbury's and Medway's men ; without those men no progress or service can be expected from the Formidable. I wish your Lordship may be able to spare time to enquire after the dispatch of those orders, otherwise time may be lost.

I hear Lieutenant Weatherel with 150 men is put into Plymouth : that 150 men here would give us another 74-gun ship.

Whilst we are out I conclude your Lordship will have very frequent occasions to send dispatches to Admiral Keppel, which will require many cutters at Plymouth. Two I think of the armed cutters are already stationed there ; and I think some of those hired in the Downs might be so employed, Lord Shuldham being directed to send an officer or trusty petty officer with the dispatches when he sends one of the *hired cutters*, for I apprehend the first and perhaps only authentic accounts of d'Estaing must be from the Admiralty.

As your Lordship encourages me to trouble you with what occurs to me upon the services in hand you will I hope excuse the length of this. I am expecting Mr Montagu to-day and have [etc.].

FROM KEPPEL

Victory, Spithead, Saturday, 11 o'clock A.M.,
30 May 1778.

The Victory is now under sail, the weather very fine and the wind but little, the Valiant and Foudroyant ready to go to St Helen's with me. The Prince George and the Elizabeth I fear will expend the day before they get in tolerable condition, and even by night will be in a state of confusion ; the Egmont will be able to go down this morning. These and the ships at St Helen's will make my number eighteen ships of the line, the Elizabeth I am afraid but poorly manned.

II.   G

The Milford is at St Helen's. The Vulcan fireship is arrived at Spithead from Plymouth but without being completed as a fireship, it now depends upon the Ordnance : I have directed her captain to write to the Admiralty upon the subject or apply to Admiral Pye.

If Vice-Admiral Byron joins me when I get off Plymouth the fleet will be thirty-one ships, supposing his squadron complete. I fear their deep condition will render them heavy cruisers ; indeed the unavoidable foulness of too many of the ships, if I should see the French and they show a disinclination to allow me to get close to them, is a disadvantage, but as it cannot be remedied I make you no complaint upon it. It will I hope be in your thoughts in time to come to have as many clean ships as possible.

The French, if your papers of intelligence of their fleet at Brest is true, are very active in their equipment and will certainly be in a very short time thirty-one or two ships of the line, and much in strength by the very extraordinary number of frigates great and small. Their fleet at home, composed as your intelligence describes, makes them exactly in number the same as that of the King's fleet when Vice-Admiral Byron joins. The French line is without the junction of Monsieur d'Estaing's squadron of thirteen.

When I have left Spithead the ships to get forward are first the Berwick and Cumberland, perhaps they may be reckoned upon soon ; in the harbour, the Terrible. Sir Richard Bickerton's own attention to that ship and her people will I hope (though I have my fears) bring her *soon* into condition. The Resolution, the Vengeance, Vigilant, Centaur, Defiance, and Lion are good ships if they were ready and manned. The Formidable, the Thunderer, and the Duke make the increased ships to be looked to as first to be brought to service, and which makes in number, reckoning the Terrible, twelve. The two ships from the River, the Duke at Plymouth, with the two ships at Spithead, I think will be the first *five* that will come into service, and will make the fleet's number thirty-six.

If Monsieur d'Estaing comes to Brest (after having made his detachments) with nine ships, the French will be forty or forty-one ships ; and after the first gun is fired and returned, if that should happen between the French ships and those of England, every place in England and Ireland will be in an alarm, invasions threatened, and I should believe real descents made, perhaps near the capital and very probably along your northern coast. God send the fleet and army safe home from America. I have long wished to see it, every hour of its absence now is critical. I must here finish upon this or I shall be led to my political ideas upon this subject, which I do not mean and will therefore confine myself to my profession, where the King has called upon me to act in.

The intelligence relative to the Spanish fleet at Cadiz makes it very formidable. Can their declarations be depended upon ? Do they yet talk the language of friendship and neutrality, or is their management with a view to get their galleons safe in port ? I hope to be gone from St Helen's before any letter from your Lordship after you receive this will catch me, but I shall hope to find one from you upon my arrival off Plymouth. Various accounts say that the French coast is lined with troops, your intelligence undoubtedly informs you at what *places* they have shipping of their own or of *neutral* bottoms which must be attended to.

Plymouth Yard and Victualling Office must be prepared for the return of the fleet in bad weather to supply their wants with fresh provisions, beer, and water, &c., with stores also that will be greatly called for. Torbay will very probably be most frequented, I mean when the fleet is obliged to seek shelter from weather or merely the recruit of three or four days. I remember the importance of Lord Hawke's having taken shelter there in the year 1759 ; it was an event that may, fairly stated, be reckoned to have enabled him to collect his fleet which he sailed with after four days' refitment and recruit to the defeat of the French fleet under Marshal Conflans. Having troubled your Lordship with so long a letter it is time to finish and I am [etc.].

FROM KEPPEL

Victory, St. Helen's, 31 May 1778, 2 P.M.

Your Lordship's letter of the 30th is this moment arrived, which mentions the intelligence of the Brest fleet consisting of 17 sail being at sea. I wish your letter had ordered my sailing without the Gibraltar convoy and I would have been at sea with to-morrow morning's tide, the wind favourable or contrary. If not bad weather with the latter I am almost inclined to risk sailing. I am sure I should not hesitate if your letter had said the account was absolutely authentic.

In one of the extracts of intelligence from Brest I observe an expression : ' On prétend que cette escadre doit aller joindre celle de Monsieur d'Estaing à la hauteur du Cap Finisterre.' Suppose it true both Monsieur d'Estaing's squadron and the Brest fleet do join off Cape Finisterre and then proceed to Ireland, have they sufficient troops on board for an effectual descent? This idea my thoughts have suggested to me, and your Lordship now reads it without any reasoning on the probability or improbability of its happening.

If I do make the signal to go to sea in the morning, I shall not prevent the Exeter with the Gibraltar convoy from sailing at the same time ; and nothing but bad weather shall prevent my sailing. Your Lordship will see that between the beginning and ending of my letter that I am determined, and I will give Captain Moore [Exeter] directions to call off Plymouth, if my fleet out-sails him which it must do, where I hope he will find directions for his proceedings upon the event in case he finds me gone. And I shall myself hope to meet explicit instructions upon this most important concern if the *intelligence requires it,* which I trust your Lordship will be so good as to send me by a messenger.[1] I am [etc.].

FROM KEPPEL

Victory, St Helen's Road, waiting for the tide—to sail.
1 June 1778.

I suppose the express I sent you yesterday, in return to your Lordship's letter of the 30th which you sent express, got to you very early this morning. The fleet only waits the tide's answering its purpose ; as the wind is westerly it becomes prudent to have an ebb to profit of in beating down

[1] On June 2 Keppel wrote : ' I am sure I feel much obliged to you for the attention you have so immediately shown in answer to the express I sent you of the 31st past. The instructions for my proceeding unencumbered with the Gibraltar convoy is a great relief to me, and my embarrassment on that particular ceases.'

Channel. I sent the Little Hazard cutter, and a few hours after her the Milford, each with a letter to Vice-Admiral Byron to apprise him of my intention to sail this day and to be in hourly expectation of seeing the fleet, which he was to join immediately if he continued under Admiralty orders to do so.[1]

The fleet now with me consists of 18 ships. The Elizabeth makes one of them, and I fear but in a bad state. As to men, the Shrewsbury I am sorry is getting very rapidly into the sickly state of the Terrible. Captain Ross, after he has landed the worst of them, will be fifty men short. If the sickness continues or grows worse your Lordship may expect that ship soon at Plymouth; she had better be docked at once, but you will be so good as to consider whether that will be a proper measure and whether she should refit at Plymouth or Portsmouth.

If you get no certain information of the destination of the ships from Brest supposed to be at sea, I cannot help making myself believe they are out with an intention to join Monsieur d'Estaing at a given rendezvous; to be cruising with 17 ships near our Channel I should not fancy they would risk. When the two fleets are together their numbers will be respectable, and perhaps they will not retire should the fleet under my command get sight of them. Monsieur Du Chaffault with his 17 ships alone will certainly run for it, if I get sight of him. Clean ships on such an event would be material to success. This letter goes by the post and I am [etc.].

[1] The Milford delivered her letter to Byron on June 5 (Byron's dispatches).

FROM PALLISER

Ocean, St Helen's Road, 2 June 1778.

I have deferred acknowledging the honour of your Lordship's letter by Mr Montagu in hopes to have been able to do it before this time from Plymouth, and at the same time to have informed your Lordship of our being on our way to look for the Brest or Toulon fleets or both ; for if Monsieur Du Chaffault has left Brest with only 18 or 20 sail of the line, I think when we join Admiral Byron we may reckon ourselves a match for both, notwithstanding their great superiority of frigates. By means of the embargo continuing I hope you will get men enough to keep pace with the enemy in increasing strength and that with the number of fine ships which we leave at Portsmouth, together with the Duke, Formidable, and Thunderer and others to be equipped, you will be able to furnish us with reinforcements and reliefs for such ships as from time to time must come in to refit.

Reflecting on the extravagant number of men said to be on board of both the French squadrons (if those accounts are true) I cannot bring myself to believe that they are going any long voyage, but think it is more probable they meditate a descent somewhere near home ; and at the same time, with a great army on the opposite coast and a great number of frigates and privateers, to attack or at least alarm and annoy us in all quarters at home at once ; and if the Spaniards have agreed to act in concert they may do the same elsewhere. But I have wearied myself, I will not weary your Lordship with conjectures about them. I am become impatient to be at a certainty : that is to be obtained only by getting sight of them, which if we once have the luck to do I trust we shall give such an account of them as the King and the public have a right to expect from us.

It is rather lucky that we did not get to sea the other day, as the wind has and still continues to blow so hard westerly that we could not have gained ground, and the convoy must have been drove to leeward.

Your son is very well. I admire his spirit in leaving his friends and the pleasures of the shore so soon after so long a voyage in pursuit of knowledge in his profession, and in hopes of soon seeing a battle. I find him very deserving of the character that Sir Edward Hughes and Captain Walters gave of him. He does the duty of a lieutenant, takes a watch with another lieutenant, for in these large ships we have two in a watch. He is quartered by me. I shall find him very useful to me, and will soon become my right hand man. I am [etc.].

June 3rd. *P.S.* I wrote the foregoing last night. I am now with Admiral Keppel, who expresses much satisfaction at your Lordship's explicitness and attention to him : this makes me happy, who am so much attached to you both. I think Monsieur d'Estaing, wherever he is, is in bad plight if he is so crowded as we are told.

FROM KEPPEL

Victory, St Helen's Road, 3 June 1778.[1]

Flying reports give out that Monsieur d'Estaing's squadron was returned to Toulon, two of his ships damaged by running on board

[1] The date of this letter is interesting. On June 2 the Proserpine arrived at Falmouth with her news of d'Estaing, and on the 3rd the Enterprise reached Plymouth with hers.

of each other, and that the French officers were much disgusted with d'Estaing's discipline. If the return of that fleet is certain, and the King's servants continue to be of opinion that Vice-Admiral Byron's squadron should be detached to Gibraltar, I think your information by the time I get off Plymouth must be clear enough for you to decide speedily your intentions so as to put them into immediate execution. It will be unlucky that Duff is senior to Byron. . . . I am [etc.].

FROM KEPPEL

Victory, St Helen's, Thursday evening
[4 June 1778].

I have desired the captain of the Proserpine to go himself immediately to London notwithstanding the express he sent from Falmouth. I am [etc.].

P.S.—Captain Sutton's information will require the order for Admiral Byron's proceedings to be speedily determined by the King's ministers.

FROM THE KING

Queen's House, 5 June 1778, 35 m. past 9 A.M.

I cannot decide whether the Toulon squadron's steering south-west is a certain proof of the West Indies being its destination. I should rather reason that it was to get in a certain track, to make the passage more secure to North America. The Cabinet cannot meet too soon, nor Byron be ordered to sail.[1]

---

[1] Captain Sutton's first report, dated Falmouth, June 2, says: ' From the regular course the fleet steered and the great press of sail they carried I cannot help supposing it is for the West Indies ' (S.P. Dom. naval).

FROM KEPPEL

Victory, St Helen's Road, 5 June 1778.

I was so desirous that you should see Captain *Sutton* that I would not detain him longer than for the line I wrote your Lordship.

The information he will give you seems to determine that d'Estaing's squadron is not at present intended for a junction with the twenty-five ships that compose the Brest fleet, but pursuing their voyage either to the continent of North America or the Sugar Islands. What you will learn I conclude will determine the King's Councils to dispatch Vice-Admiral Byron. I am glad the intelligence gives an opportunity for immediate directions without the delay that would have attended dispatching instructions to me off Brest ; I shall however proceed the moment the wind and weather permits off Plymouth to join Vice-Admiral Byron's squadron : before or by the time of my arrival there, I certainly shall have the Board's directions that will leave me nothing to doubt upon.[1]

The Shrewsbury's crew's sickness increases every day, and which must determine me to send her into port almost immediately ; from experience I think it will be advisable to recommend her being ordered to clear her hold and dock, there is no other method to bring her so speedily again fit for service. After I lose this ship the remaining number will be seventeen of the line for sea.

The winds keep me here : it is still westerly and very unpromising weather. May I hope to

---

[1] Byron was told to sail at once ; and his orders reached him at 3 A.M. on the 7th, though as it turned out he was wind-bound for two days (Byron's dispatches).

have the Proserpine added to my frigate list ?
If the Formidable is ready, the winds that detain
me here will carry her to the Downs. I am looking
out for the Lively, as I hoped from what one of
your letters said that she would have reached this
place by this time.   I am [etc.].

FROM PALLISER

Ocean, St Helen's, 5 June 1778.

According to Captain Sutton's account Monsieur
d'Estaing may be gone either to the West Indies
or America ; but, if the accounts of particular
persons and things embarked in that squadron is
to be depended on, the latter is far the most
probable. His not making a direct course may be in
order to avoid long and certain calms at this season
near to the Western Islands, and by running far
to the southward he will run across the Atlantic
in the trade wind and fine weather all the way ;
this is a material consideration respecting the
health of his men, if he is so much crowded as we
are told, and by taking that southern track it
should seem as if he means to go to the Chesapeake
or Delaware.

I have troubled your Lordship with this believing you will expect to hear from me upon this
subject.   I have [etc.].

P.S.—The westerling wind still continues to blow
very fresh, and squally weather.

FROM PALLISER

Ocean, St Helen's, 6 June 1778.

By return of the messenger which brought
Admiral Keppel's orders I have the honour to

acknowledge the receipt of your Lordship's letter of yesterday.

By yesterday's post I wrote your Lordship my sentiments upon the intelligence received by the Proserpine. I have now only to express my entire agreement in opinion with your Lordship that two frigates are a sufficient convoy for Gibraltar. The peaceable professions of Spain is very comforting at this time ; I wish them to continue and to prove sincere.

The weather now seems settled, the wind moderate at about S.S.E. on its inclining to the eastward ; we unmoored and on receipt of the orders the Admiral has made the signal to moor.

I understand Sir Thomas Pye hopes to complete the Cumberland and Berwick by Monday night.

I have a letter from Dover which says an American privateer of 20 guns is in Dunkirk Road. Such vessels may do a deal of mischief to the northward, and I expect so soon as hostilities commence the enemy will send many strong frigates and privateers to intercept our Baltic trade ; if they are successful it would very much distress us to support a fleet at sea with naval stores and masts.

I can have no objection to the Formidable's joining us at sea. I shall move into her or not at sea as I may find convenient. I wish the men to come out contented with their pay in their pockets rather than they should be discontented, but I shall be glad when they have had time to spend it, till then they will not be settled or quiet. I am [etc.].

P.S.—I am not quite satisfied at our having no watch off Brest. A. K. talks of sending orders by land for the Milford and a cutter to proceed thither which I think is right.

FROM THE KING

Kew, 7 June 1778, 17 m. past one P.M.

The letters from Portsmouth have given me infinite satisfaction, as by them I perceive everyone is doing his utmost to expedite the fitting out of the ships, and that nothing in a couple of days will be wanted but an easterly wind to enable Admiral Keppel to sail with a most respectable force.

I have given every necessary order for 600 soldiers to assist in manning the fleet for four months ; and fortunately every hour that number are expected to arrive from Scotland at Portsmouth.[1]

FROM KEPPEL

[Endorsed by Mr Stephens : ' Rec'd. 18 June 1778 by express from Lord Shuldham.']

I send this letter to Lord Shuldham, not to send it till he has a safe conveyance for it ; and it is only to suggest for your Lordship's consideration, and that of the King's servants, how far it may be advisable to extend hostility to the French flag after it is once *began*, as it may be upon *falling in with ships of the line of that nation.* I am [etc.].

---

[1] Keppel sailed on the 12th. A day or two before that, he wrote to Lord Sandwich : ' . . . I can sit down to thank you for the very explicit letter you have troubled yourself to write to me : twenty English ships of the line is certainly a formidable force, and I shall proceed when it is so strong. . . . I am exceeding glad that your Lordship has at length got the promise of the help of 600 soldiers ; they were materially wanted.'

FROM KEPPEL

Victory, at sea, 20 June 1778.

I do not well know how to explain what happened on Wednesday the 17th, Thursday the 18th, and yesterday, with more accuracy than I have done in my letters to Mr Stephens. After the action with the Arethusa and French frigate which circumstances brought on, and the extraordinary behaviour of the French frigate in the fleet, it seemed impossible for me to avoid the step I have taken ; and shall, upon having begun seizing these frigates, continue to do so till I know the King's pleasure. Believe me, my Lord, my mind has had its full share of anxiety and trouble upon this occasion ; and if I could have seen any better way to have decided maintaining the honour of the English flag, I should have preferred it to the loss of a single man on either side.

If obstinacy and ridiculous pride had not kept the French captains from doing what is almost ever submitted to when fleets meet single ships, coming to the admiral, I have no doubt with myself but a civil compliance on their part would have obliged me to wish them a good voyage, after being assured that they would not attend the fleet. But if that had been the case, I must have had the same work every day. I am informed that there is not less than eleven sail of these frigates cruising from Ushant and the Isle of Batz across the Channel. I suppose with a view of looking after the Gibraltar convoy.

The French Pallas gave the ships a long chase. The officer in her did all he could to escape ; he avoided being spoke to till he was almost surrounded and then shortened sail and did what he was desired to do, indeed he had not the power of avoiding it.

I have stood with the fleet the whole night to the northward to give cover to the Gibraltar convoy, which I am glad to say is at this moment in sight and coming down to the fleet. The damage that the Arethusa has sustained makes me wish her safe in; and I fear I must be under the necessity of sending the Stirling Castle into port with her, and the French frigates and French crews, when the wind comes to the westward, and shall order her captain to return to the rendezvous. The Formidable and Duke are seriously wanted.

I have learnt little to be depended upon from the French regarding the Brest fleet. I believe they are in port, and they say twenty-six ships of the line ready. I foresee if you are not able to cover the sea with frigates that your trade will be much interrupted.

The Milford sails most exceedingly well, but the French frigate and her getting on board each other has so disabled her that I fear she must soon leave me; and then I shall be reduced to the Proserpine and the Fox, which latter ship I think I may expect to see to-morrow. Be assured my Lord that Captain Marshall with his officers and men have done honour to the King's colours; and if the Arethusa could have kept her head the right way, Captain Marshall would have mastered the Belle Poule in a very little time longer. The Alert cutter, Captain Fairfax, did his business with the Coureur schooner very well. The French began with him, and they were on board each other for an hour before it was over.

This schooner as well as the frigates, if your measures determines keeping them, may add to your list of small ships and craft. I think if I had six more coppered-bottom frigates I should, if not unlucky, lessen very soon the number of theirs. But till the trial with the Brest fleet is over, I dare not boast ; it will be sufficient for me to promise the King and the nation that I shall do my best. But I can't help saying I wish the fleet was more in number of the line where the stake I may fight for is of that importance. I send Mr Stephens the different intelligence I have gathered : I cannot determine how far it may be depended upon, and I am [etc.].

P.S.—True or false I can't determine, but I understand that the French frigate, the Pallas, had taken a Guernsey privateer of 14 guns and carried her to Brest some days ago.

FROM PALLISER

Ocean, at sea, 20 June 1778.

Your Lordship will of course be informed by Admiral Keppel's dispatches of all particular occurrences since the fleet sailed ; but I can't help adding my testimony to his of the excellent qualities of our frigates, and the superiority they have in point of sailing over all the French frigates we have seen. Unfortunately, two of the three are disabled.

What has passed will undoubtedly be called by the French beginning hostility. If Spain is in any degree serious in her professions of wishing to keep out of the war, she will be glad to be furnished with information to show that we are not the aggressor.

The conduct of the captains of the French

frigates, I think, sufficiently shows that the purport of their orders is to provoke us to what they may pretend to construe into an insult or act of hostility, else why should they refuse to be spoken to by our cruisers at sea, where they know we have enemies cruising ? And according to the custom of the sea in all times, the cruisers of a nation at war have ever exercised a right to speak to ships that appear to be cruisers, especially when first called to in a friendly way and without molestation, or even by means of the usual signal for speaking to them, that is, by firing a gun not *at* them but ahead of them. It has never been considered an indignity to the party at peace to stop to be spoke to by those at war in search of their enemy. Our cruisers never hesitated to stop when chased by theirs, deeming it more honourable than running away and subjecting themselves to be fired at.

I have had no talk with any of the Frenchmen, but am told they say they had 14 days ago at Brest twenty-seven ships of the line, completely manned and ready to come out ; and they have near thirty frigates constantly going in and out, and six or seven more ships of the line fitting out. I have [etc.].

I can't sufficiently lament the want of more frigates.

22nd. *P.S.* I wrote the foregoing in order to be sent by the first opportunity, which I missed. This day Admiral Keppel communicated the intelligence which he lately received of the superior fleet in Brest, and in readiness for sea, with his sentiments thereon, in which I entirely agree with him.

FROM KEPPEL

Victory, Lizard bearing N. 12 E., 19 leagues,
21 June 1778.

The intelligence found in the captain of the French frigate's apartment seems, upon comparing it with the accounts received by Mr Stephens some time past (and which was by your Lordship's directions sent to me), so like truth that I do not know how to doubt of the French having twenty-seven ships of the line ready to come to sea. The fleet at present together under my command, twenty ships of the line, being so short in numbers to the French fleet of the line, besides their extraordinary superiority of frigates, obliges me to proceed as my instructions direct to St Helen's. Upon being satisfied of the force with me being manifestly inferior to the Brest fleet, I will call off Plymouth and take the Duke if she is ready, if not direct her to follow to St Helen's.

My pride might have induced me to a battle with the French fleet at all risks; but when I consider the defeat of the fleet under my command, which is always *possible* but more so when greatly inferior in numbers, would in all probability be attended with fatal consequences, I dare not put myself in the scale against so much danger to my country, though I have an unhappiness upon this occasion beyond any situation I have ever before been in. I am [etc.].

FROM THE KING

Queen's House, 25 June 1778.

I cannot conceal that I am much hurt at the resolution taken by Admiral Keppel of instantly returning to St Helen's on hearing that the Brest fleet amounts to 27 sail of the line. At the same time he says that 5 ships of the line have sailed, consequently that must reduce the Brest fleet to 22 sail. I fear this step will greatly discourage the ardour of the country : I therefore hope at your Cabinet meeting this day it may be settled to represent unto me the propriety of ordering the Admiral to return to his station. I own I think the part he has taken may enable the French to seize the Gibraltar reinforcements.

You will perceive I write the thoughts that first occur on reading the letters you have communicated unto me.

FROM KEPPEL

Victory, St Helen's Road, June [? 27th].[1]

I conclude Lieutenant Berkeley has been with you long before this with my dispatches, that acquaints your Lordship of my having judged it proper from the state of the Brest fleet's superiority of the line and frigates to return to St Helen's, as my instructions direct me in case of the fleet under my command being manifestly inferior to that of the Brest fleet. I think the more I have considered the whole information, both before and since I left St Helen's, I cannot have a doubt of the French being in force at least twenty-seven ships of two and three decks, ready to come out of Brest, and five more large ships getting forward, with frigates innumerable.

If I had ever been in sight of their fleet at sea, it would have been too late to have retired and,

---

[1] The fleet returned to St Helen's in the forenoon of June 27.

my fleet once defeated, perhaps the fate of England determined by it. This consideration is some relief to my mind, which I do assure your Lordship has had much anxiety upon it. To be always right in nice points for decision is more than can be expected : to attempt honestly ought to be expected, and in that situation I find myself. To have fought with such inferiority, and to have been totally routed, would have merited censure ; it would have been justly said that I had proper orders to return to St Helen's, and that an additional force was collecting in case of such an event. I am returned for that force, and with it I shall be ready to obey any orders sent me.

Captain Windsor saw five French ships close in with Ushant, which proves to me more that their force in Brest permits of their proceeding without fear ; if they continue to think so after the English fleet is in greater force, good consequence may come from it. Your line of battle, I hope, may and will be sufficiently increased ; but I fear you are at present without remedy for frigates, so materially necessary, and the great numbers the French have must and will operate most advantageously for them in battle. I think from the list and size of them that they may sooner or later attempt a stroke upon your guard in the Downs ; it is certainly a very tempting object, and within the probability of success, weak as it now is.

Our frigates appear in their sailing to be greatly superior to the two French frigates that were stopped, but singly not a fair match for ships of 32 guns with heavy metal.

The French officers and crews incommode the ships greatly ; and for that reason I cannot but wish Admiral Pye may be ordered to take them away directly, and the frigates secured for his

Majesty's pleasure upon them, that every ship may have their men again. Your Lordship will easily imagine, insignificant as this seizure is, that the taking proper care of it has been and is very troublesome to a fleet that is always to be kept in readiness for actual service. I am [etc.].

ANONYMOUS

My Lord—How can you go on employing Opposition admirals? Lord Howe and his brother have not done their utmost to distress the rebels, by which America is lost to this country; Mr Keppel has returned (if I am rightly informed) with the whole Western squadron consisting of 22 ships of the line, of which 5 were of 100 and 90 guns apiece, *because* the Brest fleet, from papers aboard the Licorne, appears to be of 25 ships of the line and 2 of 50 guns ready or *nearly ready* to put to sea. This our Admiral has taken upon him to do when two great fleets of merchant ships were expected from the West Indies and it is the time for the return of the East Indiamen, so that 5 or 6 large men of war with a few frigates sent out of Brest might take them all, and sweep the British Channel cleaner than Van Tromp did the Medway.

There are but two reasons to be assigned for such conduct: either that Mr Keppel is become so nervous as to have lost all his spirit, or he is so factious as to sacrifice the honour and trade and wealth of his country to party views. And I am inclined to believe the latter is the case; for I am told his Lieutenant Berkeley and his private letters immediately communicated to the Opposition the *cause* of his return, to wit, *that Lord Sandwich had sent him to sea with a fleet not capable of facing the enemy, being deficient in numbers and strength and sickly*; and the Opposition and the newspapers have everywhere been circulating the same, commending the prudence of the Admiral in returning, and condemning Lord Sandwich as wholly unfit for his post, which Mr Keppel ought immediately to be put into or the nation will be undone ; and I have heard that the same admiral, when the King and Lord Sandwich were at the naval review, contradicted his Lordship upon every naval point before his Majesty in order to impress an idea of his ignorance and insufficiency.

Now, my Lord, my motion is that our fleet was able to deal with the enemy's, if at sea ; but that if it were not equal, the commander-in-chief ought not to have returned in so critical a time, but have sent home an account of his intelligence concerning the enemy and prayed more force as *earnestly* as he thought was necessary. He should therefore be tried at a court martial for such cowardly, factious, and un-officerlike conduct, and never be employed again. You should, after the receipt of his letters by Mr Berkeley, have procured the King's permission to dismiss such an admiral ; and when at Portsmouth you should have done so, and sent out the fleet directly under the next officer, or called upon Lord Hawke, Sir George Pocock, or Mr Graves, or any other officer that it is known would fight, and not suffer yourself and the public to be thus served. If his Majesty *will* employ Opposition admirals of great political connexions and family, he will undo his ministry, the nation, and himself.

I know of no charge against you, excepting this timidity and the keeping at the Board Palliser and Mulgrave, who cannot attend it nor assist you, where one *good seaman* in time of war should always be present.[1]

FROM KEPPEL

Victory, St Helen's, [29 ?] June 1778.

The plan that your Lordship wished to be brought into execution, when you did me the honour to converse with me this morning, in order to bring the Vengeance and Defiance to join the fleet has occupied my thoughts ever since you went away ; but I foresee the distress it would in the present state of the twenty ships here bring us. Without taking one man from the ships, the deficiency from the numbers sending every day to the hospital will render them very weak, and make it imprudent to put the plan in execution ; instead of which it seems necessary to demand marines for the ships to make up their deficiencies, not less than 150 or 200. The Vengeance and Defiance I should hope to see joined before sailing, but to unman the ships of present service for it I really apprehend to be dangerous in every consideration.

I am sure I wish to be gone : my orders say I am to proceed when four of the ships are joined. I know that it is important to the last degree the fleet's getting to sea, but then it is more important that it should be in equal force to the French, ship for ship in the line, and the country have to hope and expect a happy issue. I have so often expressed my fears for my country in the danger of

[1] Hawke and Pocock were both over seventy years old ; Graves had lost the confidence of the country (see Vol. I). Palliser and Mulgrave were serving at sea with Keppel while remaining members of the Board of Admiralty. There was no other sea officer on the Board.

a battle unequally fought that I shall say no more upon [it] but to hope the King's servants will consider it seriously for the sake of his Majesty and his dominions. I shall have the honour to see your Lordship to-morrow, in the meantime, I am [etc.].

TO KEPPEL

Portsmouth, 29 June 1778.

I cannot help owning that the letter I have just received from you gives me the greatest concern. Every effort is making to give you an addition of at least four sail of the line in order to enable you to be near the strength of the Brest fleet, which we suppose to be 25 of the line and two fifty-gun ships. I know of no means of being sure of furnishing those four ships unless we can get the Vengeance and Defiance out of the harbour, which may be done by the measure I proposed to you this morning, and which I flattered myself you had approved ; that measure is founded on the rules of the service, that every ship should have the full establishment of marines, and should discharge seamen if she has a greater proportion of that class.

Let me make it my request to you that you may aid me in this point ; for if I return to London without being able to say that your fleet will be ready to sail again in a very few days, much well-founded uneasiness will appear, not only among the trading part of the nation, but with every person who has the welfare of the kingdom at heart. I am [etc.].

FROM KEPPEL

Victory, St Helen's, 2 July 1778.

I thank your Lordship for the extract you sent me of the French account of the action between the two frigates. I desire no other testimony of Captain Marshall's and his people's superior behaviour. Let us all do as well, and the nation will be well served.

I don't wonder at the alarms of the merchants, and wishing the fleet at sea ; but when they do that they should hope also that it is in force for the services required of it. The King's Councils have determined twenty-four ships' force sufficient ; I will sail when I am joined by that addition of ships. I have never lost an hour's time : I never will. My proceedings have ever been with good motives, void of fear for myself, yet full of anxiety for the King's flag and safety of his home dominions. Your public letters as yet do not tell me that his Majesty is satisfied that I have done for the best : I cannot say I feel myself well treated in this particular, and I don't think I merited it. I could not refuse myself expressing to your Lordship it's not escaping my notice.

[The Formidable has joined. Asks for any intelligence the Admiralty may receive. The French ' by their venturing large ships off Ushant believe themselves in sufficient force.']

I am [etc.].

[The 'answer to the foregoing' copied on the back of this letter runs :

I have no doubt but that when you come to any real business you will give sufficient grounds for the fullest approbation of your conduct.

Nothing has yet happened that has furnished with such an opportunity. The bringing in the French ships is, in my opinion, to be considered more upon political than military grounds ; therefore I do not think that it is advisable at once to declare publicly that it was right, though I have no scruple to tell you as a private man that, after the behaviour of the captain of the Licorne, your bringing the frigates in was perfectly right, and what I should have done myself in the same situation.]

FROM KEPPEL

Victory, St Helen's, 3 July 1778.

I have been considering very seriously the matter that we talked over regarding the rendezvous, and have formed my opinion after the most serious reflections upon it. The original rendezvous off Brest is certainly the most proper relating to the port of Brest, and as such has been heretofore preferred. Ships great and small were in no danger, though it happened, which it sometimes did, that the fleet was from the station ; but times and circumstances are changed, small forces cannot now cruise upon this station if the fleet is absent without much hazard.

For the covering of convoys expected home, a western station as far as Scilly, extending north and south from the latitude of 49.30 N. to 49.00 N., is best ; but the danger of this station, if the fleet remains long upon it, is that the Brest fleet might then run up Channel without the knowledge of the English fleet. The Lizard, for the rendezvous of junction, is certainly preferable both as to the joining and covering England, and its trade will have succour from it ; but these convoys out of the question, and the Brest fleet alone the object, off the entrance of Brest is without doubt the place. If that fleet is resolved to fight the English fleet, and will not refuse to follow it to mid-Channel, they will lose the advantage of the nearness of port, and if beat may neither get all away nor endanger our fleet with their shore.

You have here my Lord my fair and candid reasoning : do as you please with it, and I am [etc.].

FROM KEPPEL

Victory, St Helen's, 3 July 1778.

In addition to what I have troubled you with in my two other letters of this day's date, thoughts have crowded upon me which I think it proper to trouble your Lordship upon. The putting into port for three or four days' refreshments may during the cruise be necessary ; the repairing so high up Channel as St Helen's inconvenient in many particulars, and the nearness to Portsmouth, makes every officer almost believe we are in port for more time than is intended, for which reason my thoughts will be upon Torbay ; and the reinforcements your Lordship may be able to bring forward may be collected and rendezvous in Plymouth Sound.

The Shrewsbury goes into dock the 11th ; that ship, the Terrible, Centaur, and Vigilant are ships most likely to be first ready. Your Lordship will have time to consider how far you think my proposal proper long before these ships, I fear, may be quite ready. I am [etc.].

FROM KEPPEL

St Helen's, 5 July 1778.

The return to your Lordship's dispatches of yesterday informs you that the Vengeance was joined. Captain Clements is doing his best to put that ship in condition for sea and service. The Defiance is still in the harbour. My last orders direct me to proceed when I am joined by two ships of the line in addition to the Formidable. I cannot guess when the Defiance will join, the southerly wind checks her in the harbour.

When I am at sea you may depend upon my doing all in my power to cover the trade safe up Channel. I cannot take upon myself sailing with less force than my instructions determine to be sufficient; to use the force afterwards is my duty, and I hope there is not a doubt of my exerting it to the utmost for the honour of the British flag and safety of the kingdom. I wish I could be sure the French had positive orders to seek the King's fleet. I think some advantage might be made of it, I mean, if it was *certain* to encourage them to fight mid-Channel; but I fear they will be wiser and keep near their own coast, where in the end of a battle their frigates must operate very disadvantageously to the English fleet even after it had beaten the French.

I hope Lord Shuldham will have put the Duke in condition for service. I will also hope his Lordship will send her, and the other ships and vessels that are to join me, out the moment I can send notice of my being near. The rendezvous off the Lizard will be a protection to the trade and the best of all for safe junction, but after collecting all the force that is intended at present it may be advisable to stretch across the sea. The ships that remain will be getting together properly in Plymouth Sound.

I grow uneasy for the Fox and Lively.[1] Captain Windsor's taking the French merchant ships has the appearance of indiscretion, which differs from the opinion I had of him.

I am really much obliged to your Lordship for your ready compliance in the appointment of another gunner to the Victory, and I am [etc.].

FROM KEPPEL

St Helen's, 6 July 1778.

The fleet I came in with is ready to proceed to sea as soon as the Defiance joins ; the number then will be what I am directed to sail with. If the Worcester is ordered I shall have in her a ship fit for immediate service—I don't know her wants or what will detain her. The Thunderer must follow. The winds that will bring her here most probably will take the fleet to sea, as I must hope the number of ships will be made less by that time.

The Fox is arrived : I wish her captain had not stopped the French vessels. The Milford will join the fleet to-night, and I am led to hope the Andromeda will do so to-morrow : I shall then have four copper frigates. The Arethusa most probably will be left, she will soon get to the station. I am in pain for the Lively.

The Stirling Castle and Courageux grow sickly every day ; and to add to this distress I am this

[1] The Lively 20, Captain Robert Biggs, was captured on July 9 outside Brest by the Iphigénie frigate and Curieuse corvette. She was retaken in the Channel on 29 July 1781 by the Perseverance—Abstract of Progress and Lacour-Gayet, 128.

moment informed that the Victory's principal surgeon's mate must be landed with a very bad fever. I have written to Admiral Pye to ask him to assist me in this want.

I have sent Lord Amherst's letter to you to Admiral Pye. The very wretched recruits that the land officers would put into your ships must be resisted : new raised men mixed with disciplined ones seems equitable ; but wretches such as I know they have twice attempted to put into the ships in the harbour ought and must be resisted, or disgrace will come upon the flag when put to the trial.

I understand the Duke is in the Sound, which makes me consider her as in a probable situation to join when the fleet calls off the Sound for her. I am [etc.].

FROM PALLISER

Formidable, St Helen's, 6 July 1778.

Before I had the honour to receive your Lordship's letter I had had several serious and confidential conversations with Admiral Keppel upon the matters you mention, and think I can safely assure your Lordship of his disposition being of the fairest and most honourable kind, and that he is perfectly satisfied so far as relates to your Lordship's conduct towards him, of which he always speaks in terms of praise that is due to you. Therefore, let me beg of you to entertain the strongest dependence that when a proper opportunity offers he will acquit himself to the King and his country as becomes a man of honour, and that we shall all do our duties as far as we are enabled. Be well assured likewise that I shall always most readily contribute my poor but best and warmest assistance to your Lordship by every possible means ; indeed you have a full right to expect it, the numberless instances of your Lordship's friendship and good offices received at your hands binds me by every tie of gratitude to be attentive to whatever concerns your Lordship.

I don't wonder at the general wish of the nation for the fleet to be at sea. None wishes it more than those in it, at the same time wishing to be in a state to be able to perform what is expected from us. It is not your Lordship's fault that the fleet is not in more forwardness : it was no reasoning of ours that we should not equip long ago for fear of alarming France, whilst they were exerting themselves to the utmost in equipping theirs, and thus they have got the start of us. To offer battle with a great inferiority, surely, is neither good policy nor the way to make amends for being behindhand. However, I hope ere long (according to the sea phrase) we shall fetch up our leeway, put us only upon an equality or near it.

I am now in the Formidable ; and to complete her whole numbers have just received 24 young Irish landmen, with whom I am satisfied. They were raised for the Thunderer : when we meet her, Captain Walsingham may have them in exchange for my Scarborough bounty volunteers.

The Terrible and Defiance are got to Spithead. The men of the first are worse and worse, so that all men bestowed on her are thrown away ; the other ship is in the utmost state of confusion yet, men and other things tumbling headlong into her. I wish the Thunderer and Worcester with us. I understand we shall find the Duke in Plymouth Sound. All these ships together would be a fine reinforcement.

By the French equipping 5 more ships of the

line in all haste, it is evident they mean to meet us with their utmost force. The whole nation ought and I hope will contribute to enable you to keep pace with an increasing force, for whilst they forbear to divide their fleet, and it is evident they mean to give us battle with their grand fleet, every other service should be suspended till our fleet is at least upon an equality. The stake France has depending on the event is not to be compared with that of this country, whose very existence depends upon her fleet.   I have [etc.].

FROM KEPPEL

St Helen's, Tuesday evening, 7 July 1778.

I had great pleasure yesterday afternoon in the arrival of the Yarmouth from the Leeward Islands, understanding that her convoy was well forward towards the Downs, an event of much importance to the commerce and of course to the whole nation. This afternoon discovered several ships steering up Channel with light westerly winds.   I thought I observed a vessel or two among them speaking to them, which determined me to send a cutter and the Milford into the offing to give succour if wanted; and during the whole afternoon there has been seen at least forty sail steering up Channel.   The Proserpine goes to sea this evening, only with an intent to cover the rear of these ships and get in again some time to-morrow.

I have your Lordship's two letters of the 5th and 6th, and have only to observe for your satisfaction and information that the rendezvous that I have fixed upon off the Lizard is for the certain junction of the force now collecting; and as a good cover to the homeward-bound trade Scilly,

Ushant, and the Lizard are undoubtedly the most advisable points to answer the most benefit. And so soon as I am collected, the first easterly wind may carry the fleet to the opening of Brest, and if clear weather show ourselves to the fleet of France and leave it to them to come out or not.

The state of the Vengeance and Defiance I did not mean to mention to your Lordship as complaining of their confusion, but the natural consequence from the hasty equipment of them, and that time alone could bring them into order.

The Defiance has not yet joined ; the Worcester is a good recruit, she will not be able to join this day or two. If the Defiance gets to me sooner, and the wind proves fair, the Worcester must follow and so must the Thunderer ; probably the latter may get in sight to-morrow, but will have at least two or three days' business. I expect the Andromeda to-morrow, and the Arethusa on Thursday or Friday ; the Lively is now the frigate that I am in doubt about, I wish she was safe in. If the Duke sailed yesterday we must see her to-morrow morning. What to direct about the Terrible I can't determine ; the Centaur, Vigilant, and her may as well proceed to Plymouth as they get ready, and there wait for orders such as may be expedient to give them either from the Admiralty or myself.[1]

The question relative to frigates belonging to the French seems now the only matter to be

---

[1] The fleet sailed on the 9th, having been joined by the Defiance the evening before, and by the Duke soon after getting under way. The Worcester joined on the 14th, the Thunderer next day, and the Shrewsbury, Centaur, and Vigilant on the 17th. The Terrible joined off Ushant in the evening of the 19th (Master's log, Foudroyant).

On July 13 Keppel wrote to the Admiralty : ' After the knowledge I have of the different reinforcements being so near in point of time, I think it indispensably my duty to collect the whole possible force before I leave the English coast.'

II.   I

answered. I wish Captain Windsor was clear of his French seizures ; there does not show the least pretence for detaining them. I am [etc.].

P.S.—I will explain my rendezvous more largely in my letter to Mr Stephens to-morrow. If your Lordship is not prepared upon my question relative to the French frigates in future, I must hold back seizing any more of them till I am instructed, which directions, if they do not catch me before my sailing, I think can't fail of getting in time to the Worcester.

TO KEPPEL

Admiralty, 8 July 1778.

The only answer that can be given to your question, what to do with any French frigates you may meet with, is to refer you to your former instructions which direct you to take them in case they persevere in watching your fleet. The additional instructions which you have received lately will authorize you to take everything belonging to France that falls in your way, in case they commit hostilities against us ; but for some reason or other they do not seem eager to begin, therefore it is greatly for our advantage to avoid an open rupture till our preparations are further advanced and our trade got in, and it is extremely material that we should be strong in argument that we are not the aggressors, though it will not be discreet to give up any material point to that political question.

As things now stand we shall justify the detention of the frigates you have brought in from the improper behaviour of the captain of the

Licorne, which requires satisfaction to be given to us ; but we do not mean as yet to attack the trade of France, for which reason orders are given to restore Captain Windsor's prizes without delay, whose eagerness in this business is not to be justified. If he had not been an officer of whom we all of us think well, he would have met with a strong reprimand, as no orders he is in possession of can justify the measure he has taken, which possibly may draw on a war and give a strong argument from our antagonists against us.

I will sum up all I have to say upon this subject in one word : we have no objection to a war, or to being called the aggressors, if we can strike a material stroke at first. Taking a line of battle ship or some rich Indiaman would be deemed an adequate cause ; but a frigate or two or a few inconsiderable merchant ships would not come up to that idea as long as the French abstain from attacking our trade, which the safe arrival of the late convoys from the Straits and the West Indies shows to be the measure they now adopt.[1] I am [etc.].

FROM NORTH

Bushey Park, 12 July 1778.

I send you enclosed a letter of important intelligence, a great deal of which I believe, although the author towards the end of his letter speaks doubtfully of his means of information. What appears to me the least credible is that France, being in expectation of a junction with Spain, should risk an engagement with Mr Keppel's fleet. Nothing can induce her to

[1] See below, p. 126.

take such a step but a great and decided
superiority ; this she will certainly not have
if the five additional ships of the line which are
sent after Mr Keppel should join him in time.
Important, therefore, as the stake is for which
we contend, it is devoutedly to be wished that
France should try her strength with us before
Spain declares herself.

From the frequent interviews between the
rebel agents and Captain Jones, we may depend
upon some attempts being made soon upon the
coasts of this island ; and, indeed, all that part
of the letter which relates to the design of France
to insult our maritime places with fleets of frigates
agrees perfectly well with some intelligence I
received about a year ago, and therefore appears
to me very credible.[1]

This puts me in mind of an important matter
which had really escaped my memory. When
I was last in town I met the Duke of Northumberland at Court, who told me that they were very
uneasy in the north for want of two ships of war
which they expected to be furnished with by the
Admiralty. He renewed their offer of providing
the seamen, and appears to have given up his
request of a particular protection for them, seeing,
I daresay, how impossible it is for the Admiralty
to grant it.

There is certainly no part of the coast where
such material mischief can be done in as short
time as in his Grace's neighbourhood.   I am [etc.].

[Enclosure.]

INTELLIGENCE FROM PARIS, 2 JULY 1778

Captain [Paul] Jones is still here by the
connivance of Dr Fr[anklin] to assist in planning

[1] Cp. *Corr.*, 2389, 2391.

the enterprise intended by this court. A. Lee and J. Adams, not being in the secret, are angry at the delay and threaten to suspend him; the Dr says, let him answer to Congress for neglect. He is intimately acquainted with the coasts of England; and the object of France is to send several fleets of frigates on different expeditions against the east and west coasts of England with troops on board to burn and destroy all they can. And if Keppel's fleet should be beat, then to make a regular and powerful invasion.

Spain has certainly agreed to accede to the treaties with America as soon as the ratifications of Congress arrive here; and Count d'Aranda has the necessary powers in his pocket. We expect the fleets will join in the Bay and act with France immediately after. The circuitous expedition lately mentioned is laid aside for the present, for want of some ships of the line expected from Holland for French account, but pretendedly in part for Spain. They won't be ready till September: I shall know more in time.

The Court of Vienna are displeased with France on the Bavarian business. A declaration, equivalent to a declaration of war, is ready and called a declaration of reprisal and hostility.

I hear the Brest fleet will certainly endeavour to intercept your fleets and vessels, and if Keppel appears as certainly attack him. Five Guernsey and Jersey privateers have been brought into the western ports of France by the frigates. Captain Amiel is gone by Dunkirk to Flushing to fit out and command a ship of war under a Congress commission. You may depend Deane only embarked in the frigate for a day or two's concealment, and that he went on board the admiral at sea and will continue there till arrived. The passing the

Western Islands by d'Estaing's fleet, I hear, was sent by a corvette; and it is thought that the plan of their first operations was sent to M. de Sartine. I can learn nothing with any certainty, and I shall deal less in opinion and conjecture.

FROM KEPPEL

Victory, off the Bolt Head, 13 July 1778.

One of the cutters I left at St Helen's when I sailed brought me your Lordship's letter of the 8th. It describes very clearly the delicacy in commencing hostilities and the objects that might be deemed adequate; but I must observe that to speak to French frigates and not bring them into the fleet is exceeding embarrassing, and for that reason, if taking of them is rather wished should be avoided, it will be advisable not to speak to them but leave off the pursuit of them in time. The very great numbers of their frigates and their natural rights in the seas will ever permit them in peace to watch our fleets. If the Licorne and Belle Poule had joined the Victory it must have ended in the utmost civility on my part; and surely while England is in a dispute with her colonies, the English squadrons at sea have a just claim to be satisfied that what they meet upon the seas is in no way employed for the services of America. And the admiral of the fleet cruising only required first civility by his chasing ships that the ships spoke to might come to him. The Pallas was indeed seized in consequence of the behaviour of the Licorne.

As the seizing more ships of the description of frigates does not seem adopted by the explanation of Mr Stephen's letter to me upon that subject, my orders must guide me, and be assured my Lord I shall avoid plunging hastily the nation into a war upon any ideas of my own separated from the exact letter of my instructions.   I am [etc.].

FROM KEPPEL

Victory, off the Eddystone, 16 July 1778.

The prevailing calms, I imagine, detain the Centaur and Vigilant from getting down Channel. Such an additional force so near as they must be seems of the utmost importance.   This junction and the Shrewsbury's will make the fleet twenty-nine ships.   I trust with such a force we shall not complain that the French are thirty-two.

I really grow impatient for the wind's getting fresh easterly.   As yet no time has been lost, the want of wind has been such that little westing could be made.   I have got the Rattlesnake off the Lizard, and I am dispatching the Andromeda with the Alert cutter off Ushant.   The Shrewsbury I hope will be out of Plymouth this day.

Lord Shuldham tells me in this letter that he is fitting the Blenheim.   The measure is certainly proper, but I must hope that Monsieur d'Orvilliers and I shall have decided our meeting before the Blenheim can join.   The numbers of men the fleet are continually sending to the hospitals made me think it necessary in my letter to Lord Shuldham to beg some assistance, if he could give it without distressing himself too much.   His Lordship with much expedition sent me three tenders with seamen and marines : I could have disposed of the whole, but his readiness pleased me so that

I immediately returned him one of the tenders without breaking in upon her numbers; the others I gave to the ships in want, a few to each. The Courageux and Stirling Castle's deficiencies I made up with marines; I also gave the Thunderer a few.

If I had not feared giving displeasure where I don't wish to offend, I would have sent Captain Walsingham's party *of soldiers on shore* and given him a complete number of marines; indeed they would have been raw and undisciplined men as well as the soldiers, but yet as men really belonging to the fleet they must be more desirable. Walsingham's spirit in joining of me so expeditiously I feel obligation to him for, and it does him credit. If he is ill manned his numbers must tell to help him; the smallpox having got into his ship, the over complement cannot be broke in upon without the danger of spreading it.

The fleet in general are now complete, though I am kept in alarm for fear of the sickness increasing on board the two sickly ships—the Courageux and Stirling Castle.

The Victory has a few fevers, but I hope it will not increase. I am [etc.].

FROM LORD SHULDHAM

Plymouth, 17 July 1778.

My dear Lord—As I am sure it will give your Lordship pleasure to hear of the good condition of the fleet under Admiral Keppel's command, and that he has left the neighbourhood of this port perfectly satisfied, I send you copies of some letters to me from him since he has been off the

Sound, in consequence of his application to me for men to supply the places of several who had fallen sick on board some of the ships, and which was immediately complied with.

If the Board intends we should continue our endeavour in getting the Blenheim ready, which almost our whole force is employed upon, I beg to remind your Lordship to order her complement to be raised to the usual establishment and the completion of her stores and provisions, which however (to save time) the Commissioner and I have already taken upon us to order. In a conference I have had with the Builder on the subject and condition of this ship, he tells me that 'though it might not be proper to send her upon a foreign voyage or winter service, in his opinion her complaints are not so great but that she is likely to answer all the purposes of a ship of that rate at this season of the year'; and except in point of men, the arrival of which is uncertain, I think she will be ready in a week or ten days. I submit this to your Lordship's consideration and have [etc.].

I am to inform your Lordship that the Shrewsbury joined Admiral Keppel's fleet at 10 o'clock last night; and I see a large ship now going down Channel, with all the sail she can crowd and the wind at north, which I take to be either the Centaur or Vigilant.

KEPPEL TO SHULDHAM

[Copy.]

Off Plymouth Sound, Wednesday noon,
15 July 1778.

My dear Lord—I believe we have more trouble in disposing of the men you were so good as to send me than there was in the raising of them. You have a good number of marines. I could have wished to have landed the soldiers and kept the marines in their places, but that measure I don't find I have power to put in execution. I have disposed of 85 marines and 80 seamen, and I flatter myself the fleet may be called very tolerably equipped. The old-commissioned ships are capital ; the hurried ships want discipline, which every fresh day gives them.

I fear the Blenheim will not be so much worth her labour as the same force employed upon the Royal George and Defence would be.

If Captain Ross [of the Shrewsbury] comes out to-morrow he will join me here; but if later, he must look for me first off the Lizard and then off Brest. I begin to grow impatient, but the light winds are so prevalent that hitherto little could have been gained by the warmest endeavours. I wonder the two ships, Centaur and Vigilant, don't appear in sight. I am [etc.].

KEPPEL TO SHULDHAM

[Copy.]

Thursday afternoon, 16 July 1778, off the Sound.

I cannot refuse writing one line to you as a take leave. Your good men in the Joyce tender I returned you because you had behaved so handsomely to me. The officer will tell you that I did not by any officer look at them, I thought you must want men as well as I did. Ross will be out to-night ; I must give him a day to set to rights. If the French fleet continue at sea, and the two ships from Portsmouth join, I hope three or four days will give me a sight of that fleet. I have just dispatched the Andromeda and Alert cutter off of Ushant. I am [etc.].

FROM KEPPEL

Off the Lizard, Friday noon, 17 July 1778.

The Shrewsbury joined me this morning, and I feel much obliged to her captain for his extraordinary dispatch in getting out so soon. The two ships from Spithead [the Centaur and Vigilant] are in sight; and as soon as I have given the captains their instructions I shall proceed off Brest and continue upon the Ushant rendezvous.

A battle with the French fleet must depend upon them; if they are eager, I shall endeavour to get them a little from their own coast, but I am apprehensive they will not allow me to lead them from their land.

I send the Little Hazard cutter into Falmouth, that no time may be lost in giving your Lordship the earliest information of my steering with the King's fleet under my command in pursuit of the important object of meeting the fleet of France. I am [etc.].

[*P.S.*]—I leave the Good Intent cutter off the Lizard rendezvous for being in the way of ships coming to join me; his orders are to remain till next Friday and then repair to the Ushant rendezvous.

FROM NORTH

Bushey Park, 18 July 1778.

I send you a letter from Robinson and a paper which came enclosed to me in the middle of the night. The French having taken this step, I suppose no difficulty or delicacy need prevent us from giving orders to take and destroy all French vessels without exception. But upon

this one should wish to have the sentiments of
the Cabinet, and I do not know how to collect
them.   I will write, however, to those who are
within reach, and either fix a meeting or procure
their opinions without one.[1]   I am [etc.].

FROM LORD THURLOW

[*c.* July 20.][2]

My dear Lord—It is impossible to avoid
observing the embarrassment occasioned by the
equivocal situation of things between this country
and France, or to be insensible of the inconveniences, both foreign and domestic, which arise
from it.   But while it is thought necessary to
endure that situation, the consequences of it must
be submitted to—using all possible precautions
to lessen the mischief.   If I could contribute to
this, I should follow my inclination no less than
my duty.

Your Lordship takes much pains to persuade
me that the preference given to privateers, in
prizes, is inconvenient to the King's service.   In
a matter wherein I have no kind of judgment or
knowledge your opinion must decide me, even
against the invariable course of all past times.   But
it does not depend upon me to act on this occasion.

As to the rest of your papers, I have read
them, and they seem to leave the matter precisely
in the same situation in which it was the last
time I conversed with you upon it.   The paper
of the 28th of March is general, and does not

---

[1] On July 17 North wrote to Lord Dartmouth (Lord Privy
Seal) to say that intelligence had been received the previous night
from Dunkirk that France had declared war, and that Lord
Weymouth had called a meeting of the Cabinet (Dartmouth MSS.,
ii. 467).   See also *Corr.*, 2393.

[2] The Alert was captured on July 17 (Abstract of Progress).

expressly indicate the actual disposition or appropriation of the vessels to be taken *before* declaration of war. It is silent on that inter-mediate time. Either by accident or manage-ment, the same observation occurs on the letter of the 10th July. Their letters of marque and instructions, both to the King's ships and privateers, would undoubtedly speak more dis-tinctly; but the general letter goes no farther than to order the vessels to be *brought into their ports*; and if this be the extent of your intelligence, I confess I am disappointed. I thought you had known of their letters of marque being carried to the same extent as ours, namely to the appro-priation of the captures.

The material article consists, in your intelli-gence, that the Lively and Alert have been appropriated and employed in the French King's service. I suppose that in a question between States, the conduct of one settles the law, at least so far as to justify the other. I am [etc.].

I believe the usual form of proclamation has been reciting the conduct of the enemy, and making [that] the ostensible cause of your own.

FROM NORTH

Monday morn. [20 July 1778].[1]

Upon a subject on which I am not clear that the opinions of the Cabinet will be uniform, I do

[1] This seems to be the date, rather than Monday, 13th, although the Admiralty gave orders in the sense of this letter on the 19th. At 1.29 P.M. on the 18th, the King wrote to North: ' You have already this morning settled with Lord Sandwich. . . . There can be no reason to delay issuing the orders till a Cabinet is summoned; what is so clear ought never to be delayed for that formality ' (*Corr.*, 2393).

not like to have a very material measure depend upon mine. Lord Weymouth is I believe in the neighbourhood, and Lord George Germain in London as well as my Lord President and Lord Chancellor ; could not the sentiments of three or four of us be taken in the course of the day ? If the French have begun hostilities in a single instance (which I daresay they have), I think that our admiral upon receiving certain information of it should make every capture he can. Otherwise I should think it more advisable not to consider the capture of the two French frigates as the beginning of the war, and to continue as if nothing had happened to act under his instructions for a short time, until the East and West India fleets are out of danger. These are my first thoughts on receiving your letter, but I desire you not to act upon them without taking some other opinion. I am [etc.].

FROM KEPPEL

Victory, at sea, 21 July 1778.

The letter I write Mr Stephens fully informs your Lordship of the Victory's disaster in the gale of wind yesterday. I am unable to collect the defects of the whole fleet : I hope nothing but what may be set to rights during the course of the day.

I have wondered at not seeing the French fleet ; if they have not returned into Brest, they may be to the westward of the fleet, and if at sea most likely had their share of disaster.[1]

[1] On the 25th the King wrote to Lord North : ' By the note I received the last evening from Lord Sandwich, I trust Admiral Keppel will get between the French squadron and their coast, but do not think we can have [news] of an action before Monday ' [27th] (*Corr.*, 2396).

I send a cutter in with this, and shall send the ship into Plymouth whose main yard I may take for the Victory.

I am always uneasy about the junction of single ships while the French are in such force, lest accident and wind at times take our fleet from its exact station, and the French fall in with single ships looking for me.   But it is impossible to guard against everything.

The Andromeda and Alert, that I sent for intelligence, I have not seen since : I have few moments unattended with trouble.   I hope, how-ever, that all will end well, and am [etc.].

Every day I imagine will show me a French frigate.   They are out for the purpose of watching ; and without they are brought to action it cannot be prevented.   I called the Milford and Fox from chase last Sunday of one that they were within two miles of, but could not have spoke to without losing the fleet.

KEPPEL TO SHULDHAM

Victory, at sea, 24 July 1778.

I have been two days in sight of the French : the option of action has been with them.   They are at present to windward near hull down, both fleets upon a wind steering to the south-west. The French fleet seems to sail well.   The force of the two squadrons forbids my separating ; and therefore unless both are agreed to close I know not when it will happen.   We count 40 sail, great and small ; whether their line consists of 32 ships, I have never been near enough to determine.[1]

---

[1] The French were sighted and reported by the Valiant shortly after noon on the 23rd (Master's log, Valiant).

I hope the Blenheim won't attempt to join. I think if the French were accidentally between her and the English fleet, she would run much risk of being intercepted.

The Thunderer I have detained, and flatter myself her force will tell favourably.   I have [etc.].

FROM KEPPEL

Victory, 29 July 1778.

The French fleet's retiring for so many days, and the little prospect I saw of ever getting to battle in a line, determined me the moment the wind gave an opportunity to get to their rear, or any part of their line, in the best way that offered. The 27th was the first change in the wind, and my public letter relates it as minutely and truly as possible.   The object of the French was at the masts and rigging, and they have crippled the fleet in that respect beyond any degree I ever before saw.   That I have beat the French there cannot be a doubt, and their retreat in the night is shameful and disgraceful to them as a nation after the fair opportunity I gave them to form their line.   I was induced to it as a temptation that the following day might have been decisive, but they certainly were beat so much as to be without hopes for a second trial.   The Victory and Bretagne were but a little asunder ;   the Ville de Paris was as close to me as it was possible, but being upon different tacks we soon separated. I am [etc.].

Every exertion must be used to replace and secure the damages in the masts.   We are at present doing what we can, but it will be requisite for me to anchor the fleet in Plymouth Sound and Cawsand Bay for the more speedy reparation of defects.

FROM PALLISER

[Endorsed by Lord Sandwich : ' Supposed to be July 31st 1778, talks a little about the action, a good deal of reasoning not proper to be made public.']¹

I troubled your Lordship with a short letter on the 28th when I had only just time for it, understanding a vessel was going away immediately. Although I am now more at leisure I can't add much more respecting our encounter on the 27th. However, for your Lordship's private information, I send you a summary account such as I am able to give of it. I have seen your Lordship's letter of the 18th to Admiral Keppel ; and as your Lordship allows it, I can't help troubling you with my sentiments and conjectures about some matters concerning the service.

From the French stealing away in the night, I conclude they are very much damaged and got into Brest the next day or the day after.

As to the surmise that they were to go to Quiberon Bay, I think it is very probable if they had any intention to embark troops for a descent in England or Ireland ; but I am inclined to think it very uncertain whether they will now attempt to carry such scheme into execution, after they have seen our strength and felt some hard blows. However, I have no doubt but they will refit their fleet with all possible expedition,

¹ Apparently not received until after August 9. Cf. *Corr.*, 2403.

II.   K

and reinforce it to the utmost of their power ; and if you have not *very authentic* accounts of the Toulon squadron's being otherwise destined I shall believe they will join the Brest fleet, and that they will exert every nerve to dispute with us the superiority in the home seas. This I shall believe to be their plan until I know for certain that the Toulon squadron or some ships from Brest are sent abroad. Therefore, though it will certainly be right to have a squadron ready for the East Indies or elsewhere, yet I shall hope it will be thought not right to detach any ships before they do.[1]

Even with this cautionary measure for keeping their grand fleet in awe, I fear if many frigates do not speedily arrive from America our coasts and trade will be exposed to frequent mischief from squadrons of frigates and privateers. Much more caution is necessary in conducting this than any former war ; hence your Lordship will perceive that I consider the operations of the French in this war will be regulated by the schemes, informations, and advice of some able and well-informed British traitors and rebels.

A few days here and a few supplies will, I hope, put us into sufficient condition to attend their motions.

The peaceable language of the Spanish Ambassador must be pleasing at this critical juncture. I wish it may not prove as dissembling as that of the French has.

I cannot conclude without thanking your Lordship for the dispatch you gave to my

[1] There were five sail of the line under the Chevalier de Fabry in the Mediterranean ; they left Toulon at the end of July to cruise in the Levant, and returned to port on October 28 (Lacour-Gayet, 311).

request respecting the Scarborough volunteers who arrived when we were under sail. It would not have been fair to dispose of them otherwise, as that corporation and Stockton gave 10*l.* a seaman entirely on my account, and 5*l.* to landmen.

Amongst the killed in this ship fell the boatswain, who is a very great loss at this time. . . . I am under considerable disadvantages respecting lieutenants, two being very ill before the action and one wounded in the beginning ; this can't be helped, but my greatest distress of all is the want of petty officers. If your Lordship should have any recommendation for preferment who have not served their full time, I wish you would send them to the Formidable where they may not be out of the way. I have [etc.].

[A postscript about the appointment of a boatswain and a lieutenant to the Formidable.]

[Enclosure : The action off Ushant 27th July, 1778.]

After the two fleets had been four days in sight of each other, during which time we used every means to bring them to battle, and thereby crippled some of our ships' masts by carrying sail, the French always keeping directly to windward, we at last were only able to skirmish with them, for it can't be called a battle as we could not bring them to a general engagement to lie by each other. Nevertheless each of our ships that fetched up beyond their centre was closely engaged above two hours with different ships in succession, and a great deal of damage done on both sides ; on ours mostly in our masts, yards, rigging, and sails, which they chiefly aimed at and fired vast quantities of langrage ; but it may be presumed that they suffered a great deal more in men and in their hulls, as we fired at their hulls. They appeared to be 31 or 32 ships in their line.

In the evening, whilst we were forming our line, they were forming a line to leeward of us and extending themselves parallel to us, so that we made sure of engaging them in the morning; but to our great surprise at daylight there were only three of them in sight, who immediately crowded all the sail they could and steered to the S.E. It is uncertain whether those three ships had not observed the motions of the rest of their fleet during the night, or whether they were left to lie to leeward of us, and by showing lights to make us believe they waited for us in a line to leeward as at dusk and thereby deceived us and covered their retreat.

TO KEPPEL

Hampton Court, 2 August 1778.

I am very sorry you had not a more spirited enemy to deal with, but I am satisfied it was impossible for you to have done more than you did to bring on a decisive action. I cannot, however, omit joining my fullest congratulations to what I am persuaded will be the unanimous voice of the public relative to this transaction.

Our great object now must be to get out your fleet again with as little delay as possible, otherwise the French will send out detachments to intercept our trade, and the Toulon squadron will join the fleet at Brest as it is reported to be already at sea. Every measure that can be taken to supply you with provisions and stores is already executed, and we are exciting every nerve to get you a reinforcement of ships. I have hopes of getting the Suffolk round in time to join you, as she has been four or five days at Blackstakes ; at Portsmouth there is a possibility of our hurrying out the Princess Amelia, Magnificent, Resolution, and Lion, as they want nothing but men ; at Plymouth the Blenheim and Defence may probably be had, and I conclude you will consult with Lord Shuldham concerning them before this reaches you.

It seems to me that it would not be a bad measure to order two of your foulest ships to clean at Plymouth and two at Portsmouth, and to borrow 200 men or more from each of them to man the ships that are in the greatest forwardness. This however I shall leave to your better judgment.

It does not appear by your letters whether you have received the orders (triplicates of which were sent to you) to take French ships of all kinds that come in your way.

If you can get out again speedily to sea, it will add greatly to the applause you have already so justly obtained, and you may be assured that nothing that can be done on my part towards forwarding this most desirable purpose shall be omitted. If I find, or you tell me, that my taking a journey to Plymouth can be of any use, I will hasten thither as soon as I hear from you. I am [etc.].

FROM KEPPEL

Cawsand Bay, 2 August 1778.

The damages found by a strict survey and examination of the masts and yards of the ships that were engaged is very vexatious. I hope we shall be able to remedy in a great degree the defects ; but time is so materially important that I own I am in the utmost anxiety, and shall fret myself into illness if I am long delayed. The increase of my business is such that it is a difficult task to get on with it.

The Blenheim's condition has so little good in it to recommend her that we shall rather look upon her for aiding with her masts, yards, and stores than any other service.

The Toulon squadron is mentioned in your letters. I am afraid it is destined for the West India Islands. Should it get to Brest, it will be a considerable reinforcement to the Brest fleet.

We shall not wish for more than seven ships of three decks, the stout ships of 74 guns that sail well will hereafter be the useful ships.

I find your Lordship has been thinking of sending the Porcupine to me. I certainly should not be sorry you could increase my number to ten or twelve, but when I know the very many stations that should have frigates I cannot expect you to send everything of the sort to me. When those you have ordered from America get home, I trust this fleet will get their proportion. The French employ their frigates in such a line of communication from Brest that single vessels trying to join me will ever be taken, if the fleet is either by winds or chasing taken the least from the station. I wish the Alert may not have been taken. Captain Bryne [Andromeda] tells me that two French frigates chased the Alert large while two pursued him upon a wind. We have heard nothing of the Alert since.[1]

---

[1] She was taken on July 17, the day after she was sent off Ushant with the Andromeda (Abstract of Progress).

In regard to covering the convoys coming home, it is certain the Brest station will not do it. If ever I see the French again it must be their determination to fight it for decision ; if that don't become their resolution, perhaps detachment will be their next plan and will have good sense in it. I don't doubt but you have the possibility of such an event in your thoughts, but before anything new is undertaken it should be determined whether the King's Councils would prefer the continuation of the Brest rendezvous or, for the safety of the trade, having the fleet twenty or thirty leagues to the westward of Scilly crossing two degrees of latitude ; this should be well considered, and understood that the fleet cannot guard two objects and in different parts at the same time.

I left two ships of the line and two frigates at sea. If that measure is approved of, the ships' cruise being only for one fortnight will require a second detachment of the same force when this time is expired, but before I go further in it I shall wish to have your Lordship's approbation in it. I have given you my thoughts undigested as they are ; it is all I can at present offer.

I hope you will direct the Navy Board to get masts and yards completed for ships of every class and at every port. I have used every influence in the fleet to make the defective masts do for the present : some will, some can't ; the Victory's mainmast should have been taken out, but from my wishes I hope we may make a shift with it till winter comes on.

I don't imagine your Lordship can possibly suppose the fatigue of mind I undergo ; if it continues I must be knocked up, but I will endeavour to act as long as I am able, and am [etc.].

FROM KEPPEL [1]

Plymouth, 4 August 1778.

If you are so obliging as to delegate a little authority to us here I think your Lordship's coming would be only giving you unnecessary trouble, and we might fail in some things for want of your being in town ; but if you should notwithstanding think of coming, I shall be very ready to co-operate with you with pleasure for the dispatch of the fleet to the utmost of my power whatever is determined upon, either for refitting the ships or adding to its force.

I shall hope the [Princess] Amelia and Blenheim may not be of the number ; they will be to be looked after, and ever be the trouble of the fleet. If a battle was to be fought at the back of the Wight they would do for three days and no longer a service. If the Egmont can save the spring [tide] she shall be docked, and I should be glad to clean as many ships as you mention. To-morrow I shall be able to determine more. The robbing any of the old ships of their men I dread may have unpleasant consequences ; the seamen are in spirits and bold at present, but will ill brook being separated. I own I had rather go out two ships short than disturb their quiet.

You are obliging in remembering Mr Berkeley ; but I hope you will not think me unreasonable when I say that the omitting the preferring Mr Edgar, the first lieutenant, at the same time will be personally hurtful to me in the situation I am in at present. I know your Lordship's goodwill

[1] Lord Sandwich endorsed the letter thus : ' Nothing about the action. Wishes not to have the P[rince]ss Amelia and Blenheim, but says they would be of use for a few days if there was to be a battle very near home.'

towards me will excuse my solicitation. I will let you hear frequently from me. I am [etc.].

[*P.S.*]—If the fleet don't get supplied with beer, sickness must soon come on ; and your Lordship will imagine I am much alarmed about it.

FROM KEPPEL

Victory, Cawsand Bay, 5 August 1778.

I was too unwell last night to dispatch your messenger although I had wrote my letters. I can say little favourable of myself this day. Our works are going on, and be assured I want no spur nor look for a difficulty. Even health will not prevent my taking a full share of the troubles.

I hope your Lordship will upon the present occasion hint to the Navy Board the necessity there is for giving a little into a natural confusion and irregularity that so large refitting requires, more especially as expedition is of so much consequence.

Lord Mulgrave, who I must say I admire as an officer, is very anxious about the Courageux's men left at Portsmouth Hospital. I wish you could contrive to have them sent here to him.

The looking into Brest with a frigate is impossible, covered as the French are before their port. I expect the Fox from off Ushant every moment ; the Valiant &c. will be in port about a week hence. Will it be wished that I send two ships out to replace them ? I have much to do, but will not complain. I am [etc.].

TO KEPPEL

Admiralty, 7 August 1778.

I have received your private letters by the post and by the messenger, the contents of which I take the first opportunity to answer.

I am happy to understand by a letter received from Commissioner Ourry that no naval stores are wanting to supply the damages your fleet has sustained. Nothing could surprise me more than the accounts you sent of your want of beer and fresh provisions, as we had received from the Victualling Office the fullest assurances that those articles were provided in the most ample manner, and contracts made for fresh provisions both at Plymouth and Torbay. You will find that upon the receipt of your express not a moment was lost in taking every possible measure to supply your wants, and I hope that upon Commissioner Kirk's arrival everything will go on to your satisfaction. I am a little surprised that when the man at Plymouth threw up his contract, Mr Ommanney did not apprise you that there was a contract also at Torbay, which could occasion but a very small delay and little additional expense if the cattle prepared had been immediately ordered to Plymouth, besides it was Mr Ommanney's duty to see that the Plymouth man was prepared to supply your fleet and to have represented it to his superiors if he was not likely to perform his engagement.[1]

The arrival of the India fleet diminishes our anxieties for our homeward-bound trade. There is nothing of importance now near arrival from

[1] Captain Paul Henry Ourry was Commissioner at Plymouth ; Captain James Kirk was a commissioner of victualling and the Hoy-taker ; John Ommanney was the Agent Victualler at Plymouth.

the westward but the Jamaica fleet, which by a
letter from Sir Peter Parker I understand sailed
from Bluefields on the 25th June; they may
therefore probably be expected towards the latter
end of this month.   I cannot however advise your
sending a detachment to meet them till some
decisive blow is given to the Brest fleet, for I do
not think your superiority is such as to admit of
a detachment till this important struggle is over.
In my opinion the principal object is watching
and defeating the Brest fleet : if they detach, we
may do so with safety, but it does not seem to
me that that is their present [intention] ; on the
contrary my idea is that they mean to make their
home fleet as strong as possible in order to over-
power you with numbers when you next meet.
However, if you can get out expeditiously to sea,
I hope you may meet them before they have
recovered the blow you have lately given them ;
and a decisive affair between the two fleets would
have most amazing consequences to this country.

I send you everything of intelligence from
France that deserves any attention ; you will
certainly (from your knowledge of their disposition
to tell lies and misrepresent) not be surprised that
they claim the victory. If you get out to sea
before them, it will be the most striking proof
that can be given of their falsehood, but I really
believe that they will come out again, and that it
will happen without much delay.

As you do not approve of the measure of
cleaning some of your ships and borrowing their
men whilst they are in dock, I shall acquiesce in
your better judgment ; but I fear that in your
next engagement your fleet will not be so strong
as if the other measure had been pursued.

You will easily conceive that my partialities

and my inclination to oblige Lord Mulgrave have no limits, but it is impracticable to give him his recovered men from Haslar Hospital, we have no means of getting the ships at Portsmouth to sea but by availing ourselves of the men that are left behind by the ships that are sailed; if they are sent after the Courageux, they must be sent to every other ship, and then it is decided that you never can have any addition to the force you originally carried with you to sea, as the ships fitting in Portsmouth Harbour must remain there for ever for want of men.

The Army will be very glad to receive their recruits from on board the Thunderer, and orders will be given about their disposal in case you determine to land them; but surely you could make use of them if they were disposed as was originally intended, in small parties on board the several ships that have soldiers belonging to the 50th Regiment. I should think that 100 able-bodied landmen are not to be thrown away at this moment.

The first vacancies that happen that will give the rank of master and commander shall be given to Mr Edgar and Mr Berkeley. I apprehend that if there are not two sloops disposable at the same time, you mean that Mr Edgar should have the preference. Their promotions shall take place the same whether you are at sea or in the harbour, so that they will lose no rank if they sail with you in their present capacity.

I desired Mr Stephens to let Captain Faulknor know that it was necessary that he should direct his agent to solicit the Treasury for the 500*l.* his Majesty has been graciously pleased to order on account of the very acceptable news of which he was the bearer.

The Alert is certainly taken, and the French letters say that Captain Fairfax has been very ill used for having thrown his guns overboard and destroyed his rigging after he had struck his colours.

I think you have some chance of being joined by the Suffolk, as she will, in my opinion, be completely manned in the Downs. Her orders are, if that is effected, to proceed to Plymouth without calling at Spithead. There is also a possibility of getting out the Resolution, but the only means of getting men for her is by recovered men from the hospital.

I am exceedingly concerned to hear that you complain of illness, for God's sake spare yourself as much as you can. I do most sincerely assure you that I never remember a period when the health of a single man was more important to the public than yours is at this moment. I am [etc.].

FROM THE KING

Kew, 9 August 1778, one m. past 3 P.M.

I shall certainly keep the copy of the report of the Committee and the libel which gave rise unto it.

I am grieved to find so great havoc has been made in the masts, yards, and bowsprits of the fleet under the command of Admiral Keppel, but I trust your turn for expedients will soon enable him to get on his former station ; it is impossible too strongly or repeatedly to mention the necessity of getting the fleet out again.

The silence of Sir Hugh Palliser is an additional proof of his prudence, which can alone be equalled by his resolution in action.

Your letter to Admiral Keppel will, I think, be very acceptable and stimulating unto him. I never doubted d'Estaing was gone to North America; the letter from Guernsey fully fixes that affair.[1]

FROM PALLISER

Formidable, Plymouth Sound, 10 August 1778.

I am surprised at that part of your Lordship's letter of the 7th where you say you have not had a syllable concerning the action from any of your friends but Admiral Keppel. I assure your Lordship that by the post of the day we arrived here I sent your Lordship the best *summary* account I was able to give; for a circumstantial one I believe it was in no one's power to give, the fleet was so much extended, and the beginning of the action was so sudden and unexpected, that very few if any can tell what happened anywhere but immediately where he was himself.

[Unimportant remarks about Major Innes, of the Marines, and about warrant officers.]

We find a great deal more to be done to make us fit for sea than we were aware of both in our masts, rigging, and (what is very surprising) an unusual number of shot holes deep under water, so that the Robust, Egmont, Vengeance, and Courageux are obliged to go within the island to give large heels to get at them (the Egmont is docked). This ship had above 70 shot holes in her side and 5 under water: it is wonderful

---

[1] Sir Samuel Hood wrote to Mr Jackson on August 4 about reports of 'an unpleasant disagreement' between Keppel and one of the vice-admirals (*Letters of Sir Samuel Hood*, 1–2).
The King's letter is the answer to *Corr.*, 2403.

we lost so few men. No time will be lost in getting the whole ready.

I am still firmly of opinion, as I told your Lordship in my first letter (which I perceive you have not received), that the French will come out again to meet us, although I cannot persuade many here to think so. These contemptible opinions of our enemy are attended with many bad consequences ; I do all I can to correct them. Don't doubt my Lord of our bringing matters to a more decisive issue the next meeting, if our people will but believe that the French mean to give us battle and to dispute with us the command in the British seas. I can't help being very anxious about reinforcements, for I don't clearly see how you will keep pace with what I am very apprehensive France can do, especially if the Toulon ships come round to Brest ; and if the Spaniards join them God knows what will happen.

I take the liberty to inform your Lordship that our ships that are hastily equipped, and men tumbled on board them almost the moment of their going to sea, are by no means fit for immediate action in many respects ; there being so many things to be done (besides getting her under sail) for which there is not time, especially with only few able men—and more especially what concerns the gunner's matters, for the Ordnance officers do not put the furniture of the guns on board in that complete state they ought to be. I here enclose a memorandum of some particulars upon which I submit to your Lordship whether you think it right to talk with Lord Townshend [1] or write an official letter to the Board of Ordnance.

[1] The Master General of the Ordnance.

Colonel Collins[1] tells me he intends to offer to your Lordship's consideration a proposal for the marines at quarters to be exercised at great guns as well as at small arms.   I am of opinion it will be very useful, for every ship is obliged to take some of their marines to man their great guns, and it oftens happens that in ships hastily manned they may go into action without a single man at some of the guns who have ever been exercised at a great gun or seen one fired.   This is not the case of the French, who have regular companies of gunners for their ships.

I have written to Mr Stephens for a lieutenant in the room of one sick on shore : your Lordship is so obliging to say Mr Winkworth shall be appointed.

I wrote your Lordship a short letter the very day after the action to say your son was well. If I omitted saying that he had no dislike to the smell of gunpowder, it was a neglect, for I assure you no young man could behave better.   He was constantly at his post close by me, attending to nothing but the orders I gave.   I am [etc.].

FROM KEPPEL

Mount Edgcumbe, August the [blank] 1778.

[Endorsed by Lord Sandwich : 'Suppose 12 or 13th—talks about the action, and contains some reasonings, praises the activity of the three admirals.'   The date is more probably August 10.]

I am at Mount Edgcumbe to be a little in quiet from business.   I have been a couple of days most

[1] Lieut.-Col. Arthur Tooker Collins, the Marines (see vol. i. p. 122).

exceedingly ill. I hope my complaints are at their worst and that I shall be getting well every day.

I will not trouble your Lordship with all wants, neither you nor I can help them more than in what is doing. Every head and hand is at work, and notwithstanding the exertion the fleet gets forward slow in comparison to my hopes and expectation. I have great use from the pains my two vice-admirals and Rear-Admiral Campbell take ; and Vice-Admiral Lord Shuldham I feel obligation to for his readiness in doing all in his power.

When the whole fleet have their defects tolerably repaired, the next thing will be to replace the men lost in action. Your Lordship, by the Admiralty letters of this day, I find agrees to the stripping the Blenheim. The Defence I cannot hope to be ready till men come round from the rendezvous's to man her. If we can get our first fleet to sea again we must be satisfied till time adds a force for release of some of the ships that will be in great want of refitting. I conclude you have by this time some account of the French fleet's defects ; if they have not suffered greatly I shall be astonished, after seeing so many of their ships silenced in their firing, as it appeared to us.

It was unlucky for my country as well as myself that the winds were so strong in the western quarter. Most probably, had the winds been easterly, there would have been a more brilliant end to our battle, which unfortunate circumstance I almost feel as much for as if I had been the cause of the winds blowing as they did. Sure I am that I acted up to the best of my abilities : personal considerations no man will ever accuse me of. I had it in my thoughts for a moment upon my return to have divided the fleet, sending the half of it to Spithead ; but when I again considered it, the conclusion might have been in the eyes of Europe the separation of the fleet from the defects' being too like the loss of the battle, which determined my bringing them all hither, and I hope the doing it was judged prudent.

I really think it will be proper, though it may be risking, to keep two ships and a frigate constantly to the westward of Scilly crossing the latitude as far to the southward as Port Lorient. If the French are much crippled, the ships might cross the Bay. One line of battle ship and a frigate off the Lizard would be a great covering to the trade, but when I mention these different stations they depend entirely upon circumstances.

I cannot help believing that the Toulon ships are bound to their islands, and that you may soon be under the necessity of sending some additional force to your islands. If that should be so, I conclude you have in your own mind fixed upon the ships. I rather hope you will not leave it to me ; I like the captains in general so well that I should have too much difficulty in making the choice. If you send a ship of three decks to Jamaica, the Duke has no defects, and for that reason fittest for foreign service. Long-legged 74-gun ships may go into Port Royal, Jamaica, but there is no good port for such ships at the Windward Islands.

The Egmont is just cleared, and I hope will go into dock to-morrow. I have directed hurry and to fish her masts where it can safely be done. The Victory, I flatter myself, will be ready to-morrow night, beer and water excepted, and about ten other ships in the same state. I am [etc.].

P.S.—I reckon the Valiant, Bienfaisant, and two frigates will be here the 14th.

FROM KEPPEL

Mount Edgcumbe, 11 August 1778.

Your very civil and obliging letter calls upon me to acknowledge and thank your Lordship for it ; the fatigue of body and mind keeps my health rather in a doubtful state, though upon the whole rather better than when I wrote to you last. I will not complain if I can help it, but I am so much an invalid that rest, when the winter comes on, will be absolutely necessary. I have wished for wings to have waited upon the King for an hour's conversation upon the present matters, and to have frankly and freely talked over everything with your Lordship. I have no secrets about me ; Captain Faulknor had powers to talk from me to any questions you might ask him, and I hope you have found him communicative.

I expected much gasconnade from the French account of the battle, but I own I did not look for their accusation of the English fleet's having stole off in the night and putting out their lights ; the English admiral showed to his fleet and to the French the degree of sail he meant to carry, the course he steered, and lights for everybody to know where he was. The sail carried was just sufficient to preserve the weather gage, leaving it in the power of the French to be anywhere in their line except to windward ; *they* put their lights out about half-past eleven o'clock, and the morning of the 28th showing they were gone, the circumstances of which, and some rockets that were seen in the night, makes it probable that they began to run before midnight. Their excuse for going into Brest, making the island of Ushant unexpectedly, is the most paltry lie and excuse that ever was made ; they cover over their losses of men or other disasters. I will avoid all I can allowing of their lies to take my thoughts from essential business ; we are getting forward ; I am sure I feel impatience to be gone in proper repair and force ; beer is most called for.

Captain Faulknor is just arrived, and I feel thankful to your Lordship for your civilities to him. I am [etc.].

FROM KEPPEL

Mount Edgcumbe, 14 August 1778.

You are very obliging in the intelligence you sent in your letter of the 10th of August. If it is to be depended upon, the French have been severely treated by the King's fleet. After battles more is known than can be seen at the time, and consequently advantages lost. I am sure you'll do me the justice my zeal and conduct merits ; I believe there has not been a man in this kingdom whose head and mind has been so constantly employed for the public service ever since the trust reposed in me as mine has been, and I hope my whole conduct will bear the strictest examination as a seaman and officer, with all that belongs to those names.

Your Lordship very kindly expresses your hope that rest from business has had the desired effect : indeed I am much reinstated, though despair of satisfaction till I am again at sea.

Our repairs have been well executed, and I hope will answer every expectation from them. I don't quite see my way enough to inform you when I may sail. As yet I see no reason for a change of rendezvous : the Lizard is always the preferable point for collection, and after that Ushant, and towards Scilly in westerly winds, for covering the trade.

I sincerely give you joy upon the arrival of the West India fleet from the Windward Islands. The Valiant and Bienfaisant saw them safe off the Eddystone ; the two frigates I have off the Bill of Portland will cover them well up. I was glad the Andromeda was in the way to be of service to the East India convoy, but I wish Captain Bryne had found his way back to Plymouth.

I have at this moment, except the Arethusa, all my frigates upon the water, besides two of the 64-gun ships that I have this moment ordered to sea for five or six days : the Defiance with the Fox to cruise from the Dodman across the Channel to the [?] Islands, the Exeter, Pluto, and a cutter from Plymouth to the Isle of Batz. The crossing the Channel will be a great succour to the trade at this moment ; and the time is so short that they will join the fleet before it can move, which is doing all we can in our situation. The expectation of the Jamaica convoy and its being so near hangs upon my mind. The cruisers left out are now returned. I wish I dared send two or three ships of the line with the same orders Captain Leveson[-Gower of the Valiant] had. If the Suffolk, Resolution, and Lion was joined it would have but little objection to it ; but if I can't spare a large detachment, one ship of the line and one frigate may be the saving of the convoy.

I don't mention this in any other way than in free discourse—I am in respect to complaining of others exactly in your way of thinking—yet the want of beer in the beginning and ending of the refitting of this fleet is mortifying. What is worse, it may be productive of such sickness as may lay part of the fleet at the walls. Torbay will be my next port, when I shall hope to be better served. Fresh beef and water is given to us at present in plenty. Lord Shuldham does all he can to help me forward. Men to replace the killed and wounded I fear cannot be completely furnished, we must do as well as we can. The Defence is a fine ship, but will want above 200 good men to render her fit for service. Till we are quit of the American drains upon our seafaring men, we must remain distressed.

The Egmont is docked and, though she may not be ready to sail with me, a very few days will enable her to follow. The cleaning some of the ships as your Lordship proposed would have had great good in it, if we had been in numbers to do so. The Stirling Castle will be the first ship I send in for that purpose, the Worcester and Hector next. Sickness may oblige me to send the Courageux among the first, but her people have been always better at sea, and her captain [Lord Mulgrave] I have too much liking to to part with unnecessarily. I am [etc.].

FROM KEPPEL

Mount Edgcumbe, 15 August 1778.

Your Lordship does not hear so often from me as you would if the post went out every evening. The last intelligence that Mr Stephens sent me, of six ships of the line having sailed from Brest the 31st of July, I think may be true, though I do not believe they would so immediately detach. To say that they had sent six ships out and that the rest were to follow, I do not comprehend. That their whole fleet may be ordered to sea is very possible, but for what purpose unless to fight it fairly I can't imagine, no more than I can believe they will risk a battle without many advantages.

I hear much talk of Monsieur de Chartres. I can't think, unless I mistook his ship, that there was any brilliancy in his behaviour the day of the battle.

I puzzle myself much to guess, should they detach, what station they will take : most likely that which will cover their India ships, and be more or less in the way of the English trade between the latitude of 49.30 N. and 47.00 N., forty or fifty leagues to the westward of Ushant, but all this is dark imagination.

Our weather has expedited our works most favourably, but we still pray and hope for a few more days. The Valiant's foremast and mizenmast must be changed, and will be ready by Tuesday for stripping if the weather will permit. The Egmont got her new masts in yesterday, and Captain Allen promises me to use every exertion. The Vengeance is rather backward, but I hope will be ready with most of the other backward ships by Thursday or Friday next. I have fourteen ships in Cawsand Bay that will be ready to-morrow night for the sea excepting beer, six ships in Plymouth Sound, and the two in the offing make twenty-two. The remaining eight will I hope most of them be ready in three or four days after. I shall order Sir Robert Harland and Sir Hugh Palliser to proceed into the offing with such ships of their divisions as are ready to go with them ; with the rest I hope to be able to sail on the Friday.

It will be fortunate for our poor fellows if beer comes sooner from the eastward. If it does not I must proceed without it, which I will do if my number of ships make twenty-eight of the thirty I had before.

We have a party of marines ready for the Suffolk. If she and the two ships from Portsmouth arrive it will be a great reinforcement ; but my original thirty I should hope will do the business, if the French will let us place our ships as near as I would allow them without firing. The Defence will be ready in ten days, wanting two hundred seamen ; she appears to be a fine ship. I have several applications from *the English* in Mill Prison ; many Americans would be glad to come, but won't ask for fear of refusal. If we can't avail ourselves of these people in this time of want, it is our own fault. I am sure if it remained with me a day should not pass before I had the whole number distributed in the fleet.

It has been suggested to me that the brewers at Brixham, Dartmouth, and other places in that neighbourhood might be engaged to brew beer for the fleet against their putting into Torbay. I have not been informed particularly enough to say it certainly can be done, yet I judged it proper to mention it to you. The two bays the fleet now lie in cannot be used again for such a fleet after this month is over, it has too much apparent danger to venture it. I am [etc.].

P.S.—Your Lordship will be so good as to consider that it is not likely post-letters will get here before my sailing. I must observe that when I am the length of the Lizard I will send a cutter into Falmouth with my letters.

FROM MR EDWARD HUNT [1]

Plymouth Yard, 16 August 1778.

My Lord—Permit me the honour of acquainting your Lordship that the fleet under the command of Admiral Keppel is in such forwardness as to enable me with certainty to acquaint you they will be completed by Tuesday night, excepting the Valiant and Egmont. The former we are now getting ready for (with the utmost dispatch) a fore and mizen mast and main yard, and for the latter completing her quarter gallery and works incident to rigging; all of which, if the weather continues favourable, will be effected in this week.

The great exertion and zeal of the officers and workmen on the late occasion have been and is such that I could not omit mentioning it to your Lordship in this letter, and what I flatter myself will be confirmed by Admiral Keppel and the admirals of the fleet. I hope to set off from this place Tuesday or Wednesday morning and lose no time in returning to town and waiting on your Lordship. I am [etc.].

FROM KEPPEL

Victory, Cawsand Bay, 21 August 1778.

I hope to-morrow will have completed most part of the fleet in their repairs, and that this day will bring into port the beer expected from the eastward. It will be lucky if the fleet get stored in that article, but I despair of it, and fear much the consequence of it; sickness may come upon

[1] Surveyor of the Navy, in addition to Sir John Williams, since 19 March 1778.

us in the use of spirits, the forms of revenue directions in the Customs has prevented the fleet's getting wine. These disappointments will oblige the fleet to return sooner to Torbay than it might otherwise have done. I don't see anything to prevent my sailing to-morrow ; the two vice-admirals are trying with their divisions to get out this day into the offing. If the Brest fleet are ready to come out and seek battle with the English fleet it may soon be done.

The fleet will leave above 500 men at the hospital. Men killed and died of their wounds, and a large proportion deserted, will send me to sea very deficient in numbers. Lord Shuldham has given me all the men he could get. I have no remedy and must be contented.

My invalid state makes me feel my troubles and business more than I am able to do well, but as I owe my King and country the exertion of all that belongs to me I shall keep from complaining as much as possible, although my task is full of difficulty.

The prisoners taken in the small vessels off the Isle of Batz say that they understood that the Bretagne was run upon the mud upon her getting into Brest. Others say the shot did not penetrate her sides, that the Ville de Paris of 94 guns was so *shook* with the firing of her own guns (not by the English ships) that she will be laid up, that six or seven other ships are much damaged, that Monsieur d'Orvilliers and Du Chaffault are upon bad terms and many officers quarrelling with each other. I don't much expect ever to hear the real truth, and I am [etc.].

FROM KEPPEL

Victory, Cawsand Bay, 22 August 1778.

Your letter of the 19th I received late last night, and this is to return your Lordship thanks for it. The two vice-admirals and their divisions are got into the offing ; and I should have proceeded with my own division, but the wind has cast in, which will delay me till the morrow's morning breeze off the land. It is much satisfaction to me to have been able to repair the defects of the fleet so quickly. The fine weather has contributed much to it.

Your Lordship cannot have an idea of the infinite trouble I have in regard to the warrant officers in the ships, many in real bad health and many others good for nothing, that my whole time almost is troubled with the complaints of the captains and applications for officers in the room of those sick on shore. I fend off all that I possibly can, which displeases all parties. In short, I can say no more than that I fear that many very bad warrant officers have found their way into the fleet.

It is some comfort to me to understand by your Lordship's letter that in future the fleet will be in no want of sufficient supplies of beer &c. For me to complain where there is no remedy would avail little, but the small quantity the ships sail with in beer must necessarily drive the fleet into port sooner than it otherwise would return. The preservation of your seamen's health must be a principal object to attend to.

Lieutenants Edgar and Berkeley I know you won't forget, and yet your not being able to place them will make my credit appear less than I could wish it.   I have always forgot to mention to you that the overload of office business has obliged me to procure very creditable young fellows to assist my secretary, but I cannot expect them to remain with me without a view to preferment. So great a command without power to help those serving under me has every inconvenience ; and yet I would not have your Lordship believe I wish to promote, but through yourself as First Lord of the Admiralty.   I am [etc.].

FROM KEPPEL

Victory, Sunday morning, 23 August 1778.

I am now standing with my division into the offing and shall join the rest of the fleet soon. I shall then try to get down Channel, make the Lizard to pick up the Terrible and frigates off that land, and when joined by the Egmont shall stretch over to Brest.   If your last intelligence is to be depended upon, the French are lately sailed from Brest 27 ships ; if it was true they detached six, their force will be 33 ships when joined. The *happy* issue of a decisive battle with them this country looks for, and no one of it more desirous than myself ; but from experience I know, and so does everybody else, that the most promising prospect may take a change by the ships' getting disabled in their masts and rigging, and therefore I will promise nothing but endeavours.   If I see the French fleet and we don't fight close, it will be their fault and not mine.   I do not command the winds and weather.

My task has many more difficulties than action itself ; and although my Lord I feel myself as proud as an officer as I ever did, I do not go with the great load upon me with every satisfaction after all that has happened. That I might have expected; but nothing will ever cool my zeal while I am charged with the command of the King's fleet and my health permits my going upon service, so I will neither take up your Lordship's time or my own in saying more than that I am [etc.].

FROM KEPPEL

Victory, off the Lizard, 11 A.M. Tuesday, 25 August 1778.

I am made exceedingly unhappy at the cause that has given occasion for the trial of Captain Brereton. The accusation, it seems, has been rumoured among the ships some days, but yesterday was the first time anything reached me that was material. Whatever may be discovered upon Captain Brereton's trial, sure I am no conduct of his could very particularly operate to affect the day the fleets engaged. Sir Robert Harland is now sitting to determine the fate of this unfortunate gentleman. The great trust and importance of the force of the Duke is too serious a matter to leave the direction of her in doubtful hands; unpleasant as the business is to me, my duty has obliged me to direct a court martial. What happened to Captain Brereton in the East Indies operates unfavourably with the world against him, but I shall ever be ready to avow that Captain Speke, whose character as an officer and brave man was undoubted, spoke of him to me in the most favourable manner.

We think we see a large ship of war a long way to the eastward: it is most probably the Egmont. The Terrible is joining from the westward: when they are both with me I will stretch over to Ushant and look after the French fleet, and shall be well pleased if they are brave enough to quit the idea of running towards Brest till the battle has its decision. The accounts that I am able to collect differ much ; but putting all I hear together, a large squadron of them, I think to the number of twenty-two ships of the line and eight large frigates, sailed from Brest the 16th or 18th ; that seven ships were in the road ready, and were to join the fleet ; that three were in the port repairing ; that the Ville de Paris had been reported too bad to do anything with, but that the Court had been peremptory in their orders to repair her. This number makes the whole what they were before—32 ships.

I write in my public letter my proposal and intentions relative to the great ships that don't join me to-day. I think it is the best disposition of them for the present, though their being with me would be of promising service if the danger of the junction did not operate against the trial. I am in pain for the homeward bound : if ships could be spared to cover the Bristol Channel as well as the English, it would be a lucky circumstance, but till the Brest fleet is broken by a decisive battle I can aid very little in giving cover to the trade. I have hitherto done everything that could be expected. I am [etc.].

FROM KEPPEL

Victory, at sea, 8 September 1778.

My very bad fortune in not having seen or heard from any good intelligence of the French fleet since I left the Lizard is indeed very trying to the patience of an anxious mind. The vain boasting of the French Court perhaps has obliged them to send their fleet to sea ; but, although the name of Monsieur d'Orvilliers has been lent to spread to Europe a most infamous lie upon the pretended success of their fleet, they are not themselves I believe so much in earnest in looking for the English fleet as I am in my endeavours to find them.

The French King's honours and rewards to Monsieur d'Orvilliers seem political, to confirm the truth of his victory. I do not forgive the French Admiral, whose own behaviour in battle claimed the name of a brave officer, for lending that honourable behaviour to the spreading an infamous falsity.

One of my ships spoke the 7th with a Dutch ship of war that had been spoke with off the Lizard the 6th by the Resolution and Defence. I mean to stretch in a day or two towards that rendezvous with hopes of getting those two ships if the wind allows me to do so.[1] My letters to Mr Stephens will give your Lordship an account of business : you will see by them some bad luck that attended the chasing two French ships. I am unfortunate, but I have always the consolation of having never spared my endeavours, body and mind, since I have had the honour to be called upon by the King to take this command. My whole thought has been for the glory and honour of his Majesty's force and the well-doing from it of his dominions. If my labours fail of my endeavours I must be sorry and perhaps be blamed in the dark. But such censure I shall ever despise ; my conduct is

---

[1] These ships joined the flag on the 11th.

upright and clear, and will ever carry me to my journey's end.[1]

My letters will inform your Lordship that the fleet has traversed from the Ushant rendezvous to the westward of that island, between thirty and forty leagues from that to the southward into the latitude of Belle Isle, and then into the latitude of 49.30 N., a little to the westward of Scilly, the exact opening of the English Channel and track of the homeward-bound trade ; but no information to trace the rendezvous of the French fleet. Our weather has been remarkably fine, notwithstanding which there is sickness in the fleet ; and I fear the little supply we had of beer will bring complaints on sooner than we might otherwise have expected them, and may oblige me to get to Torbay to prevent an increase of sickness and get our beer, wine, &c. recruited. Indeed, if the health of the people is considered as an object, which I must think it ever a material one, no fleet of large numbers should ever be above six or seven weeks at sea. The *Courageux* is rather sickly, so is the *Valiant* and Stirling Castle ; this last ship I shall soon send in, if I find my force enables me to part with her. I hope when the other *two* next dock, that your Lordship will try the experiment of coppering their bottoms. If active war is likely to be pursued, I do think if the expense upon calculation is not too great that at least ten of your 74-gun ships should be coppered ; it should be the best sailing ships and those that are in the best repair.

[1] The Admiral wrote thus to Shuldham next day : 'My patience is worn out, and I despair except by chance seeing the French fleet. I am as yet a stranger to the object of their going to sea ; to look for the English fleet certainly has not been their business.'

I don't think I have in any of my letters to you mentioned the trial of Captain Brereton. I never was more surprised than I was to hear that he was in any degree accused on board his own ship. No observation of my own would have justified the least suspicion of bad conduct. Captain Brereton was tried at his own request, and dismissed from his ship, for having been found upon evidence to have been intoxicated with drink on the 26th and 27th of July, the day before and day of the engagement with the French fleet ; acquitted of every other suspicion, on the contrary proved to have carried a proper sail and used endeavour to get the Duke into her station. I hope as that was found so, he will be left upon the half-pay list.[1]

The appointment upon Captain Brereton's dismission of Sir Charles Douglas to the Duke gives Sir Charles great pleasure, and I believe he will be glad if your Lordship continues him to her. Captain Lloyd from the Vulcan fireship, who I have put into the Stirling Castle, is an officer of merit and very deserving the notice I have taken of him ; but as the disposing of commissions is in the Admiralty it will remain with your Lordship to determine. I had upon the hopes of some of my lieutenants' getting commands written to an officer to come to me, which he has done ; but for want of a vacancy have judged it right to order his acting as an extra lieutenant, which I am aware has irregularity in it, and yet my situation in so great a trust with so large a fleet will I hope justify such an order at such a moment as the present ; and

[1] The evidence of Captain Adair of the Marines and of some of the lieutenants of the Duke makes it plain that Captain Brereton was drunk on July 27. The first lieutenant was urged to stand by to take command ; and he ordered the officers of watches to keep a strict eye on their captain (Reports of Court Martial).

II.   M

with an opinion that I hope will be listened to that an admiral in chief command with such a fleet does require an extra lieutenant in the ship where his flag is flying.

The fleet fell in with the Lisbon convoy yesterday under the care of the Hussar. The sight of them for a moment gave spirits to the fleet ; they are lowered again. The convoy is still in sight and I shall endeavour to cover them across the Channel, which track I will take to-morrow if nothing appears to take me another way. If your Lordship gives Mr Berkeley a good coppered sloop I shall be glad to have him attached to this fleet ; he is really a most active clever lad, and will do credit to his promoters. I am [etc.].

FROM THE KING [1]

Kew, 13 September 1778, 20 m. past 11 A.M.

I had just received a similar account from the American Office, previous to the arrival of Lord Sandwich's note. It is unfortunate no means can be found of conveying to Admiral Keppel the intelligence we have received, from so many different quarters, of the French fleet's lying off Cape Finisterre for Mr de Fabry's squadron ; for if he was apprised of it, he would undoubtedly lose no time in driving it from that station.

---

[1] See *Corr.*, 2418 and 2420. The last is Lord Sandwich's answer to the King : he says that all intelligence that comes to the Admiralty is sent to Keppel, but that if it is thought proper the fleet should stretch as far as Cape Finisterre, it ought to be decided by the Cabinet before orders are sent for that purpose.

FROM THE KING [1]

Windsor, 13 September 1778, 46 m. past 7 P.M.

Nothing could be more proper than Lord Sandwich's forwarding this evening the letters from Lord Howe, as he must naturally feel how eager I am to be apprised of transactions on which the splendour, if not the very existence, of this empire depend. Lord Howe now appears in the line where he cannot but shine, though not so fit for the chicanes of negotiation. I trust, if he can oblige d'Estaing to fight, he will give a most agreeable account.

I have just seen Mr [Captain] Salter of the Hussar, on the Terrace, who dined on Monday on board the Victory. He is convinced the French fleet have quitted Cape Finisterre long before this time. He is to-morrow to wait on Lord Sandwich; I therefore think it best not to send any directions to Admiral Keppel that may probably only perplex him, and be too late to prevent the object for which the French fleet is supposed to have taken that station.

I entirely agree with Lord Sandwich as to the necessity of having the packet boats on a different construction, and will direct the strongest directions to be given for that purpose unto the Postmaster General.

FROM KEPPEL

Victory, at sea, 13 September 1778, wind easterly.

The Andromeda joined me this morning. I received by her the Admiralty dispatches and your Lordship's letter of the 27th of August.

Mr Stephens's letter informs me that you have

[1] This letter is the answer to *Corr.*, 2420, which begins ' Lord Sandwich is always fearful of being too troublesome to your Majesty.'

thought proper to reinforce the little squadron for the protection of the islands of Guernsey and Jersey. I observe the name of one ship that I had hopes would have been sent to this fleet, the Jupiter : I understand she is coppered, had she been with me the other day when the fleet had a run after the two French ships I think we must have had them. Coppered bottoms, both of large and small ships, will be of infinite benefit. The West India convoy's arrival, as well as that from Gibraltar, are surely most fortunate events ; this fleet has covered the sea for them, which the French expected who have, if at all, been but for a moment in the Chops of the Channel. The Romulus's arrival will add a forty-gun frigate to your number, and if you so please might enable your Lordship to give me the Jupiter.[1]

My letter acquaints the Board that I have been informed that the French fleet were seen cruising off Cape Finisterre the 29th of last month, a very

---

[1] A squadron of two frigates and two cutters, under Captain Philip Boteler of the Actaeon 44, was formed in August for the defence of Guernsey and Jersey. It was afterwards joined by the Jupiter 50, another small frigate, and two sloops (S.P. Dom. naval and List Book).

There is an undated letter from Lord North on this subject : ' The lords of the Cabinet who stayed at my house yesterday evening, after your Lordship left us, expressed in very strong terms their anxiety about Jersey and Guernsey, and seemed to consider the preservation of those islands as the most pressing of services ; and, as it appears by the intelligence we have received that Admiral Keppel is at present superior to the French fleet, they wished either the ships which are destined to join him, or if they are not fit for this service a part of their crews, may for a time be employed in the protection of Jersey and Guernsey. I perceive by Mr Smith's letters that there is a new frigate arrived at Plymouth, and I suppose there are some ships under the line now at Portsmouth. The addition of one or two ships immediately to the Actaeon's squadron may preserve the islands ; and the retarding, for a few days, the junction of a large ship of the line or two to Mr Keppel's fleet does not appear at present likely to be of any fatal consequence.'

extraordinary station to find the English fleet. I fear making so long a departure without having some knowledge of the probable time the French fleet are to keep the sea. What can Monsieur d'Orvilliers be to do off Cape Finisterre ? Is it in expectation of their East India ships' coming in that track ? Or is it a rendezvous to join the Toulon squadron ? It surely cannot be with any hopes that d'Estaing can be upon that coast before they must return. I hope they never will be so strong as the junction of those two squadrons would make them ; they would be upwards of fifty ships of the line. You will stand in need of Lord Howe and Admiral Byron's getting home with their ships very suddenly.

If the French admiral gets joined by all his ships from Brest and the Toulon ships, he will, he must, fight this fleet. He may be thirty-seven ships, if he fails of complete junction and only gets six or seven ships from Brest to the number twenty-six that he sailed with. I think it likely that he tries to play the same manœuvre that he did in July. A westerly wind blowing fresh and a tolerable nearness to Ushant will, I much fear, give him the power of practising the paltry game of fighting at a distance, not for decision ; I hope however that my good fortune is to come, and that I shall be able to catch whatever favourable is offered me.

The junction of the Resolution and Defence I am much pleased with, but it requires several days to have reliance upon very good service from them. They are manned with twenty different ships' men and large drafts of miserable recruits ; so equipped, much cannot yet be expected from them, but the scarcity of seamen makes their condition for the present unavoidable.

I much wish for tolerable good weather.

I think it will operate for the English fleet in many views, and I am sure my own infirmities require it very much—I stand in great fear of my usual complaint's rendering me unfit for winter's service in the sea. Indeed wisdom must direct the ships into port as soon as the bad weather months come on. As far as depends upon me the day is fixed : after that period it will depend upon the King's servants in council to determine what will be most advisable, whether to be forming a respectable fleet at Spithead or blowing and dispersing the fleet we have to pieces by cruising in stormy months to no other purpose. Be your resolutions what they will, the sickly ships must refit upon my next return, at least five or six of them. The French can have no better wish than to know you keep your large fleet collected at sea in the winter : their fleet in port quiet, recruiting and waiting the moment of the storm's separating and demolishing your fleet, while theirs remains perfect to go upon some settled service when the English fleet is in port from disaster and sickness.[1]

But some plan must be adopted, though it cannot be done as largely as necessary till your Lordship gets force from America, I mean for cruising and covering the opening of the Channel as well as annoying the enemy's ships passing. Without some precaution the trade must suffer greatly ; and besides this service, if your Lordship had ships enough to establish a flying little squadron at Kinsale it would be of the greatest utility—some chosen well-thinking officer to command it. If it became the determination of the Admiralty that it should be distinct from the

[1] The Admiral had written, on the 11th, to say he fixed October 12 as the day he must go back to Torbay to recruit.

Cp. Kempenfelt's similar views a year later (*The Barham Papers*, i. 303).

command of the Western squadron, it will be more requisite to put an able officer to command it. The chief object of this squadron would be to cover the Irish and Bristol Channels, and when cruising stretch across from the latitude of Cape Clear to the latitude of Scilly, and when not cruising there to attend to eventual matters not at the present foreseen. The force should be at least six sail of vessels : a ship of sixty [or] forty [or] a large frigate, a smaller, two sloops, and two cutters. I make your Lordship no apology for opening my thoughts to you for the public welfare, I do not believe you expect me to make any. I fear more that you have not spare craft enough for my proposition ; but sure I am that you have no other effectual method of protecting tolerably the trade of the Bristol and Irish Channels.

Sir Charles Douglas I have seen : he has much content and pride in his present appointment to the Duke, rather inclines to continue, yet begs he may have a little time before he determines. I am [etc.].

FROM THE KING

Windsor, 15 September 1778, 27 m. pt. 4 P.M.

I cannot help looking on Admiral Keppel's return to Torbay, if previous to his meeting the French fleet, as a most untoward event.

Admiral Keppel seems to have compassion for Brereton, which is a strong proof that he believes him guilty of drunkenness ; for he shows half pay is going as far as possible in the Captain's favour.[1]

[1] This is in answer to the following from Lord Sandwich : ' Your Majesty will observe that though Admiral Keppel exculpates Captain Brereton of misbehaviour in the action, the utmost he points out in his behalf is that he should be put upon half pay ' (*Corr.*, 2422).

FROM KEPPEL

Victory, at sea, 21 September 1778,
latitude Ushant, wind E.S.E. fresh.

Since writing my letter of the 14th [13th ?] I have been crossing the latitudes as far southward as 46.42 N. in the line towards Cape Finisterre, but no sort of information relative to the French fleet. I sent the Porcupine yesterday to stretch in the same line as far as the latitude of 45.00 N. and so back again to the Ushant rendezvous. The very long run of easterly winds keeps most ships bound to Europe a long way to the westward.

Our sickly ships are growing bad every day: the Victory has the distemper in a degree, but not like the Valiant, Courageux, Conqueror [Centaur?],[1] and Stirling Castle. These ships should be docked as soon as possible. I shall venture of myself, when I bear up with the fleet for Torbay, to order the Stirling Castle to Plymouth to clean and refit immediately; and I think it probable that I send three or four more of the 64-gun ships into the Sound to complete their provisions etc. there. If your Lordship should incline to order any of them to clean, the Exeter should have the preference than the Worcester and America. I could wish to find your orders relative to the sickly ships.

It is possible that I send the Valiant to Portsmouth with orders to clean, and I should hope that she will be ordered eighteen-pounders for her upper-deck guns in the room of her present twenty-four pounders; and if after that you like to copper her, she will outsail the coppered frigates and be the completest ship in the world. I think the best of our 74-gun ships that would do credit to your

[1] The Conqueror was with Byron in North America.

choice for coppering are the Valiant, Foudroyant [80], Courageux, and Thunderer of my division ; the Monarch, Berwick, and Cumberland of the vice-admiral of the Red's division ; the Ramillies, Elizabeth, and Robust of the vice-admiral of the Blue's division. The Hector has merit, or much is due to Sir John Hamilton, who generally contrives to be among the foremost of the chasing ships.[1]

I now come unpleasantly to my own personal situation. For these five last days I have found my health promising unfavourably, and yesterday I was so thoroughly crippled with the spasms that I know not what I should have been able to have done if the moment had called upon me to direct the fleet properly in sight of the enemy ; perhaps the seeing them might have operated pleasantly, but if not, and any deficiency in myself, you will easily allow me the credit in supposing I should have been miserable beyond a cure. I am sorry to think that I am obliged to apprise your Lordship so early upon this subject, but I should not act an honest part if I did not. If the command of the fleet continues with me while I am on shore in the winter for my health, I shall exert my poor abilities whilst I can do so with honour to myself and good to the public : having said so much I would not be understood

---

[1] The Valiant and another ship, the Triumph, were designed after the French Invincible, taken in 1747. They were nearly two hundred tons bigger than normal 74s; and like some of the French ships they carried 24- instead of 18-pounders on the upper deck. Both were reduced to 18-pounders during this war.

It was thought inexpedient at this time to copper the ships referred to, and Keppel wrote as follows on the 27th : ' Your Lordship's reasoning in opposition to the coppering the great ships is sufficient to stop my further application upon it.' A year later, in a letter to Barrington of 5 August 1779, the First Lord was able to say that coppering ships of the line ' is now become almost general.' See below, p. 365.

that in what I have explained I request being continued in the command.   I have from the first moment the King thought proper to call upon me considered myself devoted to his service and to the public, however difficult, and at times unpleasant, my task.

I had near forgot to observe that the Ocean is complaining as an old ship ; the Sandwich not so bad, but getting into that state.   I am [etc.].

P.S.—I enclose your Lordship the state of the ships in point of foulness, but the sickness of some of them not so long off the ground will make it advisable giving them the preference. [See p. 171.]

FROM KEPPEL

Victory, at sea, in sight of Scilly, 24 September, 1778.
Wind north.

I intended to have sent the Little Hazard cutter with my letters, though they have not the importance I could wish they had, but as I have always considered it a right measure to keep your Lordship as much informed as possible I think it is time you should hear from me.   The French brig prize sails so remarkably well that I am venturing to send my dispatches in with her ; they are slung for the deep in case of her being taken.

The wind as it is encourages me to get easting and look at the entrance of the Channel.   I hold it prudent to do so occasionally, lest the French should at any time get within me and up the English Channel, a measure that I do not, however, believe has been either in their power or intention.   If the wind gets to the N.N.E. again,

STATE OF ADMIRAL KEPPEL'S SQUADRON.
[Enclosed in his letter of 21 September 1778.]

Ships foul out of all expectation of getting up with the ships of the enemy that make away at a distance: Off the ground, some of them, eighteen months and more, the rest out of dock in the end of last year.		Ships foul and want docking that have been from six to nine months out of dock.		Ships four months out of dock and cleaner.	
Ships	*When docked*	*Ships*	*When docked*	*Ships*	*When docked*
Stirling Castle	9 Jan. 1777	Valiant	14 Jan. 1778	Terrible	10 June 1778
Exeter	27 ,,	Robust	14 ,, ,,	Defence	12 ,, ,,
Victory	9 Apr. ,,	Ocean	31 ,, ,,	Resolution	9 July ,,
America	5 Aug. ,,	Foudroyant	30 ,, ,,	Shrewsbury	11 ,, ,,
Monarch	8 ,, ,,	Thunderer	23 Feb. ,,	Egmont	11 Aug. ,,
Hector	1 Sept. ,,	Defiance	3 Mar. ,,		
Ramillies	20 ,, ,,	Duke	13 ,, ,,		
Elizabeth	4 Oct. ,,	Formidable	14 ,, ,,		
Berwick	24 ,, ,,	Vengeance	16 ,, ,,		
Courageux	29 ,, ,,	Bienfaisant	11 Apr. ,,		
Worcester	13 Nov. ,,	Sandwich	13 ,, ,,		
Cumberland	2 Dec. ,,	Centaur	6 May ,,		
Prince George	30 ,, ,,	Vigilant	25 ,, ,,		
Queen	30 ,, ,,				

and the weather is not foggy, I will look into Brest. I have not done it hitherto, believing from every information that the French fleet was most certainly at sea, and that it would be wasting time too much in a vain bravado ; but as I cannot find them, and five weeks are past since they sailed from Brest, I shall feel satisfaction in knowing for certain they are out. I think, as I have said in my letter to Mr Stephens, that the first settled westerly wind will bring them near their home.

I shall dispatch the Little Hazard cutter to Plymouth in about one week. I am [etc.].

P.S.—The southern latitudes is full of French ships ; three have been taken by the fleet, and if I had not had a business in view more honourable, I suppose in ten days' cruising the fleet might have caught as many French trading ships as days.

FROM KEPPEL

Victory, at sea, 27 September, 1778.
Wind N.N.W. strong.

My public letter to Mr Stephens gives your Lordship information upon the alarm I am under for the safety of the fleet. If in the time of recruiting at Torbay it should be caught with a gale of wind to the southward of the east, it is more than probable that, a gale coming from that quarter, nothing would get round from Torbay to Plymouth ; it is more certain that if the vessels did come no work could be carried on, if the sea was up, and I am told the small craft would most likely if it blowed be driven on shore. I do not know how to persevere in my first proposition of Torbay for refitting the fleet in such large wants as they will require. In the summer months the difficulties were to be met, and the danger for the fleet little to what may be in the middle and end of October. It is the opinion of other experienced seamen that has alarmed me ; and if it becomes absolutely necessary to put out from Torbay when the wind gets easterly I see the possibility of the fleet's dispersing, and that much time will be wasted with disappointment.

I must therefore beg most earnestly to be relieved from my anxiety, and that I may find a cruiser off the Start Point with your orders, and also in case of my missing her an officer may be at Torbay from Lord Shuldham awaiting there my arrival with a duplicate of my instructions. The fears I am in about Torbay will make me endeavour to keep one week longer, if I possibly can, beyond the 12th of October. The Peggy cutter is dispatched with this letter.[1] I am [etc.].

FROM KEPPEL

Victory, at sea, 1 October, 1778.
Wind N.W., nearly the latitude of Ushant.

The ship is rolling so very much that it is not easy to write ; our weather is getting winter—dirty, blowing, with large seas. The Defence crippled her bowsprit yesterday in a hard gale at S.W., and I fear the patched masts in the fleet are generally complaining.

I send Mr Stephens a duplicate of my letter to him upon the alarm relative to the fleet's riding

[1] Keppel wrote the day before to say that his ' patience and hopes of ever seeing the French fleet again ' were quite gone.

in safety with the S.E. winds so late in the year at Torbay. I must confess my own fears at first were but little ; but now the experience of others has operated strongly in alarming of me, and therefore it is my duty to alarm you as much. Sir Robert Harland, Sir Hugh Palliser, Admiral Campbell, and many others that I talked with the day before yesterday upon it, are every one of them decided against Torbay so late in the year in any other than stopping for shelter in hard S.W. winds, and using such time in getting as much provisions as may be sent in the time before an easterly wind requires the fleet's putting to sea for safety. It is their opinion the fleet should proceed to the eastward for recruit and refitting. I confess if I dared give the orders I should carry the fleet to Spithead and direct six or seven of the ships into Plymouth Sound to refit, from whence they might rejoin the fleet again at Spithead before they could proceed to sea.

If the increasing sickness of the fleet don't with other defects make me bear up for the Channel the 12th, I shall be well pleased to take the chance of five or six later days ; I will do so if it remains tolerably prudent to do it.

The Thunderer's sick list is up to 160, the number in the fleet exceeds 1000. How are these numbers to be made up ? If by cruising with the fleet in the winter months they become really sickly, you will have no fleet to depend upon for service in the spring. Or should the French fleet come up Channel in the winter or go to Ireland, how is it to be opposed to effect—not with crippled ships from late cruising, and broken disheartened crews with sickness. My thoughts whilst such a great charge is in my hands I am obliged to give your Lordship without reserve. I ever have been open where the good of the service has required it ; and I hope not only in this particular, but upon every other occasion, my conduct towards your Lordship has been fair and satisfactory to you.   I am [etc.].

FROM THE KING

Windsor Castle, 3 October 1778, 20 m. past 10 A.M.

My opinion entirely coincides with Lord Sandwich in approving of the change in Admiral Keppel's sentiments as to where he ought to assemble the fleet.   I do not state my thoughts but as grounded on what I have frequently heard Lord Hawke state as the most effectual and ready means of having a fleet ready to defend this country.   Certainly a considerable part of the fleet must refit at Plymouth, as it will be impossible in any moderate time to refit the whole at Portsmouth.   I hope you will acquaint Lord North that I entirely concur in the mode proposed, and you may state on whose general authority.

I desire the state of Admiral Keppel's fleet may be on Wednesday returned unto me for further inspection.[1]

----

[1] This is evidently the answer to *Corr.*, 2414, though Lord Sandwich's letter is dated September 2 (instead of October).   He writes : ' Your Majesty will perceive Mr Keppel has changed his opinion about the fleet's coming to Torbay.   The reasons he gives, Lord Sandwich was always apprised of, and thinks Mr Keppel's second plan much safer and better than the first.   He would therefore wish to order the fleet to Spithead instead of Torbay, but cannot presume to think of proposing that measure till he knows whether it coincides with your Majesty's sentiments.   It may perhaps be advisable to send some of the ships to Plymouth, as there will otherwise be too much business for one port.'

TO KEPPEL

Admiralty, 3 October 1778.

I have now before me your several private letters from the 13th to the 27th of last month inclusive. Many parts of those letters are already answered in the public dispatches and in the letters with which I have already troubled you as a private correspondent ; but I will now take up very little of your patience upon the points that still remain unanswered.

In your letter of the 13th you mention it as a matter of consideration whether your fleet will not be better at Spithead during the stormy season. I think there is much good sense in that idea ; but the whole of that matter must depend upon the operations of our adversaries more than on our own councils, and the Western squadron must be at sea if the French leave their port either in large or small force.

It will be a very great misfortune to the public service if your old complaints should return upon you so as to make you unfit for winter service, but I will not reason upon this subject, as I will not persuade myself that we shall have such an addition to our other misfortunes.

The idea of a squadron off Cape Clear to rendezvous at Kinsale has been long in agitation, but we have not ships to execute that and many other desirable schemes ; when we get part of our fleet from America, our hands will be more at liberty, but till then it will constantly happen that a service ordered one day must be countermanded the next for something that presses more.

I am sorry that the Jupiter can't be put under your command, but she must go to protect our

Newfoundland trade that is now pushing for the coasts of Spain and Portugal.[1]

I congratulate you upon the success of the Porcupine, and remain in hopes that before your return you will pick up some more Indiamen, as they will in the course of this month be all coming to Lorient or perhaps push for some other of the French ports deeper in the Bay.

The Valiant is ordered to have eighteen-pounders on her upper deck.

There will be two more fireships ready for sea by the time your fleet will be able to sail. I own I think that when great fleets are likely to meet, they are a very useful engine of war. I should not be so confirmed in that idea if I had not from reading and from conversation with many very able sea officers found them in the same sentiments, particularly Lord Howe, who when he left England left it with me as a sort of legacy that that useful though horrid instrument might not be laid aside.[2]

If the brig that you have taken is fit for our service she shall be purchased and employed in any manner you think proper.

There are eight ships of the line ready for sea in all respects but men, 2500 men would complete them all : the ships I mean are the Britannia, Royal George, Namur, Magnificent, Russell, Lion, Yarmouth, and Medway. I could wish to put them all immediately under your command, and that must be done if Monsieur de Fabry comes into these seas ; but if he continues in the

[1] The Jupiter was replaced in the Channel Islands by the Thetis 32.

[2] See *Signals and Instructions*, especially pp. 106, 116, for Howe's orders for fireships in action, and *The Barham Papers*, i. 296, for Kempenfelt's views. A class of fireships as big as 20-gun ships was built during this war. See also below p. 311*n*.

Mediterranean, it is absolutely necessary that five of them at least should be sent immediately to reinforce Admiral Duff, and to enable him to face the Toulon squadron, otherwise our whole trade in that part of the world is at an end.[1]

I wish just to throw it out to you whether it would not be a good scheme to shift the men and officers of the Victory into the Britannia for the next cruise while the Victory is cleaning, and to turn over the men and officers from the Queen into the Royal George in the same manner ; this will give you two first-rates not long off the ground. The Namur will also be ready to sail with you, as she has men enough to carry her to Portsmouth, and is now under orders to sail from the Nore. These three capital ships will be no small addition to the strength of your fleet, and will in a considerable degree compensate for the loss of three or four of the smaller ships while they are in the dock to clean.

I most entirely agree with you in opinion that Torbay is not the proper place for your fleet to come to, especially at this time of the year ; from what I have heard in conversation with the ablest seamen I was long ago confirmed in these sentiments, but I would not venture to controvert your first idea, as I can never presume to set up any superficial notions I may have formed against those of a person of your knowledge and experience. However, there is no occasion for discussion on this subject, and you will find that the orders you now recommend will be immediately sent to you.

[1] Fabry had five ships of the line. For reasons explained in the next letter, no ships were sent to Duff. The Magnificent, Lion, Yarmouth, and Medway sailed for the Leeward Islands in December.

We are in hourly expectation of good news from America, but nothing that in my opinion deserves attention is as yet arrived, though there are stock-jobbing reports that Lord Howe has destroyed d'Estaing's fleet.   I am [etc.].

TO NORTH

[Draft in Lord Sandwich's writing.]

15 October, 1778.

The situation of our affairs is at this time so critical and alarming that my mind will not rest, without I collect my thoughts and put on paper the ideas I have of the danger we are in, and what exertions we can use to guard against the storm that is hanging over us.

From the present conduct of the Court of Spain I am convinced that they mean to go to war with us without much delay, unless they are bought off at a very high rate : their objects are Gibraltar, Minorca, and perhaps Jamaica.   They will content themselves with more or less as circumstances shall turn out and the state of our affairs lay us in a greater or less degree at their mercy.   I conclude that it will be the determination of this government to struggle to the utmost to avoid submitting to any part of these disgraceful and hard conditions, which would occasion the utmost confusion at home and possibly be attended with very disagreeable consequences to those who have the conduct of the King's affairs at this fatal period.

If we had been early enough in our naval preparations, and by that means had had a fleet ready for sea and superior to the combined force of France and Spain, little danger (except to our finances) would in my opinion have been to be apprehended ; but I fear that if Spain now engaged in the contest they will, when united with France, be superior to us in naval strength at least for a time, and will soon find out our vulnerable parts. Jamaica is at their mercy, if a squadron is not immediately sent to defend it. So I think is Minorca, unless a reinforcement of troops is immediately sent thither ; for though Governor Murray does not make a formal demand for an increase of his garrison (at least that I know of) he mentions his weakness, and says that he will in case of an attack do everything he can to defend the island with the *inadequate* force under his command. As to Gibraltar, it would in all probability stand a long siege, but must fall unless relieved by a superior fleet.

In this situation with regard to Spain it seems obvious that we should not offend them on any account, and that we should temporize with them as long as we can, but I cannot conceive that they will suffer themselves to be amused with fair words and professions of friendship only. The great expense they have been at in equipping their fleet is felt by them, and they do not hesitate to declare to us that they mean to procure some advantage to indemnify them for the expense they have incurred. I would therefore go so far with them as to say that our differences with France are in a very narrow compass, and that that Court may be very easily accommodated if they will relinquish the support they are giving the Americans in their claim to independence, and also desist from any pretension of liberty to trade with the King's subjects ; and that with regard to the matters to be discussed with Spain, it is impossible we can enter into any explanation upon that subject till we know from them what points they wish to discuss with us.

This language will gain at least two months, which time might, I should imagine, be very advantageously employed in increasing our strength both by sea and land. As I have already said, some troops should be immediately sent to Minorca and, if possible, a squadron to Jamaica.

Now that there is a probability that Spain will act against us, I much doubt whether it will be judicious to carry our late determination into execution by sending a small squadron into the Mediterranean which must be cut off the moment the Spaniards commence hostilities. The naval force of France in Europe at this time, including their squadron in the Mediterranean, is I suppose near 40 sail of the line in actual commission ; that of the Spaniards, as appears by a late account at Lord Weymouth's office, of about the same number.[1]

Our strength at home consists of 33 ships with Admiral Keppel, 8 more nearly ready for sea, 1 expected soon with the East India ships, 1 from Newfoundland, and 6 others now are or will be ready to receive men before Christmas next. There are besides these about 5 old ships that are now fitted only to receive pressed men, which on an apprehension of an invasion might be usefully employed for our home defence. If we can gain time in the course of another twelve months, that is to say from January 1779 to 1780, we may have 14 more at sea and many coming in every

---

[1] Instructions to Admiral Duff, dated 16 May 1778, promised him ' a considerable reinforcement ' ; but a note in the Hinchingbrooke summary of these instructions says that no reinforcement was sent for the reasons given here by Lord Sandwich.

successive year. It will be proper in this place to observe that the largest number of ships of the line that were ever at one time in commission in the last war was 97, in which 7 taken from the enemy were included.

In this unpleasant situation every exertion ought to be practised. I have already pointed out some things necessary to be done without delay, in addition to which every possible means should be used to increase our number of seamen, upon which the whole naval part of the business absolutely depends. But I cannot think that pressing again from protections would answer that purpose, some new method must be struck out, possibly by calling in the assistance of the military when in winter quarters or by some other means to get the seamen from their lurking holes ; for I am persuaded there are men in the kingdom that cannot be got at for want of better regulations and more strength in the executive part of the government. Lord Howe, or whoever commands in America, should be positively ordered to send home all Admiral Byron's squadron as soon as ever d'Estaing has left those seas ; and in proportion, if he sends away any of his ships, he must also be told on no consideration to detain the marine battalion.

More troops should be raised by every possible means, for everything is now at stake.

I should not think it unadvisable to send a messenger directly to St Petersburg to try whether by communicating the Spanish Memorial to them, and apprising them of our danger, they might not be at least prevailed on to send a fleet to our assistance early in the spring, for surely it is a great object to them not to suffer France and Spain to be superior to us at sea.

If these and other measures to strengthen ourselves are pursued without delay, something favourable may turn out to us that we do not now foresee, and at all events the door of negotiation will be open. If fate then decides against us, we shall be less blameable if we are obliged to submit.

Your Lordship, I flatter myself, will be convinced that nothing could have induced me to trouble you with this long letter but my zeal for the cause in which we are mutually concerned and the attachment I bear to you both as a public and private man.   I am [etc.].

STATE OF SHIPS OF THE LINE

[Not signed.]

Admiralty Office, 24 October 1778.

	No.
East Indies and going thither . . .	4
In North America	19
Newfoundland	1
West Indies	3
Mediterranean	1
Coming from St Helena	1
With Admiral Keppel	33
At home nearly ready	8
May be ready by Christmas if men can be got	6
Supposed may be ready in the course of next year	14
Old ships lying as guardships . . .	5
	95

The greatest number of the line of battle ships at one time in commission in the last war was 97, in October 1759, when hostilities had been commenced above four years, in which were included 6 old ships that lay as guardships and 7 that had been taken in the course of those hostilities from the enemy.

FROM PALLISER

Formidable, 26 October 1778, working in to Spithead.

It gives me real concern that the occurrences of our cruise have not been such as to countenance me in troubling your Lordship with an account of particulars ; for, not having had the luck to meet the French fleet, everything else has been unpleasing. The first part was extraordinary fine weather, the middle and latter very boisterous and bad, by which many of the ships have suffered much in their masts and sails and the fleet has been dispersed. Some of them are very foul, and others leaky, particularly the Ocean, who has been so to a dangerous degree, owing chiefly to her sheathing having been kept on too long ; it is so rotten it washes off in bad weather.

Our chief has at times been very much afflicted with his disorder, and appears to be much chagrined at his bad luck.

I wish I could give a better account of myself. I assure your Lordship I never underwent so much anxiety about anything, as I have done this cruise about the object of our pursuit ; nor more vexation at any disappointment ; nor more fatigue and pain from the disorder in my foot, which about two months before I left town broke out afresh, and instead of healing again as I expected, and as upon former occasions it had done, it has been constantly growing worse, insomuch that if after a little rest it does not grow better I fear I must undergo the like operation as I did several years ago. During the cruise it rarely permitted me to get an hour's sleep at a time.[1]   I have [etc.].

[*P.S.*]—The Admiral, though being in a situation not to fetch in, he made my signal to come in notwithstanding.   It is probable I may save this day's post, but I think he will not be in time.

FROM KEPPEL

Victory, Spithead, 27 October 1778.

The distance between Spithead and Portsmouth will not allow of my sending my dispatches by the post, and I must therefore trouble your Lordship with another express with them.   My public letters state the complaining condition of the fleet that is arrived here with me ; I flatter myself the ships at Plymouth and the Torbay rendezvous are not so complaining.   I believe it will be found both expedient and wise to collect as many ships together at Spithead as soon as possible ; and however the fleet may in future be employed, great men sitting round a council table cannot get it ready without time and the means that are requisite.   For myself, I must repeat what I have said before, that the fleet in a large body will be more properly collected at Spithead than driving in the seas in quest of an enemy that may

---

[1] Keppel wrote on October 28 : ' Sir Hugh Palliser talks of leaving Portsmouth the day after to-morrow.   He has, poor man, suffered most exceedingly in his old complaints during our cruise.'

perhaps the whole time be in port during the winter months ; and how my frame can undertake a cruise, I am well able to judge to be almost impossible doing my duty as becomes me.

Your Lordship's proposition relative to moving the Victory's people into the Britannia would break their hearts and make them believe their duty would have no end. The inconvenience, was I able to undertake winter's cruising, would be great to myself, changing about from ship to ship. Your Lordship will say, What is there to be done ? I answer, if the Sandwich is unfit, her men may go into the Britannia ; the Victory may be refitted at Spithead without *docking*, which had better be deferred till the spring.

I have talked to Sir Robert Harland ; and he will be pleased to have the Ocean's crew in the Royal George, and leave the Queen as she is now manned, except taking a very few favourites.

I am really in so much pain at present that it is with difficulty that I am able either to collect or write my ideas to your Lordship ; indeed my thoughts are fitter for several conversations than communicating by letters.'

More ships than are now ordered into harbour cannot be undertaken till those that are gone in are in forwardness for getting out, though there are very many that require it much.

I shall wait in expectation of the King's promise to go to London. It will take me a few days after my leave reaches me before I can set off.

What of the new ships you join to this home fleet, you will be the judge : I did upon a former wish hope to have Captain Cornwallis of it, I understand he is now captain of the Lion. I am [etc.].

FROM KEPPEL

London, 16 November 1778.

The various services that naturally call for ships may oblige your Lordship to take from the Home fleet for foreign detachments. Every officer commanding these ships is so well thought of by me that I should certainly prefer them to any new set of men and ships ; but as it is probable you will not allow of the whole number of them being employed in the home seas, I have taken the liberty to enclose a curtailed list that I solicit may be looked upon, if I remain in the command, as ships belonging to the fleet employed in these seas.[1]

I found much service from those cutters that sailed well ; those that sailed ill were of but little utility. Whenever a great fleet assembles again, more of these cutters, as well as such like the Rattlesnake, will be necessary ; little fast-sailing brigantines may be of much use. It is necessary to hint to your Lordship that some larger ships of the frigate sort are wanted, and the number should be many more than you have hitherto been able to attach to the fleet. I beg to be understood that I am only mentioning matter that relates to your Grand fleet. I have [etc.].

[1] These eighteen names appear with their ships in Keppel's writing on a small strip of paper that is presumably the list he refers to : Captains Rowley, Ross, Stewart, Lord Mulgrave, Walsingham, Leveson-Gower, Jervis, Bickerton, Maitland, Digby, Macbride, Goodall, Nott, Lord Longford, [Alexander] Hood, Cosby, Peyton, and Hamilton.

CHAPTER II

THE COURTS MARTIAL
November 1778—May 1779

INTRODUCTION

THE first four letters in this chapter concern Lord Sandwich's appointment of Palliser to be Lieutenant-General of Marines, in succession to Sir Charles Saunders. The jealousy caused by this appointment largely accounted for Keppel's distrust of a man who with him was a favourite disciple of Saunders, a beneficiary under his will, and with whom until now he had always been on friendly terms. When Palliser resigned his appointment in 1779 the King, as acute in his observation as he was sound in his judgment, described the original appointment as ' the real source of all the mischief that has now broke forth.' [1]

It was unfortunate too that Palliser and Keppel should have been *political* opponents, but when their lives are considered it is obvious that this was inevitable. Keppel was an aristocrat. He had had quick promotion and had seen the most interesting service in the last war. Engaging in his manners, fluent in speech, and popular with everyone, he was well fitted to become the national hero, although the indecisive engagement off Ushant certainly did not prove him a great commander-in-chief. Palliser, on the other hand, was a practical seaman and a person of high professional intelligence. Possessing no influence, he had had to fight his way up step by step, and although three years older than Keppel he got his flag thirteen years later. Compared with Keppel, he was a self-made man and therefore particularly sensitive to public criticism ; and if he had once been a Roman Catholic, as was stated, he was particularly subject to it.

[1] *Corr.*, 2540.

We have seen above how after the first cruise Palliser worked to dissipate the distrust between Keppel and Sandwich. After the second cruise—that is to say, after the action—there were rumours at Portsmouth and Plymouth and veiled references in the London press to a misunderstanding between Keppel and Palliser.[1] If Keppel wished for an official inquiry into Palliser's conduct (and we can find no evidence that he wanted this at the time) he was perfectly right to keep silent about it, since a court-martial at that time would have delayed the sailing of the fleet, giving the French command of the sea and delivering the year's trade into their hands.

So the fleet sailed, and the circumstances of that long cruise, as we have seen, were very trying to both Admirals. Palliser suffered much from his foot, an old wound caused by an explosion in the Sunderland thirty years before. Nevertheless, it appears from the letters of October 26 and 28 that their relations were still friendly.

Unfortunately on October 15, while the fleet was still at sea, a paragraph appeared in *The General Advertiser and Morning Intelligencer*, blaming Palliser for Keppel's failure to re-attack the French fleet on July 27.[2] When shown this on his return to Portsmouth the over-sensitive Palliser reacted violently. Keppel left Portsmouth for London on October 30,[3] and when he arrived Palliser asked him to sign a denial of the charge. He refused, so Palliser inserted in the newspapers of November 5 a lengthy explanation with a covering letter over the signature Hugh Palliser. After an acrimonious debate

[1] See *Letters of Sir S. Hood*, p. 2, and daily papers, *passim*.

[2] This newspaper was violently anti-governmental in policy, and its pages throughout the winter are full of attacks on Sandwich and Palliser. The ministerial writers replied in *The Morning Post*, which criticises all Keppel's actions from July onwards.

The offending paragraph appeared beneath a covering letter signed 'E.' It was not copied by any of the usual morning papers.

[3] 'Our Admiral set off for town this morning, and I fear will resign if not well received.' Lord Robert Manners to the Marquis of Granby, Rutland MSS. iii. 14.

PLATE III.

VICE-ADMIRAL SIR HUGH PALLISER, BART.

from a mezzotint of a portrait painted and engraved by
J. R. SMITH in 1787.

in the Commons on December 2, in which both Keppel and Palliser spoke, Palliser demanded, in a letter dated December 9, a Court Martial on Keppel for misconduct and neglect of duty.   The charges may be summarised as follows :

1. That he attacked in disorder.
2. That after the van and centre divisions of the British fleet had passed the enemy's rear ' he did not immediately tack and double upon the enemy . . . ; [but left] the vice-admiral of the Blue engaged with the enemy, and exposed to be cut off.'
3. That he hauled down the signal for battle too early.
4. That he ' wore and made sail directly from the enemy,' which ' had the appearance of a flight.'
5. That he did not ' pursue the flying enemy.'

It cannot be denied that to demand a Court Martial on Keppel was not only extreme but unwise ; for the right way to clear his own character was to ask for a Court Martial on himself.

The following letter is typical of sensible contemporary opinion : ' . . . while Keppel was considering whether he should ask for a C.M. on Palliser, behold Palliser has asked for a C.M. on him, charging him with bad conduct, and all the world is full of this.   I think something must come out somehow in it that will pull down Ld Sandwich. . . . There is no doubt of Keppel's coming off with honour, even though he should at first not have managed the attack to the highest perfection ; and Sir H. P. can never find an excuse for not obeying signals.' [1]

On December 16 a Bill was passed through Parliament allowing the Court Martial to be held on shore, since it was thought that Keppel's health was too poor to stand the confinement on board ship, a proceeding which was without precedent.   Though inevitable, it was most unfortunate, for the ensuing publicity emphasised the *political* quarrel

[1] Lady Pembroke to Lord Herbert, 13 December 1778. Pembroke MSS.

and undoubtedly exposed the judges to influence.   The leaders of the Opposition filled the town and attended in court, where they did not hesitate to applaud or to hiss.[1]

Twelve admirals signed a Memorial protesting against Palliser's conduct, and presented it to the King on December 30.   Nevertheless the order for the trial was dated December 31, and the Court assembled on board the Britannia on January 7.   It adjourned immediately to ' the House of the Governor of his Majesty's Garrison at Portsmouth,' and was composed as follows :

President—Sir Thomas Pye, Admiral of the White.

Matthew Buckle } Vice-Admirals of the Red.
John Montagu

Mariot Arbuthnot } Rear-Admirals of the White.
Robert Roddam

Captain Mark Milbanke   Captain Francis Samuel Drake
        Taylor Penny   John Moutray
        William Bennett   Adam Duncan
        Philip Boteler   James Cranston

Sir Samuel Hood, Commissioner at Portsmouth, suggested that Government should provide for the members of the Court by ordering ' their dinners etc. to be sent from the Mountain Tavern, otherwise a cook and housekeeper or steward with kitchen furniture etc. etc., must be provided.'   To this Middleton, the Comptroller of the Navy, objected ; would it not ' give a handle for abuse to those who are seeking the means of finding fault with your Lordship's administration ? '   Nevertheless Hood provided a cook and steward to ' give the gentlemen a good dinner every day,' and having kept ' a register account of every disbursement ' had spent £300 by January 18.[2]   Sandwich himself attended the trial on January 28 (' Your Lordship may be assured of a well-aired bed,' wrote Hood), but did not give evidence. The trial was concluded on February 11 and Keppel ' unanimously and honourably acquitted,' the charges being described as ' malicious and unfounded.'

[1] *Corr.*, 2497, Pembroke MSS.
[2] From Hood, January 1, 6 and 18 ; from Middleton, January 2.

A processsion was formed and marched through the streets of Portsmouth, wearing light blue ribbons with the word KEPPEL in gold letters, and headed by a band playing ' See the Conquering Hero Comes.' ' The whole concourse and ladies from the windows supplied the vocal part, and the crowd closed each period of the harmony with a choral cheer. . . . It is impossible to paint the joy that possessed every face. Holiday was expressed in every look, and the hearts of the people were in their eyes.' [1] ' All of which, if he is a sensible man,' wrote Lady Pembroke, ' must have distressed him terribly.' [2] In London the mob looted Palliser's house and broke all the Prime Minister's windows.

During the course of the trial the King proposed to strengthen the Board of Admiralty by making Howe First Lord and promoting Sandwich to be a Secretary of State vice Lord Suffolk. An account of the suggested re-arrangements will be found in Fortescue.[3]

Palliser resigned his offices, and the Admiralty asked Keppel whether he intended to continue in the command of the fleet. Keppel replied on March 15 that no one was more willing than himself to risk his life and forgo his ease in the service of his country ' when I can at the same time be secure of my honour,' but that ' the public will not be well served by any officer, unless he is confident that his reputation and upright endeavours will be well supported by his Majesty's ministers,' and he concluded ' that it is next to impossible for me to render creditable and beneficial service to the King and the nation by my continuing in the command of the Western squadron, under the direction and authority of those whose approbation in the execution of my duty and support afterwards, experience has taught me, I cannot depend upon.' [4]

Lord Thurlow, in two hurried letters to Sandwich, both undated, but one endorsed by Sandwich ' March

---

[1] *An authentic and impartial copy of the Trial.*
[2] To Lord Herbert, 18 February 1779. Pembroke MSS.
[3] *Corr.*, pp. xviii–xxii, 2470–2611, *passim.*
[4] Keppel to Stephens, March 15.

1779,' expresses his fear that Keppel may after all agree to remain in command, ' which however it may disgrace him will I think disgrace us more,' and wonders if the Admiralty may not treat the words ' next to impossible ' (in Keppel's letter) as a definite refusal, and by accepting them as such, give him no chance of withdrawing them. The Admiralty evidently decided to adopt this plan, for on March 18 a letter was sent to Keppel with the approval of the King (see p. 236), expressing their ' surprise and concern ' that he should find it necessary to resign, but ordering him to strike his flag. To this Keppel replied on March 21 that he was glad to be relieved of further correspondence with the present Board of Admiralty, but that he must observe that ' there is so much offence conceived in the expression of your letter, written by the Lords' directions, that nothing less than the deference due from me to the Board of Admiralty would prevent me replying in terms that would not be pleasing to their Lordships.' [1]

Sir Charles Hardy was given command of the fleet with Kempenfelt as his first captain. Vice-Admiral Robert Man took Palliser's place at the Admiralty.

During Keppel's trial several matters respecting Palliser's conduct and behaviour on July 27 and 28 were given in evidence, so that it was obvious from the first that he too would have to be tried. Keppel refused to act as prosecutor, and as there were no fixed charges, the Court was ordered ' to enquire into the conduct and behaviour of the said Vice-Admiral,' Mr Jackson, the Judge Advocate of the Fleet, conducting the inquiry.

This mode of ordering the Court Martial was approved by Thurlow, who wrote to Lord Sandwich in an undated letter : ' According to the best judgment I can form of a matter which I understand so little I think this mode of ordering the Court Martial will do, and to this opinion I am much determined by Lord Mulgrave's judgment who is well acquainted with such business.' [2]

[1] Keppel to Stephens, March 21.
[2] But Mulgrave's opinion on Courts Martial was not always accepted, cf. *Parl. Hist.*, xx. 59–73.

The Court assembled on board the Sandwich in Portsmouth Harbour on April 12. The members were as follows :

President, George Darby, Vice-Admiral of the Blue.

Robert Digby, Rear-Admiral of the Blue.

Captain Sir Chaloner Ogle	Captain Richard Kempenfelt
Joseph Peyton	William Bayne
Mark Robinson	Adam Duncan
Samuel Granston Goodall	James Cranston [1]
Robert Linzee	John Colpoys
George Robinson Walters	

On May 5 the Court acquitted Palliser and found that his ' conduct and behaviour on those days were in many respects highly exemplary and meritorious : at the same time cannot help thinking it was incumbent on him to have made known to his Commander-in-Chief the disabled state of the Formidable.'

This was the end of the proceedings, but the results, owing to the publicity of the first trial and the violence of Keppel's partisans, were far-reaching. The question divided the Navy and had a marked effect on discipline. As late as 1785 Captain Leveson-Gower abused Henry Bazely, one of his midshipmen and a son of Palliser's flag-captain, with harsh reflections on his father's character.[2]

Keppel did not serve at sea again. At the fall of Lord North's ministry in March 1782 he became First Lord ; except for a few months when Howe took his place, he remained at the Admiralty until December 1783.

Palliser spent £3000, which he could ill afford, in his defence, and by resigning his offices lost an income of £3000 a year. He asked North to restore him to the Marines, and when that failed he petitioned Sandwich to give him a seat at the Admiralty.[3] In May 1780 he

---

[1] Cranston retired from sickness after the third day.
[2] *Letters of Byam Martin*, iii. 292 n. See also below, p. 236, l. 9.
[3] Palliser to North, 13 August 1779. From Palliser, 18 March 1780.

was made Governor of Greenwich Hospital—an appointment which created a storm in Parliament, and which led Palliser to make a very spirited defence of his conduct in a speech delivered before a Committee of the House on December 4. The draft of this speech was sent to Lord Sandwich on June 22 and is among the papers at Hinchingbrooke. We have not printed it here because it resembles, in the main lines of the argument, the printed version.[1]

Finally, in a pathetic letter of February 28 [1781 ?], he again asks for his half-pay, and points out that the granting of this request could not *increase* the attacks of Sandwich's enemies.

The alterations in the Robust's log book, discovered during Keppel's trial, involved her captain, Alexander Hood, in serious trouble, many important people accusing him of deliberate dishonesty. There are naturally a number of references to this among the Bridport papers. Hood evidently felt bitterly towards Keppel. ' Should an officer dare,' he writes in an undated draft, ' for his own justification to say a word, or to alter a word in a log book, those words are to be construed, by the admiral, into atrocious crimes. They must be meant to affect his life, and what on evidence is delivered under the oath he takes, is deemed falsehood, if that evidence does not come up to the admiral's feelings and those of his *party*.'

There is a very frank letter from Palliser to Hood, dated 18 March 1779, asking to see him before he goes abroad, which certainly does not suggest that there had been any collusion between them. ' The principal thing for me to establish is, the true situation and condition of myself and of the several other ships of my division at different periods, in order to justify myself and division and to detect and expose the wicked plot for my ruin

---

[1] The speech is important because of the beneficial effect that it had on public opinion. In it he points out the differences between the Official Minutes of Keppel's Trial and Almon's edition of them. See above, p. xi.

formed on the day of action : be assured my dear Sir I shall not require anything that can be improper, inconvenient or disagreeable to you.'   More interesting than these is a letter from Mrs Hood to Lady Chatham, in September 1782, describing his reception by Keppel on being appointed Kempenfelt's successor as commander of a division in the Channel fleet—his first employment since leaving the Robust. ' His Lordship received him at his bedside early on Monday morning, and was pleased to wish that what had passed might be forgot, which I think was a tacit acknowledgment of the injustice done to Mr Hood. . . . I think that Mr Hood's restoration to the service being on the ground only of his *merit* in *it* and owing that entirely to Lord Keppel and Lord Howe, with the approbation of the King, are very pleasing circumstances and I thank God.   Though his sufferings, and mine, have been great for above three years back, yet his conscious integrity has carried him through ; and he made a stand not only against party rage, but against a weak government and the last Naval Lord at the head of the Admiralty, who would have had him gone out in the Robust, degrading his rank as an officer, which he had the spirit to resist, and chose to face his enemies at home rather than fly from them in so disgraceful a way, though absolutely without support from any person whatever.' [1]

A final flicker of the conflagration of 1779 can be seen sixteen years later when Palliser writes, 6 July 1795, to congratulate Hood on his victory off Ile Groix. ' Your victory in the view of all is great and important, and in the minds of many must appear wonderful that you should obtain such a victory on that *lee* shore so much dreaded by a former *renowned* hero, and what adds lustre to the action is your remaining on that coast to block up the enemy's fleet and perform other services to your own country.'

. In spite of what the King and Lord Sandwich thought,

[1] See below, pp. 237–41, 243–5, for Sir Samuel Hood's argument on behalf of his brother.

as far as his own interests were concerned Hood acted wisely in declining to go to North America as a private captain in the Robust. His presence at home seems to have convinced his enemies that he had not acted dishonestly, and public opinion by 1782 seems to have condoned the fault so violently assumed after the disclosures of 8 January 1779.

FROM ROBINSON

House of Commons, 5 o'clock [8 December 1775].

My dear Lord—We are brought into a situation of great distress by Lord North's acquiescing with your Lordship's recommendation of Sir Hugh Palliser to be Lieutenant General of Marines and his having kissed hands for it to-day. [Rear-Admiral] Lord Howe had some time ago applied to Lord North for it, which had slipped Lord North's memory, the thing coming so suddenly upon him, and Lord Howe has now told him that he will resign his flag immediately. Lord Howe has left the House this instant after having told Lord North this; and if something is not immediately done you will probably in an hour or two receive a letter for this purpose from Lord Howe. The only thing that strikes at present to remedy the evil is to make Lord Howe General of Marines, and to prevail on Admiral Forbes to resign on a pension on the Old Store Fund.[1]

Something must be done without loss of time,

---

[1] On December 8 and 9 respectively, when they heard that Sir Charles Saunders was dead, Sir Charles Knowles, who was senior to Forbes, and Sir John Moore, a vice-admiral of the Red, asked to succeed him as Lieutenant-General of Marines. Lord Howe evidently asked for this dignity while Sir Charles was still alive, which takes away the sting from his friend Captain Leveson-Gower's remark that Palliser was appointed ' before he was cold ' (Cornwallis Wykeham-Martin MSS., p. 315, and Cornwallis-West, *The Life and Letters of Admiral Cornwallis*, p. 56). When Forbes refused to resign, Howe was pacified with the command in North America, at Shuldham's expense (see vol. i., pp. 45, 119–20).

or all will be blown up. Let me entreat your Lordship to give this your best attention and most serious consideration. The consequences are great ; but I so well know your Lordship's abilities that gloomy and distressing as appearances are at present and must be if not removed directly, that I have hopes you will be able to chalk out the way to remove them.

The debate here is just coming on and I write this in great haste, but ever am [etc.].

FROM KEPPEL [1]

Bagshot Park, 17 December 1775.

It is much credited that Admiral Forbes is to retire from the post of General of Marines and that Rear-Admiral Lord Howe is to be appointed his successor. I am not used to feel disgrace or affront ; but indeed, my Lord, I must feel cold to my own honour and the rank in which I stand in his Majesty's service, if I remain silent and see one of the youngest rear admirals of the fleet promoted to Lieutenant General of Marines, and a few days afterwards another rear admiral made General of Marines.

It is not for me to say who should or should not be appointed to those honours ; but I may presume to say to your Lordship, and through you as head of the sea department beg leave to have it laid before his Majesty with my humblest submission to him, that little as I am entitled to claim merit, yet a series of long service may, I hope, permit me to observe that such a repetition of promotion to the junior admirals of the fleet cannot but dispirit every senior officer jealous of

[1] Keppel had lately become a vice-admiral of the White.

his own honour, as it tends to manifest to the whole profession the low esteem he stands in, which allow me to say may at one time or other have its bad effects. Juniors cannot complain, nor are they dishonoured, when their seniors are promoted.

My Lord, I must hope I stand excused for writing in such plain terms. But when I am writing or speaking from facts and feelings of honour, I cannot allow myself to express those sentiments in a doubtful manner. I have [etc.].

TO KEPPEL

Admiralty, 20 December 1775.

I have laid the letter with which you have favoured me before the King, but did not receive any particular commands from his Majesty relative to its contents.

I am sorry that the appointment of Sir Hugh Palliser to be Lieutenant General of Marines is considered by you in a different light from that in which it appears to me. No one is more sensible of your merit both as an officer and in every other particular than I am; but as seniority has never been attended to in the appointment either of a General or Lieutenant General of Marines, I cannot be of opinion that those admirals who are higher on the list than the person to whom his Majesty gives the appointment have any just cause of complaint.

When Sir Charles Saunders was appointed Lieutenant General of Marines, he was the youngest vice admiral and had been the youngest rear admiral within the same year; and I never heard that the many distinguished officers above him complained of his having been honoured with that mark of his Majesty's favour. I am with great regard [etc.].

FROM KEPPEL

Bath, 27 December 1775.

The letter your Lordship has done me the honour to write directed to Bagshot, I did not receive till this morning or should sooner have acknowledged it. The very indifferent manner with which my remonstrance is received, however mortifying, does not make me repent of having made it; I have done my duty to my profession and to myself, which is a comfort I hope always to feel and never to depart from. Your Lordship is pleased to reason different from myself, which by no means heals the affront or can allow me to see the senior officers of the fleet but in a neglected light.

The situation you remind me Sir Charles Saunders was in, when appointed Lieutenant General of Marines, is in a degree correct; but your Lordship has avoided mentioning the whole about that officer, which I am obliged now to do, though I am almost certain your memory furnishes you very completely upon the subject. Admiral Boscawen had beaten the French fleet and Sir Charles Saunders just returned *from taking Quebec* when it was judged proper to reward them with honours, and the marine posts of generals was created to be given to those two most excellent officers. Afterwards the General of Marines fell vacant by the death of Admiral Boscawen: Admiral Forbes, one of the very eldest flag officers of the fleet, was his successor. Sir Charles Saunders unfortunately for this country dies, and Sir Hugh Palliser, one of the very youngest flag officers of the fleet, is his immediate successor. What is to follow time will discover. Your Lordship must wish me to finish, and I am [etc.].

FROM PALLISER

Formidable, 26 October 1778.[1]

It is impossible for me to express how much I feel myself honoured by his Majesty's being graciously pleased to think of me in the disposal of the Britannia, which is certainly a preferable ship to the Formidable. As some things arise for consideration upon which I wish first to be honoured with your Lordship's friendly advice and opinion, therefore, if there is not a necessity for immediately determining, I shall be glad to defer it till I have the pleasure of seeing your Lordship. I have [etc.].

FROM PALLISER

Portsmouth, 28 October 1778.[2]

By Admiral Keppel's *first express* I had the honour to write to your Lordship, for we both got in too late for the post. Since that time I have learnt more about the condition of the ships, and

[1] It should be noticed that an interval of three years separates this letter from the last.

[2] In a letter received this day endorsed by Lord Sandwich, 'Nothing about the action, chiefly about Finch's prize,' Keppel wrote: 'I must be glad [Captain Finch] has done so well, but indeed my Lord my wishes and pursuits were of a more honourable description. However, I have failed, and have been the subject of slander; my intentions and the purity of them must carry me through. But although I may have cause to complain, I have avoided putting in any of my letters upon business to you this complaint of unjust usage *from some*, and will not even in this note dwell upon the subject.'

although I am very imperfectly informed of anything I fear we have brought you in a fleet almost all unfit for service at present.

I have seen Lord Howe only for a moment, so I know nothing about the state of our ships in America.

I came on shore last night for the sake of a little rest and quiet, which is very much interrupted by a paper put into my hands at landing containing a paragraph to justify Admiral Keppel's conduct for not continuing the battle on the 27th July last, and laying the whole blame on me and my division. After such a publication I think the nation has a right to know, and I am determined it shall be rightly informed, whether I or anyone else are blameable for what passed that day; nevertheless I shall not do anything rashly, although I think on the absurd assertion with the highest indignation. And although I have ever resolved to disregard anonymous papers, yet the quarter from whence this reflection evidently comes makes it exceeding alarming, and together with many other disagreeable things too numerous to mention in a letter makes me a very miserable being at present.

Admiral Keppel is not yet on shore; but the moment he is so, I shall speak to him upon it in very serious terms. I have only one favour to hope for, that is that I may not be out of the way when the Parliament meets. I am [etc.].

FROM PALLISER

Pall Mall, 31 October 1778.

Your Lordship will not be surprised that in my present unpleasant situation I am not in condition to think on anything else but the measures that may be best for me to take.

Amongst the many things that successively come into my head, I have for the present fixed on two for further consideration as expedients for obtaining that satisfaction I ought to have (and without which I can neither serve nor live) : the one an easy quiet way without disturbing the quiet of anyone else, the other a more direct way of coming at the point and matters of fact, but which may be productive of many things disagreeable to others which had better be avoided if possible. I have put my thoughts together on these two methods merely to take time to reflect thereon before I take any steps whatever, wishing to avoid anything that may be deemed rash.   I have [etc.].

FROM THE KING

Queen's House, 5 November 1778.

Though rather late and unwillingly, I am glad to find Lord North is coming into the right path [for obtaining a better attendance of ministerialists in Parliament].

Sir Hugh Palliser's account of the action, published in the newspapers of this morning,[1] is a clear proof he did all that could be expected of him, and that the dispersing his division made the French fleet escape. This must make an eternal breach between the two admirals, and occasion much ill-humour among those concerned in that day ; but

---

[1] The letter was dated November 4 and appeared in *The London Evening Post*, November 3–5 ; *The Morning Post*, November 5 ; *The London Chronicle*, November 3–5 ; *The Morning Chronicle*, *The Morning Intelligencer* and *The Gazeteer* of November 6.

Palliser could not avoid the step he has been drove to without the greatest blame.

FROM PALLISER

Pall Mall, 6 November 1778.

I have had a most gracious reception indeed from his Majesty, which (as it ought) makes me perfectly easy.

Admiral Keppel was about half an hour in the closet. I guess from some things that dropped that he declined conversing about the engagement, reserving himself (in case any enquiry should be called for) till then.

Lord Howe was in a much longer time. I had a little conversation with his Lordship and was sorry to find by him that it is very doubtful whether the expedition will proceed to the West Indies; amongst other reasons he speaks of the ships' not being able to proceed if these westerly winds continue. I hope something will arrive before the convoys sail that may inform us for certain whether the expedition goes on and with what ships.[1]

I am very uneasy about the state of our provisions in America. I am afraid they have not enough to carry them through the winter; and the ships now going out with supplies, the odds is against them that they will not get hold of the coast or that they will be blown off the coast.

I will wait on your Lordship in the morning. I am [etc.].

[1] See chapter iv. The expedition sailed on November 3.

FROM CAPTAIN WALSINGHAM [1]

Portsmouth, 11 November 1778.

My Lord—I am much flattered by your Lordship's friendship and good opinion, both [of] which it shall be my study to deserve.

As soon as any plan is formed for procuring men I am sure my brother officers will give it *firm* support and assistance. I have conversed with them on the subject on receiving your Lordship's first commands and find them unanimous; when I have your permission to go to town I will stir in it amongst my friends in Parliament.

I am cleaning my ship as fast the few hands I have will admit of, keep up constant fires and fumigations, but nothing can be done effectual till my hold is swept. I mean to dock her the last thing for two reasons: the first to take her out as clean as possible, the next if possible totally to eradicate the disease.

I take in the most friendly manner your Lordship's kind advice. *Everybody* laments it, and I can assure you no one more than Mr Keppel did, or strove to suppress it. Whenever it is mentioned amongst us it is talked of as a most unhappy affair which rose from nothing and may end unpleasantly; but there is *no party* in the case, indeed there is no grounds for it. I believe I have traced the author of the letter. I have great reason to believe that he is a foolish boy, and from his own production confessedly a fool and a lubber.

[1] The Hon. Robert Boyle Walsingham, a captain of 15 June 1757. He was lost with his ship, the Thunderer, in the West Indies in the famous hurricane of 1780.

II.   P

I hope in God it will drop. I shall be happy to contribute to it, wishing all parties well.[1]

My gunner is upwards of seventy, has been for some time past his service, but since the last voyage has had the fever settle on his lungs and ended in addition to other disorders in an asthma; he begs for superannuation and is entitled to it. I shall be much obliged to your Lordship if you will let me have Daniel Martin gunner of the Portland as he is well recommended to me and a good man in that department is of the utmost consequence. I am [etc.].

FROM THE KING

Queen's House, 10 December 1778, 47 m. past 6 P.M.

On the present very unpleasant business the public must have approved of Lord Hawke's presiding; I am sorry his health gives him so fair a plea to decline. It will deserve some consideration whether Sir Thomas Pye ought not to take that part of course, or whether Sir Charles Hardy shall be ordered to Portsmouth. Sir Thomas Frankland and the Duke of Bolton seem no ways fit to be sought out on this occasion; Admiral Forbes, I should suppose unable to undertake the fatigue.[2]

[1] On December 11, during Mr. Temple Luttrell's motion for the trial of Sir Hugh Palliser, Captain Walsingham said he was ' perfectly satisfied ' the anonymous letter was written by a lieutenant in Palliser's own flagship (*Parl. Hist.*, xx. 56). Hunt (*Life of Palliser*, 234) attributes it to Captain Hon. George Berkeley, Keppel's nephew, who was fifth lieutenant of the Victory in July, and afterwards master and commander of the Firebrand fireship.

[2] The order of seniority of the admirals was as follows : Lord Hawke (Admiral of the Fleet), John Forbes, Sir Thomas Frankland, the Duke of Bolton, Sir Charles Hardy, Lord Northesk, Sir Thomas Pye . . . Admiral Pye, Commander-in-Chief at Portsmouth, was president of the Court that tried Admiral Keppel.

FROM PALLISER

12 December 1778.

As I am of opinion it will be proper I should strike my flag and come on shore in case Admiral Keppel should do so, I submit it to your Lordship whether I should do it by request from myself or in pursuance of an order from the King ; but if Admiral Keppel should not be put out of commission, I suppose it will not be necessary that I should.

Enclosed I have taken the liberty to send a letter for Mr Stephens, to be used or not as your Lordship may think proper. I have [etc.].

P.S.—I have desired Mr Astley to prepare a case for taking an opinion whether captains called as evidences can sit as members on a court martial. I will inform myself of the Judge Advocate what has been the practice of the service in that respect.[1]

I now think it will be necessary to employ privately some good writers in the papers.

FROM THE KING

Queen's House, 13 December 1778.

It was very natural to foresee, when so strong a charge was brought against Admiral Keppel, that he must be desirous of having the testimony

---

[1] Walsingham, although a witness, insisted on his right to take his seat. The Law Officers decided that ' if any officer entitled by his rank to sit is either prosecutor, party, or witness, the officer next in seniority must supply his place ' ; and in conformity with this decision the Court was composed. Sir John Laughton states that ' it was not and never had been unusual for even the prosecutor to sit as a member of the court ' (*Letters of Sir T. Byam Martin*, iii. 294, 294 n.).

of an officer so much concerned in the action, and whose character is so well established.[1]

The strengthening the squadron with the addition of the one destined for the West Indies seems highly expedient. Lord Shuldham seems well qualified to take the command of this fleet.

FROM SIR SAMUEL HOOD

Portsmouth Dockyard, 26 December 1778.

My Lord—The Memorial brought to Lord Shuldham by Captain Robinson with a letter from Lord Bristol had the name of Lord Hawke and twelve others, and Lord Shuldham and Admiral Gayton made the number fifteen, when Captain Robinson returned with it to London. Admiral Pye declined to sign it, and it was not carried to Admiral Montagu. I find the Memorial contained a great deal about the Admiralty and more than was necessary ; it was not meant to be mischievous to the Board, or rather to your Lordship.[2] I do not find it was offered to any captain.

I was much alarmed, my Lord, last night by Captain Truscott, who came at ten o'clock to tell me that the crew of his Majesty's ship Elizabeth had mutinied and refused to weigh the anchors until they were paid a part of the wages due to them. Upon talking with Captain Truscott I found the ship had not been in commission a year, and

---

[1] This must be Captain John Jervis of the Foudroyant, in which ship Lord Shuldham flew his flag during the service mentioned in the second paragraph. On December 11, Admiral Keppel wrote to the Admiralty asking that Jervis should be kept at home, so an acting captain was appointed to the Foudroyant.

[2] The King described it to Lord North as ending ' without any request consequently shews only great wrath at Sir Hugh Palliser and the Admiralty ' (*Corr.*, 2495).

two months' advance had been paid on board before she went to sea in the summer. I therefore advised him to turn the people up and acquaint them that he had been with me, and that I would be on board early in the morning to explain to them how much they were mistaken in their conduct, and that it was not in my power to make a further payment but that every man might remit six months' wages so soon as he had twelve due; and upon my going on board I found not the least difficulty in satisfying them of their error. They very cheerfully got the anchors up, and the ship is now at sea. I went to St Helen's in the Elizabeth, and seeing Lord Shuldham he gave me the enclosed to be forwarded to you to-day, but the post being gone before I reached the shore I have sent it by express, and have [etc.].

FROM SIR SAMUEL HOOD

Portsmouth Dockyard, 31 December 1778.

I never saw the memorial, therefore cannot speak the particular matter of it ; but from what Admiral Pye and Lord Shuldham have said, it bears very hard and conveys strong censure upon the Admiralty. Lord Bristol seemed certain that it would not only overset the Board but the ministry ; at least he so expressed himself in his letter.

The underneath eleven names were to it. Who were the other four signers I cannot find out at present, but probably may from Admiral Gayton, whom I mean to see as soon as I have finished the dock pay.[1]   I have [etc.].

[1] The memorial as presented was signed by Hawke, Bolton, Geary, Young, Moore, S. Graves, Gayton, Harland, Pigot, Shuldham, Bristol and Barton ; and not by Frankland or Campbell.

Lord Hawke	Sir Robert Harland
Sir Thomas Frankland	Admiral Pigot
the Duke of Bolton	Lord Bristol
Admiral Geary	Lord Shuldham
Sir John Moore	Admiral Campbell
Admiral Gayton	

TO PALLISER

Admiralty, 4 January 1779.

Admiral Keppel has written to Mr Stephens to mention his intention of calling me as a witness in order to my producing such letters as I received from you from the 27th of July to the 23rd of August.

I find in my possession two letters from you during that period, in one of which you mention your sending me a summary account of the action ; but I can find no such paper, unless that of which the enclosed is a copy was the said summary, which I can hardly believe. Pray explain this matter to me by the return of the messenger, whom I send to Sir Samuel Hood that less notice may be taken.[1] I am [etc.].

FROM PALLISER

Portsmouth, 6 January 1779.

The summary account alluded to in my letter to your Lordship is that of which you have sent me a copy.

Mr Keppel having called upon your Lordship to produce my letters to you, I must also when

[1] The summary is printed above, p. 131.

you are examined desire you will produce such letters as you have received from him containing any accounts of the engagement on the 27th of July last. I have accordingly wrote to Mr Stephens to desire he will give you notice of it, and I have [1] [etc.].

FROM MR. JACKSON

Portsmouth, 8 January 1779.

My Lord—It was yesterday requested by Mr Keppel that all masters summoned to give evidence should be required to bring in their log books to lay on the table. Sir H. Palliser thought it would be sufficient for the Court's information if each master after giving his evidence was then to leave his log for that purpose. The request was agreed to be granted. The masters this morning in court produced their logs. It was agreed to swear them that they were in point of time between 23rd and 30th July without any alteration or addition. The master of the Robust objected, saying his book had been altered and added to, respecting what had passed between the days named, by order of his captain. His examination to this particular has given a strong impression ; it was agreed not to examine him as to the nature of the alterations and additions. He was only required to ascertain that such had been made *since it was known Mr Keppel would be tried.*

Captain Marshall has been under examination all day and comes on again to-morrow. Hitherto,

[1] Lord Sandwich appeared before the Court on January 28, having received the King's permission. The Court resolved that it could ' not take cognizance, in point of evidence, of any matters contained in letters of private correspondence,' so Lord Sandwich withdrew, after agreeing with the Court's decision.

in my judgment, his evidence has not produced what was expected from it.

Your Lordship will not I hope forget the liberty I took in begging your excuse for such rough and hasty hints, nor refuse me the indulgence at a moment so peculiarly due to one who has not time for even necessary refreshments.[1] I am [etc.].

FROM THE KING

Queen's House, 10 January 1779, 43 m. pt. one P.M.

The express to Mr Jackson to send his accounts in a more expeditious manner was highly necessary.

I am surprised Captain Hood should have altered the log book, he has always borne the character of a man of strict honour. I therefore trust that affair will be explained, and that his conduct will rather be proved to have been actuated by over niceness than any inclination to alter the complexion of his document. Till it is cleared up, it certainly is a most favourable event for Keppel.

FROM THE KING

11 January 1779, 35 minutes P.M.

Lord Sandwich must have been surprised at the very extraordinary question put at the close of Captain Marshall's evidence to him by the Court. The newspapers lay it at the door of Vice-Admiral Montagu; if that is true, Lord Sandwich need

[1] Jackson, the Judge Advocate, wrote a less restrained letter to Stephens the same day : ' You cannot conceive the impression the alteration in the Robust's log book has made. A loud hiss took place below the Bar, which was not rebuked by the Court ' (*Corr.*, 2498).

have no scruple, if he by the failure of others should become president, being thought to stand under his influence.[1]

FROM THE KING

12 January 1779.

Lord Sandwich must see that but very little progress is made by the court martial; that if soon the business is not put into some shorter mode, that it may last for four or five months.[2]

FROM PALLISER

Portsmouth, 16 January 1779.

I beg to know the time when Admiral Keppel's journal was delivered into the office. I think I show [up] a most contemptible trick, in entering an erroneous account of the distance the fleet was from Ushant according to the ship's reckoning

[1] On January 9 Admiral Montagu asked Captain Marshall of the Arethusa, repeating frigate, this question: '. . . do you, from your own observation, or knowledge, know of any act of Admiral Keppel's behaving or conducting himself unbecoming a flag officer ? ' Palliser, as prosecutor, objected to the question as being a matter of opinion rather than fact ; but the Court allowed the question, and the witness answered, ' No, as God is my judge ! ' (*Trial of Admiral Keppel*, Official edition and Almon's edition).

Vice-Admiral Buckle resigned, owing to sickness, at the end of the session on January 13. This left Montagu the senior member after the president. The Court was adjourned on January 18, owing to the indisposition of Admiral Roddam.

[2] Sir Samuel Hood also was impatient. He wrote to Lord Sandwich on January 18 : ' As the Court aim at making every evidence to give judgment upon his own testimony instead of judging upon the facts that are produced, the shortest way of coming to a conclusion would be for each captain to be called to declare at once whether the Commander-in-Chief did right or not, and let most voices carry it.'

on the 27th and 28th July last, to favour the pretence that it would have been dangerous to have pursued the French till we had seen them into port. If it comes out as I expect it is a subterfuge that must prove disgraceful. I have [etc.].

Captain Hood has most manfully resisted the must cruel attack that can be imagined.

FROM PALLISER [1]

It is very probable it is intended to ask Lord S. some leading questions to discover whether his Lordship advised the charge's being made. Sir H. P. has declared in Parliament that he advised with no person living whether he *should* or *should not* make a charge. His Lordship can safely say that he did not advise it. Sir H. P. can safely say that he expected Admiral K. would bring a charge against him, therefore he deferred it till he found Admiral Keppel was determined to ruin his reputation without a trial. Sir H. P. then drew his charge, and advised with Counsel about the form and method of proceeding.

About the same time he told Lord S. that he had long had reason to expect that A. K. intended to endeavour to fix the blame on him for not re-attacking the French fleet ; therefore he had kept in his bureau a paper addressed to his Lordship, containing some particulars for his information to the purport of the present charge, that in case he should be killed in the expected engagement on the following cruise, his Lordship might be enabled to contradict any reflections on his memory.

[1] In Palliser's writing : no date or signature, but endorsed by Sandwich ' recd Jan. 25. 1779.'

Lord S. should examine whether A. K., on his going to sea, expressed in his letters a discontent at the fleet's being ill manned, and whether he expressed being satisfied on this head.   There is reason to suspect he will draw from many of the captains upon evidence a complaint about their men.   Did he not return a number of men sent out to him off Plymouth ? [1]

Lord S. would recollect his letters to A. K. In one he says : ' You may take the Blenheim and Amelia for appearance sake.'

I must beg the favour of your Lordship to furnish me with copies of my letters to you, also Mr Keppel's to your Lordship as soon as may be.

The business here goes on very heavily and disagreeably.   The consequence of granting a sea court-martial to be held on shore is felt very severely :   besides the ill effect of the court's being filled with the great leaders of party, every good purpose is defeated that was intended by the regulations for courts martial.

It is proposed to examine very few more evidences, as scarce any more are to be found that *will know* anything relating to *the points* in question.   It is proposed (if you don't desire to be excused from appearing) to finish with your evidence, and as soon as ever you can make it convenient, letting me know the night before when you will be here ; and if you come into town between 10 and 1 o'clock you may be called in immediately.

An apology will be made to you for desiring to produce private letters ; but as the other party has set the example, shall hope you will not object.   I am advised the letters will be very

---

[1] See above, p. 122.

useful.   I wish for your answer as soon as possible, and that you will let me know the night before you come ; if you come in any time between 10 and 1 you may be called in directly.   If I don't call you now I can't do it after closing my evidence, nor call upon you for anything when you appear at the summons of the other party.

FROM PALLISER

[In his writing : no date or signature : on or after 2 February 1779.   Harland gave evidence on February 1, Campbell on February 2.]

Admiral Keppel's defence, and the evidences of Admirals Harland and Campbell, amount to a charge against all the captains of the centre division for disobeying the admiral's signal for forming the line whilst he was standing towards the enemy after the engagement ;   none of his ships came near him, therefore he was prevented renewing the attack at time.

Admiral Keppel pleads that he was again prevented attacking in the evening by the Vice Admiral of the Blue's not getting with his division in their stations in the line.

If one person is to be tried upon what arises out of the evidences of Admiral Keppel's trial, why not the whole who are charged in like manner ?

TO PALLISER

Admiralty, 4 February 1779.

As I imagine that the court martial is now drawing to a conclusion, and as it is not difficult to judge what will be the issue of it, I cannot avoid suggesting to you that it seems to me inevitable that you must undergo a trial also. It is universally believed that some one of Admiral Keppel's friends in the House of Commons will move to address the King that your conduct may be inquired into ; I therefore think it will be much better that this office should take it out of their hands by ordering a court martial to be assembled to examine into your conduct in consequence of what has appeared in the evidence given upon Mr. Keppel's trial. I am persuaded you do not wish to avoid such inquiry ; but I think it my duty as a friend to tell you that, was it otherwise, I do not believe that as things now stand it could by any means be avoided ; and in that case I am sure you will join with me in opinion that it will be advisable to proceed in the mode which is least liable to objection.

If these matters are first agitated in Parliament during the present ferment, I think it most likely that several resolutions may be carried very hostile to you ; but it should seem to me that if the matter is taken up by the Board, it will check the warm attack of your enemies after the conclusion of the present court martial, when you must expect that the stream will run strong against you. I am ever [etc.].

P.S.—You will observe that if motions are made to dismiss you from your employments etc., it will be an argument against them to say that your cause is now under trial, and that therefore it will prejudge it if any question is previously carried against you.

FROM PALLISER

Portsmouth, 5 February 1779.

I am truly sensible of your Lordship's friendship, and have long been of the same opinion
with your Lordship that a court martial on me
is necessary. As to its being ordered by the
Admiralty, grounded upon what has appeared
upon Admiral Keppel's trial, I have reasons to
wish to avoid, as that would be calling upon those
who have given evidence against me to appear.
I think it would be more proper to be ordered upon
my own request.

It is a very disadvantageous time for me, as
the public prejudice and the stream is so strong
against me; its being ordered to come on at a
little distance of time will give me a chance for
the prejudices produced by the violence of party
subsiding a little. I am [etc.].

P.S.—I think it is probable Admiral K. will
close his evidence to-morrow. Whether the Court
will allow me to reply to his defence and observe
upon the evidences I know not; but it will be
the most extravagant partiality if they do not,
and in that case I shall be prevented setting the
strongest things against Mr Keppel in their proper
point of view, and will amount to a condemnation
of me. In short such is the present disposition
of people that I consider my life as in danger, and
I tremble for the consequences of the party poison
which the officers of the fleet are infected with.

The moment the Court pronounces I will dispatch a letter desiring a court martial.

FROM JACKSON

Portsmouth, 5 February 1779.

There is no command of your Lordship's which from inclination I would not use my utmost endeavours to comply with. The business of the summary, which has been (though hastily) the produce of my own pen, has not only made the labour of afterwards revising the Minutes very great, but it has obliged me to have in view the postponing the correction of the copy till I could get a few days for it in town. Your Lordship may, however, depend on receiving a copy (corrected in part) by the time you receive the sentence. I will not guess whether I shall have the option of conveying that by the same express.[1]

Noise, hurry, interruption, and excessive labour will plead in excuse for inaccuracies. I will promise there shall be nothing deficient in point of fact. I cannot resist apprising your Lordship of the labour of a bare reading, expecting the contents will not fall much if at all short of 1200 pages.

Your Lordship may look for the copy by Thursday, the Admiral having gone through all his witnesses except one to invalidate the charge and vindicate himself. In doing this he drives the nail quite home, nor are his witnesses less willing in their endeavours.

Your Lordship will receive to-morrow a letter from the *Corps* on the subject of expenses while in attendance on the court martial. Your ready penetration and great experience will point out the object of the application ; but as a duty I owe

[1] Published by order of the Admiralty by Strahan & Cadell, 1779.

your Lordship I must observe that I have privately understood, if the application is not attended with a compliance, it is meant to be a ground for *an* application to Parliament.

By to-morrow's dispatch I may add with certainty the day your Lordship may receive the copy ; what I have said is upon conjecture only. With [etc.].

I do not attempt to apologize to your Lordship for the hurry in which I write. I do it through necessity.

FROM PALLISER

[In his writing : no date or signature : on or after 5 February 1779.]

It is not possible to describe the violence of party and prejudice in the course of the business in hand here ; but the most astonishing thing is the addition to the message sent by the Fox, which is vouched by Admiral Campbell, the captain and lieutenant of the Fox, though never heard by any one in the Formidable. Besides the absurdity of it, if true, considering the circumstances and the time when sent, and the pains taken to conceal the true time when it was sent, altogether plainly shows a conspiracy to destroy Sir H. P.

The rancour which Campbell and four or five of the captains have shown is wonderful. Captain Jervis in order to turn Lord M[ulgrav]e's contest with the Court into contempt or ridicule, desired the general question might be put to him, saying he thought himself bound by his oath to answer it. God knows to what length they will carry things against Sir H. The court is daily filled with opposition noblemen and members of Parliament, ladies and townspeople, who upon every occasion of anything being said against the prosecutor or in behalf of the prisoner express their approbation by clapping etc.

Mr. K.'s letters to Lord S. being refused by the Court has been a great disadvantage to Sir H. towards proving the alleged intention of re-attacking to be a mere pretence.

FROM PALLISER

Portsmouth, 8 February, 1779.

Admiral Keppel has closed his evidence. I immediately addressed the Court to be permitted to reply to Admiral Keppel's defence and to observe on the evidence, as was granted to the prosecutors upon the trial of Admiral Knowles, but this the Court refused; indeed, from the very beginning, everything has been heard which was offered by the accused at any time, so almost everything which I have offered at any time has been refused. Perceiving myself abandoned and sacrificed to party rage, I am at a loss what steps to take, nor do I know with whom to communicate or advise; the only hope I have is that, if his Majesty has not been so much prejudiced against me by the partial proceedings at this place, his friends will not suffer me to be condemned without a hearing.

The reply I should have made I have already prepared, and think I ought to send it to the Admiralty as the Court have refused it, but this I shall defer for the present.[1]

[1] Eventually published as *The Defence of Vice-Admiral Sir Hugh Palliser, Bart., at the Court Martial lately held upon him, with the Court's Sentence.'* London, T. Cadell, 1779.

II.   Q

I think it probable the Court will give their judgment very soon ; whenever that is done I shall set out the next moment for town, and have the honour to pay my respects to your Lordship. I am [etc.].

FROM PALLISER [1]

The addition made by the master of the Victory in her log book is exactly similar to that of the Robust, being the entering a signal (of consequence to the Admiral) that had been omitted, which omission was put in a few days only before the book was given into court.

The Ramillies's log had two leaves torn out for the very same reason as those in the Formidable, viz. because they had been ruled in too small a space to contain the occurrences.

The Shrewsbury's log book has the day's works of the 27th and 28th crossed out because there was not room for the whole, and those day's works are entered anew, but without tearing the leaves out.

The above particulars may be proper to be published to obviate reflection on any particular book.

FROM ROBINSON

9 February 1779.

Lord North desires me to ask you whether the proper steps are taken to give orders, the first proper moment that can be seized, for the trial

[1] In Palliser's writing : perhaps an enclosure to his letter of 8 February 1779.

of Sir Hugh Palliser. Has your Lordship any guess when the sentence of the court martial may be given, that we may be prepared to repel the attack which I hear from all hands is to be very violent and to go very great lengths ?   I have [etc.].

FROM JACKSON

Portsmouth, 10 February 1779.

Yesterday and this day have been employed in settling the sentence ; and it is now fixed it shall be pronounced to-morrow at 11 o'clock.   It is declared that the charge is malicious and ill founded ; that Mr K., so far from tarnished the honour of the British Flag by his misconduct and neglect on the 27th and 28th July, behaved as became a judicious, brave, and experienced officer. He is unanimously and honourably acquitted.

My Minutes and the Sentence shall be forwarded the moment I return from the court, that if possible they may reach your Lordship by 11 o'clock at night.   If the messenger cannot be at the Admiralty by that hour, he shall be with Mr Stephens by 7 o'clock the next morning. I shall follow the moment I have collected my papers, but fear I shall not be able to reach your Lordship to know your commands till Saturday morning, after which I shall hope for your Lordship's indulgence for a few days to recover the effect of a fatigue which would have been indifferent to me if it had not been accompanied with so rare a noise, and such incessant interruptions.

The Duke of Bolton has written to the President telling the Court he means to move in Parliament for leave to bring in a Bill to release the members of courts martial from their confinement; on which I fancy your Lordship will be solicited, the Court having already told me they shall ask my assistance to-morrow.   I am [etc.].

FROM SIR SAMUEL HOOD

Portsmouth Dockyard, 10 February 1779.

A memorial to the King has been handed about here to be signed by the captains, praying his Majesty to remove Sir Hugh Palliser from all his employments.   It was carried by Captain Jervis last night to Captain Robinson, who begged to be excused signing it, as did Captain Digby also. Captain Robinson does not know all the names that had signed; but on throwing his eye over the memorial as Captain Jervis was reading it, he saw the names of Sir Robert Harland and Admiral Campbell, and the Captains Sir John Ross, Edwards, Walsingham, Maitland, Clements, Carter Allen, Laforey, Leveson Gower, and Marshall.   Captain Jervis said eighteen had signed it and six or eight more had promised.

What a glaring proof is this, my Lord, of the malevolence and rancour of party; and what presumption to attempt to prescribe to his Majesty who he shall or shall not employ.   Let Sir Hugh's fate be what it may, the King never had a more brave and able officer, or a more zealous and faithful servant.   I have [etc.].

FROM CAPTAIN WALSINGHAM

Eight o'clock, Wednesday [10 Feb. 1779].

I find the paper includes *all* his places, and I am told that the intention is to deliver it *to-day* by the admirals and officers in town. Though I think he merits every mark of displeasure, yet I shall remonstrate *against* its being delivered till a more proper opportunity or till it is found absolutely necessary. I give your Lordship this hint in consequence of the conversation I had the honour of having with you yesterday : when it is finally determined I will send you a line, till then I am [etc.]

You will be so good as not to mention my name on this occasion.

FROM PALLISER

Private.

[In his writing : no date or signature.]

Captain Peyton[1] has just been with me. He is very friendly. I find that during the trial he struck his name out of the list of the captains' mess, giving for reason he could not concur in their plans of parties etc., that the other day he put an entire stop to a scheme formed for objecting to sit at a court martial with Captain Hood. The intended memorial has not been offered to him to sign, his sentiments being so well known.

I find his ship is under orders to be fitted for foreign service. It would to my knowledge be exceeding detrimental to him in some interesting

---

[1] Captain Joseph Peyton of the Cumberland. He was a member of the Court that tried Palliser.

family affairs to go abroad at this time ; if it is not intended to send him abroad, would your Lordship enable Mr Stephens to say so, to whom I know he intends to apply for information on that head.

PROPOSAL TO THE CABINET

[Endorsed by Lord Sandwich : 'Proposal laid before the Cabinet, Feb. 13th 1779, for the dismission of Sir H. Palliser.']

. Memo. of naval officers to remove Sir H. P. added to its coming from the Houses of Parliament must end in his losing his offices, therefore strongly recommend his being instantly removed from Lieutenant General of Marines and the nominal government of Scarborough : to give notice of it in this night's Gazette.[1]

FROM ROBINSON

15 February 1779.

Lord North directs me to acquaint your Lordship that Mr Fox told him in the House to-day that he (Mr F.) would move in the House to-morrow for a copy of the order for a court martial to try

---

[1] The 'prevailing sentiment' of the Cabinet seemed to be 'that a court martial is unavoidable, and that it would not be right to send him to his trial under the prejudice of a censure and dismission on the part of the Crown' (*Corr.*, 2542). The King, though not in agreement, wrote : 'I will not insist upon [the dismission]' (2548). Under pressure from the petition of the admirals and captains, Sandwich and Robinson met Sir Hugh on the 17th 'at a small distance from town, in order to persuade him to resign his offices voluntarily' (2547). The King very naturally thought this 'a mean subterfuge' (2549), but accepted the resignations on February 18.

Sir Hugh Palliser. Mr Fox does this, knowing that there is *no such order* at present existing, on purpose that he may argue from thence that he will not be tried, and so get some ground for the principal motion he proposes to make, viz. the expulsion of Sir Hugh. Lord North directs me to mention to your Lordship this, that you may be prepared with some answer to give to Mr Fox; and he will be glad to be apprised of the ground that the Board of Admiralty think most proper to be taken. I am [etc.].

TO ROBINSON

Admiralty, 15 February 1779.

Dear Sir—No orders have been issued for assembling a court martial; but Sir Hugh Palliser has been written to by Mr Stephens to inform him that it is the intention of the Board of Admiralty to order his conduct to be enquired into by a court martial.

Admiral Keppel is written to to ask whether he has any charge to exhibit against Sir Hugh. If he answers in the negative, as I suppose he will, the Board of Admiralty will order the Judge Advocate to summon the necessary witnesses to prove the matters of accusation that appear against Sir Hugh Palliser in the minutes taken upon Admiral Keppel's trial. This is the only mode that can be pursued where there is no prosecutor, and will be carried into execution as soon as Admiral Keppel's answer is received. If this mode is not approved, it may not be too late to ask the opinion of the Law Servants of the Crown in what mode he shall be brought to his trial, as there is no prosecutor.

You will observe that the proceedings against Admiral Keppel was exactly the same as that now proposed against Sir Hugh Palliser as far as relates to the time of ordering the court martial; for he was told on the 9th of December that a court martial would be held for his trial upon the charge exhibited against him by Sir Hugh Palliser, though that court martial was not ordered in form till the 31st December, when they were directed to assemble on the 7th of January.

The ordering the court martial so late, which seems to be the general usage, is to give time to the parties to collect their evidence; and Admiral Keppel was told that if he did not approve of the day proposed, it should be ordered on a later day. I am [etc.].

P.S.—If Lord North wishes for any further information from me on this subject, I shall be ready to attend his Lordship any time to-morrow morning after 11 o'clock.

FROM PALLISER

London, 18 February 1779.

After duly revolving in my mind the present state of things, the confusion into which his Majesty's service is thrown by the present violent measures and proceedings of a deluded mob against me, and having long perceived a spirit of envy and jealousy drawn upon me by the favours and honours which his Majesty from time to time has been graciously pleased to bestow upon me as rewards for long and faithful labours in the service of my country, I think it best, in order to abate the rage of prejudice raised against me and to

favour measures for restoring tranquillity, humbly
to beg your Lordship will intercede with his
Majesty to permit me to resign my commission as
Lieutenant General of Marines and the nominal
government of Scarborough Castle ; at the same
time I must beg through your Lordship's favour
that his Majesty may be assured of the continuance
of my loyalty, duty, and zeal to his Majesty to the
last moment of my life whatever may be my fate,
and to whatever low situation I may be reduced.
I have [etc.].

FROM THE KING

Queen's House, 25 February 1779.

Until I saw the copy of Sir Hugh Palliser's
letter unto Captain Bazely, I had supposed
Admiral Keppel's assertion to be groundless.
I am sorry [he was ?] well authorized for what he
said in the House of Commons.[1]

FROM ADMIRAL GRAVES

Hembury Fort, 27 February 1779.

My Lord—Upon the present occasion, when so
many admirals seem disgusted, I should think
myself wanting in my duty if I did not renew my
application for employ. The late appointment of
Lord Shuldham to a command in the Channel
hurt me beyond measure, as I trust my services,

---

[1] During the debate on 23 February 1779, on Mr. Fox's
motion for papers respecting the state of the French fleet in
Brest, Admiral Keppel said that Sir Hugh Palliser had written to
Captain Bazely, saying that the King had thanked him for the
conduct of the Blue squadron on July 27 (*Parl. Hist.*, xx. 155).

pretensions, and character equal his and my rank certainly places me before him. I had no seat in Parliament to attend and was in town when he received that appointment.

Your Lordship may perhaps wonder at my troubling you with any application after setting my hand to a late remonstrance. The truth is that I refused signing at first, notwithstanding your Lordship's long total neglect of me, and had I lain under the obligations which Lord Shuldham did I should never have subscribed from the mere principle of gratitude.

Nevertheless I must confess that I think no commander in chief should be subjected to a trial on a stale charge from a subordinate officer who voluntarily and without complaint has served under him subsequent to the ground for that charge ; and I do not see that a protest against such a proceeding can be made but to his Majesty and against the Board who has ordered it. Upon these considerations I joined in it, and yet I did so with reluctance, as wishing never to be personal to the members of a Board which I always desire to honour and respect. Had the Vice Admiral prayed a court martial upon himself to wipe off aspersions recently thrown, there would have been a strong ground for granting it : such at least is my sincere opinion ; and saying that I trust your Lordship will not deem me indecent if I again entreat your favour for some active command, and I can assure you that if I obtain one I shall hold and profess myself to be personally obliged to your Lordship, I am [etc.].

FROM THE KING

Queen's House, 4 March 1779, 23 m. past 9 P.M.

By the minutes of the proceedings of the House of Lords this day, I find the Greenwich Hospital business is postponed for a week. I understand the Opposition in general think nothing can be gained by the enquiry, that perhaps it will entirely fall to the ground.[1]

I desire Lord Sandwich will go to-morrow morning to Lord North, and inform him that I am clearly of opinion that no further time ought to be lost in offering the command of the fleet to Vice-Admiral Man. Many difficulties have arose from employing men adverse in their political opinions. This step is absolutely necessary, or further time will be lost ; and in the end the sending to Admiral Man will be the only measure, and perhaps means may be employed by ill-designed persons to prevent his accepting.[2]

FROM PALLISER

14 March 1779.

I am not able at present to put on a shoe, or I would wait on your Lordship to express my wish to be informed what steps will be taken in consequence of Mr Luttrell's motion for the charge

[1] On March 11 the Duke of Richmond moved that the House of Lords resolve itself into a committee to inquire into the management of Greenwich Hospital. A motion to print the evidence given before the House was rejected on June 14. These motions arose out of the trial of Captain Thomas Baillie for a libel on the inferior officers at Greenwich in November 1778. Thomas Erskine defended Baillie and delivered his famous indictment of Sandwich. Baillie was discharged.

[2] Man politely declined the offer ' from the present bad state of my health,' on March 7.

upon which I am to be tried.[1] I am inclined to think it will be an advantage to me to have a specific charge made against me for disobeying orders, as Admiral Keppel calls it in his letter. I hope to be duly informed of every step taken that concerns me, that I may be better able than I now am to know how to prepare for my defence.

I hope your Lordship does not forget my wish to be permitted to reside on board the Formidable during the trial, and if possible that the court may be held on board her : this indulgence I hope may be granted in consideration of my particular circumstances and of my infirmities. This indulgence I hope will not be thought less reasonable than that of passing an Act of Parliament to hold the court martial on shore upon Admiral Keppel on account of his ill state of health. I have [etc.].

FROM THE KING

Queen's House, 17 March 1779, 46 m. past 6 P.M.

It is impossible to draw up a more proper answer than the one transmitted by Lord Sandwich to the letter received yesterday from Admiral Keppel, and I thoroughly approve of its being sent to him this night.

Sir Charles Hardy ought to have notice that he must kiss hands to-morrow for the command of the home fleet ; the promotion of admirals should take place at the same time, and the colonels of Marines.[2]

I desire Lord Sandwich will have copies pre-

[1] The Hon. Temple Luttrell, M.P. for Milbourne Port, Somersetshire, moved the trial of Sir Hugh Palliser on 11 December 1778 (*Parl. Hist.*, xx. 53–73).

[2] The promotion was dated March 29.

pared for me of the letter wrote on the 12th to Admiral Keppel, of his enclosed answer, and of the letter to be sent this night unto him.

FROM THE KING

Queen's House, 20 March 1779, 46 m. past 4 P.M.

The resignation of Captain Leveson[-Gower] is no more material than as it shows the faction in the fleet is more rooted than was expected from Lord Sandwich's language yesterday. It is impossible to have made a more judicious choice than in Captain Goodall as his successor. I hope the Valiant will be sheathed with copper, that she may appear in the most successful light in the hands of so excellent an officer.[1]

Should any other captains resign, I trust Lord Sandwich will without loss of time supply them, and as much as possible by the advancement of men as creditable as this last appointment. Captain Elliot, though at present intended for a ship that is fitting out, may with great propriety be placed in one now in commission and ready for sea, should more resignations ensue.[2]

FROM SIR SAMUEL HOOD

Portsmouth Dockyard, 29 March 1779.

The unexpected arrival of my brother under my roof yesterday greatly alarmed me, and upon

[1] Captain Samuel Cranston Goodall was appointed to the Ramillies *vice* Captain Digby promoted. He went later to the Valiant, and distinguished himself on the 12 April 1782, and with Hood a week later at the capture of the stragglers in the Mona Channel.

[2] Lord Mulgrave suggested that Lindsay and Jervis might resign (*Corr.*, 2584).

being informed of the motive of his coming I was filled with the deepest concern.

He tells me your Lordship will allow him no alternative to his going to America as a private captain in the Robust, which must be very distressing to him in the rank he has now the honour to hold in his Majesty's Navy ; and more particularly as for some years past officers of inferior rank have had broad pendants with captains under them on that service.   The going to North America distinguished as his juniors have been would be truly flattering and honourable, and what he would rejoice in, but to go as a private captain must give him feelings totally the reverse.   Had he been ordered abroad *alone*, to any part of the world, he would most cheerfully have gone without saying a word, but to sail with a vice admiral for the purpose of acting under him must, I think, fully justify him in humbly stating to the Board his present oppressed situation.

The idea of clamour against him that may have been whispered to your Lordship is not well founded, as I know the unbiassed, dispassionate and respectable part of our corps think as highly of him as ever (and I may be bold to say no officer stands higher in reputation for zeal and attention to his duty, or has more strenuously exerted himself for the honour and dignity of his Majesty's crown and government) ; but admit, my Lord, that a clamour is against him as high as may be, he is ready to meet it *all*, both as a public and private man, supported as he is by conscious innocence.   And under such an idea of clamour as your Lordship suggests, the sending him to America as a private captain would not only be very unpleasant and distressing, but disgraceful in the extreme in his present advanced rank ; and I entreat your Lordship, if you cannot be prevailed upon to distinguish him, you will not put him in a situation that will be dishonourable to his standing in the service.

Upon the home employ his situation will be honourable, he must in the Robust have the leading his Majesty's fleet into action on the starboard tack, or if your Lordship should be pleased to appoint him to a second-rate he will probably be as honourably placed by being second to the commander in chief. I therefore most humbly hope and trust, my Lord, you will not compel him to retire from a service he so loves, and has so distinguished himself in, by insisting on his going to America under the command of Vice-Admiral Arbuthnot as a private captain, when he is the oldest upon the list employed, either in Europe or America, and so many his juniors in rank have had captains under them upon the same service he is now under orders for ; and if he is not worthy of those marks of distinction his rank entitles him to, and have been given to others, he is certainly unworthy to command the Robust.[1]

[1] On February 7 Captain Alexander Hood wrote to Lord Sandwich reporting a rumour of an intended promotion of flag officers, which was said to stop at Sir John Ross, only six places senior to himself. He went on : ' I am extremely anxious at this moment to have some mark of favour from Government, which I trust my services will entitle me to. I therefore most earnestly request of your Lordship that I may be included in the promotion of flags, if his Majesty shall be graciously pleased to order one. But, my Lord, if I cannot be honoured with my flag, I hope your Lordship will not think me unreasonable in requesting the Marines, as three colonels will be vacant by the promotion to Sir John Ross.'
. The promotion of March 29 did stop at Sir John Ross, and Hood got his flag in the next promotion, 26 September 1780, at the same time as his brother. The vacancies in the Marines were given to John Elliot, Walsingham, and Hotham, all of whom were a long way junior to Hood. Elliot and Hotham had already been serving for some time in America as ' established ' commodores.
Lord Sandwich afterwards offered the Union 90 to Hood, but for some reason the arrangement fell through (Sir Samuel to Lord Sandwich, 20 August 1779).

Your Lordship must imagine my feelings to be very strong on my brother's account, and must therefore, I flatter myself, forgive my troubling you with so long a letter. I have [etc.].

TO SIR SAMUEL HOOD

Admiralty, 31 March 1779.

Dear Sir—I am much distressed at the receipt of your letter, not having it in my power to make such an answer to it as will be satisfactory to you. Every argument used by you is almost word for word the same as what was used by your brother in our last interview, to which I replied to the best of my ability.

It is a little hard upon me that this matter should be treated as if the mode of employing Captain Hood depended solely upon my will and pleasure; for I told your brother what I now repeat to you, that there were other persons besides myself whose opinions it was necessary for me to attend to, and that had I thought it a right measure to give him a broad pendant at this period of time it is what I had not the means of executing. After having said thus much I must add in my own behalf that the ordering the Robust to America was meant by me as the most friendly act I could do to Captain Hood; if he had been my own brother I should have done the same; and if it was a wrong step in me, it was owing to my want of judgment and not to any inattention on my part to his situation or interests.

When I last saw Captain Hood, I said everything I could think of to dissuade him from quitting the Robust; and I think that on consideration you will join with me in endeavouring to preserve to the service as good an officer as any in it, who if he takes a precipitate step at this important crisis in his affairs will, I am persuaded, be soon sorry for what he has done, which it will be very difficult ever after to retrieve. I am [etc.'].

FROM LORD THURLOW

[Endorsed by Lord Sandwich : 'Ld Chancellor, March 1779.']

My dear Lord—In Jackson's examination there were two points which seemed to press at least till explained : why the order for holding the court was not or should not be more extensive, so as to comprehend the whole period of that service or at least the 27th and 28th, the second as to the witnesses. Mr Jackson's answer to that was that he took the strongest omitting the rest, and that he confined himself to the witnesses who had spoken materially to affect Sir Hugh Palliser. It is obvious that there may be great difficulty in going further, and judging either from situation or otherwise who can speak materially ; but within a certain extent it is better to go too far than too short, and with this caution Mr Jackson has sense enough to be trusted. I entirely approve the line he has prescribed himself of taking his witnesses from the charge, omitting nothing material and adding any other witnesses whom the narration makes obviously material. It was perfectly right to summon Keppel.[1]

---

[1] On March 31, during the Duke of Richmond's motion respecting the trial of Sir Hugh Palliser, Jackson was called to the bar of the House of Lords and examined for nearly two hours (*Parl. Hist.*, xx. 410–14).

II.   R

Have you taken as much notice of [Captain George] Johnstone as he deserves and as many considerations require ?   Yours etc.

FROM SIR ROBERT HARLAND

Portman Square, 31 March 1779.

My Lord—After the communication your Lordship did me the honour to admit me to, and desiring now to decline the favour of any ornament for my person, it does not become me to say more than that I am ready to continue in the fleet under the command of Sir Charles Hardy, and to use my greatest exertion to fulfil the expectations of your Lordship, notwithstanding I have not the like opinion of the abilities of that gentleman I had of Admiral Keppel, who I came into service with in the same fleet.   My friendship and my opinion of that officer will ever remain the same, although I have not the same reasons for following him in declining service, nor will it hinder my being a respectful and obedient subaltern to my commander in chief.   What I aim at is the good opinion of his Majesty, the world, and my profession ;   to merit it shall be the latest endeavour of my life.[1] I have [etc.].

[1] Both the King and Lord Sandwich were delighted. ' It is impossible to pen a more becoming letter,' wrote His Majesty. ' It is very fair and shows he deserves the character universally given of him.'   Unfortunately Harland changed his mind, and on May 10 wrote a violent letter to Stephens, declining to serve, ' which seems,' wrote the King, ' rather dictated by passion than reflection.'

FROM PYE

Portsmouth, 31 March 1779.

Notwithstanding the letter I received last post from Mr Secretary Stephens to direct the captain of the Formidable to proceed into the harbour and to hold himself in readiness to prepare her for the dock, I have taken upon me to detain her at Spithead till further orders till I acquaint your Lordship of a report that prevails here, and I have reason to believe too well-founded to doubt, that should the Formidable's and Victory's ships' companies meet it would be fatal to many of them as there is such an inveteracy towards each other, which I wish to prevent as much as possible by begging leave to recommend her remaining at Spithead until the Victory gets there, which your Lordship may depend no time shall be lost in hastening her there. I have [etc.].

P.S.—The captain of the Victory has this instant been with me and acquaints me she will be ready for dock to-morrow.

FROM SIR SAMUEL HOOD

Portsmouth Dockyard, 1 April 1779, ½ past 3 P.M.

I was full of hope that what I took the liberty of stating to your Lordship in my letter of Monday [29th] would have been more favourably attended to, and your Lordship would not have been so determined against my brother.

The calling of Captain Kempenfelt to the honours and emoluments of a rear admiral by appointing him to be first captain to Admiral

Sir Charles Hardy makes it impossible for Captain
Hood to serve at home ; and as he is the oldest
captain in full pay, either in Europe or America,
he must serve under Admiral Arbuthnot as a
private captain with a label of disgrace about his
neck. This is the light every officer of my acquaint-
ance here sees it in, and must compel him to retire
on half pay : hard and cruel alternative, to which
however he must submit unless your Lordship will
do him that justice his services merit. But I now
pledge myself to your Lordship that the day is not
far distant when he will be acknowledged by the
voice of the nation to be an honourable, innocent
and oppressed man.[1]

Let the minutes of Admiral Keppel's trial
be attentively considered. It will appear that
Lieutenant Lumley swears the alterations in the
Robust's log book were made on the *sixth* of
December, the master on the *twelfth* and in the
presence of the first lieutenant. Now it is well
known the first lieutenant was in London by
Admiralty leave from the 5th to the 16th of
December, which he has made oath of ; and one
of the master's mates has also sworn that the
alterations were wrote in the log book between the
6th and the *10th*, that he bought the paper for the
book on the 5th and that previous to that day
the alterations were wrote in a rough sheet by the
directions of the master, and that no other alterations took place after that time but what were
occasioned by the master's omitting three day's

[1] ' Reflecting upon Captain Hood's situation I would not by
any means stand in the way of anything that may be his inclinations therefore if your Lordship is disposed to send him abroad
and he inclined to it I beg he may not be stopped upon my
account.' From Palliser, March 9. As we have seen, Hood did
not go to North America, nor did he give evidence at Palliser's
court martial.

works in October, on which account some leaves were taken out of the book. Where, therefore, can the criminality be against Admiral Keppel? I have [etc.].

FROM THE KING

Queen's House, 3 April 1779, 40 m. past 2 P.M.

The conduct of the Admiralty towards Captain Hood seems very proper, and he has taken a very injudicious step which I fear he will have reason to repent of. His enemies could not have chalked out a path for him more exactly than the one he has chosen to follow. Lord Sandwich warned him of it, therefore may very composedly let the affair rest where it does.

How has the last negotiation with Johnstone ended ; has he accepted of the Alexander ? [1]

FROM THE KING

Queen's House, 5 April 1779, 49 m. past 8 P.M.

The idea of removing Lord Longford to the Alexander, Captain [George] Montagu to the America, and thus appointing Captain Johnstone

[1] Captain Johnstone had recently attacked Lord Howe's management of his campaign with d'Estaing in the House of Commons, arguing on most unseamanlike grounds that Howe's force was superior to the French. The Government appear to have proposed him as Palliser's successor at the Admiralty (and to command the Alexander at the same time) ; but Lord Mulgrave wisely insisted that there must be at least one admiral on the Board, and he also insisted that the post must be filled before Palliser's trial began. Johnstone eventually took command of a small squadron of cruisers on the coast of Portugal, with his broad pendant in the Romney. Cp. *Corr.*, 2601–2.

to the Romney, I think the true test whether the latter gentleman is serious in wishing to be employed. I desire Lord Sandwich will without loss of time put this into train.

I knew before from Lord North that he would not object to Sir Charles Hardy as successor to Sir Hugh Palliser at the Board of Admiralty, but that he will not consent to its being put into execution until Johnstone is satisfied by being put into a ship and command. This hint will I trust show Lord Sandwich that concluding with Johnstone will also forward the filling up the Board.

[H. M. has already appointed majors to the three new regiments of light dragoons, so he cannot appoint Lord Mulgrave's brother. ' I am as desirous not to give real reason of complaint to the Army as to the Navy.']

The draft of the orders for assembling the court martial is very judicious. I am glad it is directed to Vice-Admiral Darby, as I should not choose that Sir Charles Hardy should in the least be mixed in this unhappy business.[1]

I shall be ready to receive Lord Sandwich at half hour past two to-morrow, and trust he will by that time have received a final answer from Captain Johnstone.

---

[1] Having received orders to assemble a court martial to try Palliser, Darby wrote to the Admiralty on the same day : ' On so particular an occasion as this, from my own diffidence, I find myself inadequate to such an undertaking. And as there are several senior flag officers to me employed on the home service, I most earnestly press you to move their Lordships to appoint some one of them to be the President at this time who has had more experience in the duty of courts martial than myself ' (Channel Fleet disp.).

FROM PALLISER

Thursday evening.   [? 8 April 1779.]

If your Lordship can't secure the Formidable's being in the harbour before the trial I shall go to it under very disadvantageous and disagreeable as well as dangerous circumstances.

It would be very much to be wished Captain Duncan could be out of the way.[1]

I understand a letter was received last night from Admiral Montagu at Bath to his secretary, in which he says he knows for certain that Sir Robert Harland does not intend to go to sea. I have [etc.].

[1] Captain Adam Duncan was a member of both courts martial. It was proposed to send his ship, the Monarch, to sea with Vice-Admiral Arbuthnot, who was about to sail for North America with a few ships of the line and a convoy, to strengthen his force until he was clear of the Channel, a common enough procedure. On April 6 Sir Thomas Pye wrote to Lord Sandwich that Duncan thought it 'impossible to be ready for the sea soon enough to sail with Admiral Arbuthnot, but hopes you will give me leave to order [the Monarch] to St Helen's, or give him a few days' leave of absence till after the 12th.' On April 9 Arbuthnot was ordered to take the Monarch, Centaur, and America to accompany him 100 leagues west of the Lizard. On the 11th Duncan wrote to Arbuthnot that he had prepared to drop down from Spithead to St. Helen's, 'though the ship was in no condition to put to sea'; but 'the people refused [to unmoor] until they were paid. I immediately went to Admiral Pye, who has directed me to acquaint you with it.' There is nothing in Duncan's journal (a detailed one) or his master's log to suggest mutiny; Pye's dispatches do not mention it; nor can we find any orders that refer to it. The Monarch was paid on May 8, and sailed with Darby for a cruise on May 11.

It seems that Duncan outwitted the Admiralty. (See also *Considerations on the Principles of Naval Discipline and Courts Martial*. Anon, Almon, 1781.)

FROM NORTH

Downing Street, 9 April 1779.

I have seen Sir Charles Hardy, who declines the seat at the Admiralty Board unless he can at the same time enjoy the commission of Lieutenant General of the Marines, as Sir Hugh Palliser did. He said that upon the return of peace he with his large family would feel very sensibly the diminution he would suffer by having exchanged the government of Greenwich Hospital for a seat at the Board of Admiralty. He added that he should be very happy to have both the offices, but he did not seem to think that he should be much benefitted by quitting the Hospital for either of them separately. I did not offer him the Marines, so I cannot say whether he would not accept of that employment, but the Admiralty he declined, and I took my leave. I am [etc.].

FROM THE COMPTROLLER

10 April 1779.

My Lord—The enclosed state of our stores is in no shape exaggerated, and our provision for the current service may be equally depended on.[1]

I have wrote to Captain Cornish by this post, for the chance of the wind being out of the way, to give the House list his assistance at the election.

Admiral Man is much disposed to obey your Lordship's commands ; and I shall be much disappointed if your Lordship does not find him disinterested in his views and not thirsty after

---

[1] This refers to ' Paper D ' in chap. iii. below, pp. 262–3.

emoluments. If I had thought otherwise I should have been silent, as I flatter myself you will at all times find, when I take the liberty of offering a character to your consideration, that the interest of the party is but a secondary motive to your Lordship's credit. I am [etc.].

FROM THE KING

Queen's House, 11 April 1779, 44 m. pt. 3 P.M.

I have received Lord Sandwich's two notes. I entirely agree with him and Lord North that Sir Charles Hardy is unreasonable in declining the Admiralty unless he gets the Marines. I am glad to find Vice-Admiral Man has been sounded and approve of his being immediately placed at the Board. He may be presented on Wednesday. I think the arrangement much better, as he will be attending the Board in summer.[1]

Sir John Ross has wrote a very proper letter, and I trust an opportunity may soon offer of employing him.

I am sorry Lord Sandwich has met with any severe blow of a private nature. I flatter myself this world scarcely contains a man so void of feeling as not to compassionate your situation.[2]

---

[1] Admiral Man remained at the Admiralty until September 1780, when he was replaced by Admiral Darby, then commanding the main fleet. Thus for about one year, and one only during the European stage of the war, Lord Sandwich was assisted by a sea officer who had no appointment at sea to distract his attention from the work of the Board.

[2] Miss Ray was murdered on April 7.

o

FROM PALLISER

Formidable, 20 April 1779.

The time is approaching for me to begin my defence. In a very short time I shall expose the wickedness and malice of my enemies, and I trust fully justify myself in every point. In the meantime I have only to entreat your Lordship and my friends not to condemn me before I have made my defence. I have already been condemned by one court without being heard, which has served the purpose of my enemies ; it would be too much indeed to be served so by my friends, whose countenance and protection I trust to if finally I acquit myself. I have [etc.].[1]

FROM THE KING

Queen's House, 22 April 1779.

. . . The letter from Sir Hugh Palliser rather shows the anxiety of his mind than a confidence of being able to remove the impressions which the very uniform and clear answers of the gentlemen produced on this court martial cannot fail to have made on the minds of impartial men. No one will more sincerely rejoice than I shall, if his effort may prove successful ; but after his being so very short of what, from his character, might have been expected in his proofs to confirm the strong charge brought by him against the Admiral, one cannot help doubting whether he

---

[1] In a letter of April 19 Jackson urges the importance of Captain Keith Stewart's return to Portsmouth to give evidence, and says that ' the desire of witnesses to be got forward in their examination in preference is very great.' Stewart gave evidence on May 1.

may not be mistaken in those he thinks will remove the proofs brought against himself by his enemies.

FROM PALLISER

Formidable, 2 May 1779.

I trust your Lordship will have made an excuse for me in your own mind for not sooner acknowledging the honour of your Lordship's very kind letter, very kind and friendly indeed to think on my situation, so similar in many respects to your own. We have each undergone the severest trials in the power of envy and malice to invent, unsupported by anything but innocence and the rectitude of our conduct. Believe me, my Lord, I interest myself as much in the issue of your persecution as my own. Whatever turn things may take, I shall remain to the last day of my life, my Lord, [etc.].

Copies of my defence are printing in order to be given to friends in Parliament to furnish them with arguments against General Conway's motion : one of the first printed will be sent to your Lordship.

FROM PALLISER

Admiralty, 9 May 1779.

I have applied by letter to Lord North for his good offices with his Majesty to be restored to the lieut.-generalship of marines, and I venture to flatter myself with having your Lordship's aid therein. I beg your Lordship and Lord North will understand that I do not mean to be pressing at this time but to wait patiently till the time may be favourable.   I have [etc.].

FROM ADMIRAL GAMBIER

Queen Street, Berkeley Square, 14 May 1779.

Absorbed, my honoured Lord, in the joy of being restored to a beloved family and affectionate attention to a poor invalid wife, I learnt not that any post of honour and emolument was vacant in your Lordship's department that my rank and services, and present delicate situation from my late *recall*, could with any degree of propriety authorize my solicitation, until some of my friends, affectionately zealous for my welfare, communicating to me the Marines' being quitted, partial in their ideas of my services and pretensions, encourage my presumption to think I should in justice to my numerous family and forty-two years faithful unremitting service at sea to become a candidate under the auspices of your Lordship's other particular arrangements.[1]

But however susceptible of thankful sensibility for the apparently kind solicitude of my friends for my advancement, my first pride and wish is that of being governed in every part of my conduct by that respectful and grateful attachment of your Lordship's friendship and patronage I would wish to stamp my character and conduct, happy in your permitting me to continue to confide in your disposal of my fate, in every respect, being most truly [etc.].

[1] The post of Lieutenant-General of the Marines was not filled until 29 September 1780, when it was given to Admiral Sir Thomas Pye, an appointment which his seniority made unexceptionable.

CHAPTER III

A DEBATE IN THE HOUSE OF LORDS 23 APRIL 1779

INTRODUCTION

THIS chapter relates to Vice-Admiral the Earl of Bristol's motion in the House of Lords for the removal of Lord Sandwich from the office of First Lord of the Admiralty. The debate on the motion took place on 23 April 1779, and was rejected by 78 votes to 39—a rout of the Opposition which may be due in part to Lord North's having lately accepted responsibility on behalf of the whole Cabinet for Admiralty measures, by saying that a vote of censure against one member of the Cabinet involved the whole.[1]

The position is stated in the following minute, which was copied on a sheet of notepaper and is now among the papers at Hinchingbrooke [2] :

' Every expedition, in regard to its destination, object, force and number of ships, is planned by the Cabinet, and is the result of the collective wisdom of all his Majesty's confidential ministers. The First Lord of the Admiralty is only the executive servant of these measures; and if he is not personally a Cabinet minister he is not responsible for the wisdom, the policy, and the propriety of any naval expedition. But if he is in the Cabinet, then he must share in common with the other ministers that proportional division of censure which is attached to him as an individual. In no situation is he more or less responsible to his country than his colleagues from any misconduct which flows from a Cabinet measure.'

[1] In the House of Commons on March 3 (*Parl. Hist.*, xx. 197–8).
[2] It is written on a double sheet of quarto paper with a half-width margin. There is neither date, signature, endorsement, nor other sign of origin ; the writing looks like a clerk's.

The speeches made during the debate may be read in Volume XX of *The Parliamentary History*, columns 426–67. Most of the papers here are notes in Lord Sandwich's writing for his answer to the motion, some of them evidently inspired by recent speeches in the House of Commons, especially Mr. Fox's motions on March 3 and 22, and April 19, and Dunning's on March 15. Since the MSS. have no labels, we have arranged them in five parts (Notes I to V), as far as possible as they appear in Lord Sandwich's speech; and the supplementary papers that go with them have either been placed after the appropriate Note, or summarised at the foot of the page.

After the Notes, which were prepared beforehand, we have printed 'Points Raised in Debate.' Lord Sandwich jotted them down during the speeches and embodied them in his replies; they are a useful supplement to the *History*, which does not report the First Lord's speeches as fully as those made by speakers against him.

The last paper is Lord Bristol's written protest against the rejection of his motion.

On April 7, a week before the date originally fixed for the motion, Martha Ray was murdered by James Hackman outside Drury Lane Theatre. She had been Lord Sandwich's mistress for sixteen years and had borne him two sons (see vol. i. p. x). Her death was a great loss to Sandwich, who wrote that he had been 'robbed of all comfort in the world.' The first two letters in this chapter describe the way in which the debate was postponed in deference to his feelings.

TO LORD BRISTOL

Richmond, 11 April 1779.

My Lord—You will doubtless be surprised at receiving a letter from me ; but the situation I am in will, I hope, plead my excuse for the trouble I am giving you.

It is understood that Navy matters are to be discussed in the House of Lords on Thursday or Friday next. I am at present totally unfit for business of any kind and unable to collect any materials to support the side of the question that I must espouse. I perceive impropriety in putting off the business by a motion from anyone with whom I am politically connected ; I have therefore recourse to your humanity, to request that you would contrive that this point is not brought on till after this day sevennight, by which time I hope to be as fit for public business as I ever shall be.

The friendship that has formerly subsisted between your Lordship and me will, I flatter myself, incline you to enter so far into my feelings as to be convinced that I am sincere when I assure you upon my honour that I have no other cause for wishing to postpone the enquiry than that which is now given you. I have [etc.].

FROM BRISTOL

Ickworth Park, 12 April 1779.

My Lord—I have this moment the honour of receiving your Lordship's letter of yesterday ; and though I had not such an application from your Lordship, yet, from the very instant I heard of your misfortune, I felt too much for it not to have determined that no consideration should induce me to bring on any business that might be disagreeable for your Lordship to attend to till it was more convenient for you.   I am at present not very well with a slight touch of the gout, and shall therefore desire some of my friends to give that as my reason to the House for desiring to put off the business alluded to till I am able to attend.

I must also beg that your Lordship will do me the justice to believe that there is no man in this world who felt more for you on this occasion, nor who can be more concerned than I am for any interruption to your domestic felicity.   I have [etc.].

NOTES FOR THE SPEECH—I

[In Lord Sandwich's writing and endorsed ' Introduction.']

Was it not for the consciousness of my having done my duty in the station in which I am placed with the truest zeal for the service of my country and with the most upright intentions, it would have been difficult for my mind to have upheld itself against the many persecutions both of a public and a private nature which I have lately experienced.   However, feeling within myself that the charges brought against me are ill founded, and knowing that all my time and attention have been given to the business of my office ever since I have been in it, and that attention has not been useless to the public, I am rather pleased than otherwise that my conduct is this day become the subject of your Lordships' examination.

But before I proceed any further let me ask one question, and that is why the First Lord of the Admiralty is supposed to be the only person that is to be answerable for the not having ships enough at sea, and not having furnished the commanders of these ships with proper instructions. Do my lords imagine that the First Lord of the Admiralty equips fleets whenever his own fancy leads him to do so ?   That it is his duty to do his utmost to have ships and stores ready for equipment I will allow, but it is the business of the King's administration at large to judge when it shall be advisable to put the nation to the expense of that equipment.

The same thing is to be said about instructions. The First Lord of the Admiralty is only one among many who are to approve those instructions ; nay in matters of much importance the instructions generally come signified to the Admiralty in an official letter from the Secretary of State.   If this is the case why is the First Lord to be considered as the only responsible person ?   If blame is due I am willing to bear my share of it, but there is neither reason nor justice in making me the single object of public censure.

My Lords, when I first came to this office, 1771, the fleet was in a most deplorable state, the ships decaying and unfit for service, the storehouses empty, and a general despondency running through the whole naval department from an idea that these calamities were not to be remedied. I was one of the few that did not despair : I set my hand and heart to the work, and now have the satisfaction to say, and to be able to prove, that the fleet is in as good a condition as it ever was since this was a kingdom, and more forward in the equipment than a fleet ever was taking your date from the time that equipment began, which I will state to be in the year 1777 ; for I do not consider our utmost exertions as having taken place till we saw a near prospect of a war with France. The American war required very few line of battle ships ; frigates and small vessels fully answered that purpose, but it is the line of battle ships on which we are to depend for the defence of this country and for its power and credit as a nation.

On the 1st of January 1777 we had only 36 of the line in commission ; in January 1756, the first year of the last war, they set out with 61.

Turn to the paper.

NOTES II

[In Lord Sandwich's writing and endorsed: ' Comparative state of the fleet and state of stores.']

Considering the state in which it came to me, and the losses we have sustained, surprising it should be in the condition it now is.

55 lost or taken. Now in commission, March 1, 314 ; December 1759, 301.

At the highest period of the last war 97 of the line—the 4th year of the war, December 1759, [including] 7 French prizes.

The second year of the war, we have 80. [It is 79 altered into 80.]

And in the course of this year shall have 9 more. [10 altered to 9.]

They set out in January 1756 with 61 of the line.	Vide paper B.[1]
We in January 1777 with 36.	Vide C.[2]
Our 90 stronger than the 97— 29 of 60 guns, we only 5.	Vide comparison I.[3]
The fleet came to me in a deplorable state in 1771.	
Blame nobody.	
21 line of battle ships broke up since 1771, and 60 frigates.	Vide paper A.[4]
20 more that can never go to sea.	
The fleet in a manner to be rebuilt.	
No timber. Despair of getting any. Broke the combination [of timber merchants].	
At this moment, double quantity of stores of every kind and no want of anything.	Vide papers D., E., F.[5]
If, therefore, the having no stores would be a crime, the being well supplied claims some degree of merit.	
More men now employed than at the highest period of the last war.	Vide paper G.[6]

[1] Two first-rates, seven second-, thirty-three third-, and nineteen fourth-rates.

[2] Two second-rates, thirty-three third-, and one fourth-rate (of 60 guns).

[3] In 1759 : 97 ships, 6850 guns, 51,980 men. By the end of 1779 : 89 ships, 6548 guns, 51,987 men.

[4] Two second-rates, fifteen third-, four fourth- (60) ; two fourth- (50), eight fifth-, eight sixth-rates ; ten sloops and thirty-two smaller vessels—81 in all.

[5] See below, pp. 262–5.

[6] See below, pp. 265–6.

In the year 1770, only 18 ships,   Vide paper H.[1]
large and small, building. In
1779, seventy-seven.

Paper D.[2]

Foreign Stores

Hemp.   So large a quantity as is now in store was
never known at this season of the year.
It amounts to upwards of one year's
consumption exclusive of 1000 tons on
board the neutral ships. 5000 tons more
are contracted for and will be delivered
within the present year. This state of
the store obliges us to make temporary
places for receiving the neutral cargoes,
and to supply the contracting rope-
makers with our own hemp.

Masts.   At least three years war expense in store
and near two more contracted for.

Pitch.   Two years expense in store and one year
contracted for.

Tar.   Three years in store and one year contracted for.

Iron.   Four years expense in store.

Timber.   We have at this time in the Yards and
due on contract 72,000 loads, and
which is upwards of three years expense at the highest rate of consumption. This increase of timber has

[1] In March 1770, of the line 14, under 4 ; in March 1779, of
the line 27, under 50.

[2] This paper is in Middleton's writing. He wrote on April 10
as follows : ' The enclosed state of our stores is in no shape
exaggerated, and our provision for the current service may be
equally depended on.'

induced us to caution the contractors, and particularly at Portsmouth, from making any new bargains without our advice and consent.

The above is a true state of the Naval Stores. The contracts for the present year are concluded and the foreign stations fully provided. The western yards are prepared for accidental and current services ; and we may safely assert that on a comparative view the naval arsenals of this kingdom never have been so fully supplied as at present. 7000 tons of stores have been sent abroad within these four months, and 1500 more are provided and shipping. This is a circumstance on which a great stress may be laid, as it is extraordinary. The particular services are underneath.

	Tons.
Admiral Byron's Squadron . .	875
Antigua	2219
Gibraltar	284
Minorca	219
Jamaica	1608
New York	1170
Halifax	673
	7048

Preparing and shipping :

West Indies	600
East Indies	700
New York	500
	1800

PAPER E.

Navy Office, 17 April 1779.

State of the Masts at the periods against each expressed, viz. :

Ins.   *No.*

Masts, New England and Riga in store and due } 34 to 14 31st December 1770 1,759
31st December 1778 3,263

Annual Expense in War   .   .   793
in Peace   .   .   285

Hands

Masts, Norway, in store and due } 16 to 6 31st December 1770 3,308
31st December 1778 6,084

Annual Expense in War   .   .   2,141
in Peace   .   .   1,130

N.B.—To the account of masts in store 31st December 1778 may be added the Riga contracted for with John Henniker Esq.   .   1,350
and with Messrs Durand & Bacon   .   .   600
And to the Norway, those contracted for with Messrs Sanders & Henniker   .   .   1,520

PAPER F.

Navy Office, 17 April 1779.

State of the following Stores at the periods against each expressed, viz. :

Loads

Timber in store and due 31st December 1770   31,366
31st December 1778   72,317
Annual expense in War   .   .   22,936
in Peace   .   .   23,618

	Tons
Hemp in store and due 31st December 1770	6,135
31st December 1778	7,150
Annual expense in War . .	6,978
in Peace . .	2,413

	Barrels
Pitch in store and due 31st December 1770	4,674
31st December 1778	6,812
Annual expense in War . .	3,464
in Peace . .	2,578
Tar in store and due 31st December 1770	12,072
31st December 1778	30,780
Annual expense in War . .	13,968
in Peace . .	7,500

	Tons
Iron in store and due 31st December 1770	3,588
31st December 1778	4,255
Annual expense in War . .	945
in Peace . .	681

PAPER G.

Admiralty Office, 20 April 1779.

The number of seamen borne on the	
1st January 1778 was . . .	50,174
31st December 1778 was . . .	68,253
Increased in the year . . .	18,079
which upon a medium amounts each month to	1,560
Supposing the increase this year to the 31st March equal to the increase of last year, it will be reasonable to add to the number borne on the 31st of December last, viz.	68,253
three months' increase at 1,560 men per mensem	4,680

The number therefore now borne may be
supposed to amount to about   .   . 72,933

The number of marines now borne amount
to about   15,277

So that the number of seamen and marines
employed at this time in the service of
the Royal Navy amount to about   . 88,210

N.B.—The greatest number of seamen and marines
borne in the last war was in the month of July
1760, and amounted to 87,819.

NOTES III.

[In Lord Sandwich's writing.]

Bad condition of Admiral Keppel's fleet.

By what did it appear to be in
bad condition ?

Many of them
had been long
in commission.

No ship kept out of the line because she was bad.

Two of them only have wanted
any material repair.

The worst manned ship behaved
as well as any of them.

Some few had been hastily
manned, but they were at
least as good as those of the
French in the same state.

In the equipment of large fleets,
there must be always some
on each side that have been
hastily equipped.

11 of his best ships drafted from
him, but very speedily replaced.

Adm. Keppel said he found only 6 ships when he first went down.

What reason had he to expect more ?

Came first to Portsmouth on March 25.

Enter dates. Sailed the first time with 20 ships, June 13.

His ships were assembling from different parts, soon amounted to 30.

Every admiral at first takes possession of a small fleet.

Returned to St Helen's June 27. Sailed again July 9 with 24, and was joined off the Lizard by 6 more.

Sir Edward Hawke did the same.

Adm. Keppel's fleet not despicable soon after he had taken the command.

Had not frigates enough.

Vide No. 5.[1]

No. 3 : his own private letter.[2]

As many as the French, but why detach ?

Suffering Admiral Keppel to go to sea with an inferior force.

Not true : was always superior when at sea.

Greatly superior in size of ships and weight of metal and number of guns.

Sir E. Hawke sailed with an inferior force.

French had two of 50 guns.

[1] Hawke had 18 of the line put under his orders on 9 May 1759. He sailed on the 17th with 12, and was joined by 6 next day, and by 2 more on the 27th ; the French had 21.

[2] See below, p. 268.

Sir E. Hawke ordered to return   No. 20.[1]
to Torbay after examining the
strength of the French fleet :
did not return, but I never
heard he had complained of
his orders so to do.

PAPER NO. 3.

[In Lord Sandwich's writing and endorsed : ' Ex-
    tract from Admiral Keppel's letter to Ld S.
    May 5th 1778, No. 3.   Proves that his fleet
    was not despicable when he first took the
    command.'   The whole letter is printed in
    Chapter I.]

The pressing and essential service that the
detached fleet is going upon must have every
well-wisher to his country's assistance in ;   and
I am sure no man in England will be more anxious
for their success than myself.   However, their
being taken from my command renders my force
reduced, and indeed feeble for the numbers left
me ;   I mean that of having so many raw ships
in lieu of ships of old crews and habituated to
the sea for these twelve months past.

PAPER NO. 20.

SIR EDWARD HAWKE'S ORDER, 18 MAY 1759.

States that it is given out that the French
intend an invasion upon either G. Britain or
Ireland.   And as it is of the utmost consequence

---

[1] See below.

to prevent any such design taking effect, he is directed, as soon as he shall be joined by Sir C. Hardy, to proceed off Ushant to cause accurate observation of the state of the French to be made, and to return to Torbay in fourteen days.

NOTES IV.

[In Lord Sandwich's writing.]

Declaration made of 35 ships that were ready November 1777.

Has been proved to be true over   Vide papers 60,
and over again in both Houses   70, 80.[1]

Want of frigates at home last year.

Upwards of seventy in America : 20 ordered home but not sent : upwards of 50 lost or taken : yet have now more in service than in the highest period of the last war. It is the vast extent of coast we have to attack and to defend that makes our fleet appear inadequate to the services required from it.

Not allowing Admiral Keppel to produce his instructions.

Not true : the objection was that he should not produce his *whole* instructions.   He well knew that those parts that it was wished he should not produce could have no concern with his conduct in the action on the 27th of July.

[1] See below, pp. 270-4.

Admiral Byron's first destination.

The orders he sailed under were for New York ; destination varied according to the intelligence we received of d'Estaing's destination.

PAPER 60.

[Endorsed by Stephens thus : ' Admty 16 Dec. 1778. An account showing how the 42 ships of the line which were stated to be ready in Nov. 1777 have been disposed of.']

Of the . . 42 ships of the line which were stated to be ready in Nov. 1777,
    1 (the Mars) was paid off being in want of repair,
    1 (the Torbay) was set on fire by accident ;
    ___
of the . . 40 ships remaining
[Papers] A. & B. 12 sailed 9th June with Byron,[1]

    14 sailed 12th June with Keppel;
    3 had sailed before for the West Indies,
    2   do.   North America,
    1   do.   Newfoundland,
    2   do.   East Indies and St. Helena,
    1   do.   with convoy to the Mediterranean ;
    ___
in all . . 35

[1] See below, pp. 271-4, Papers ' A. 70 ' and ' B. 80.'

5 remained in port when Keppel sailed—of which, 3 sailed with him the 9th July, the second time he put to sea ; 1 sailed to join Keppel after the action ; and the other (the Burford) was detained for the East Indies :

—

which accounts
  for the   . 40
exclusive   of
  which   the
  Monmouth .   1 sailed with Byron 9th June,
  [Paper] C. . 6   do.   Keppel 12th June.[1]

So that there were when Byron sailed, including his squadron . 47 ships of the line actually at sea or nearly ready to proceed to sea.

PAPER A. 70.

[Endorsed by Lord Sandwich : ' a week later.']

Admiralty
  Office,
  19th November 1777.

{ List of thirty-five ships of the line in commission at home with the number of men wanted to complete them, distinguishing the seamen and marines.

[1] Victory 100 ; Elizabeth, Robust, Cumberland, and Berwick 74, America 64.

Ships' Names	Compt	Borne	Short of Compt		[Disposal]
			Seamen	Marines	
Sandwich	750	673	—	77	Keppel, sailed 12 June.
Prince George	750	648	3	99	K.
Pss Royal	750	442	203	105	Byron, sailed 9 June.
Ocean	750	653	1	96	K.
Queen	750	459	188	103	K.
Foudroyant	650	566	4	80	K.
Cornwall	600	553	47	—	B.
Valiant	650	540	27	83	K.
Invincible	600	529	—	71	B.
Resolution	600	490	13	97	[Joined K. *after* the action.]
Mars	600	522	—	78	Paid off.
Royal Oak	600	546	—	54	B.
Culloden	600	532	—	68	B.
Egmont	600	516	6	78	K.
Hector	600	503	18	79	K.
Monarch	600	542	—	58	K.
Ramillies	600	528	—	72	K.
Centaur	600	570	—	30	[Joined K. *before* the action.]
Terrible	600	535	—	65	
Courageux	600	587	—	13	K.
Albion	600	540	15	45	B.
Conqueror	600	508	11	81	B.
Torbay	600	564	10	26	Set on fire— paid off.
Pr. of Wales	600	574	7	19	Barrington— W. Indies.
Bedford	600	600	—	—	B.
Boyne	520	458	4	58	Barrington— W. Indies.
Burford	520	446	14	60	[Detained for E.I.]
Stirling Castle	500	403	30	67	K.
Exeter	500	455	—	45	K.
Ardent	500	478	—	22	North America.
Worcester	500	403	56	41	Convoy to Mediterranean.
Trident	500	452	—	48	North America.
Bienfaisant	500	430	13	57	K.
Asia	500	485	9	6	East Indies.
Belleisle	500	443	3	54	St. Helena.
	20,890	18,173	682	2035	

PAPER B. 80.

Admiralty Office, 19 November 1777.

List of seven ships of the line which have been since added to the thirty-five ships in the separate list.

Ships' Names	Compt.	Borne	Short of Comp.		[Disposal]
			Seamen	Marines	
Russell	600	179	311	110	Byron 9 June
Grafton	600	116	360	124	B.
Shrewsbury	600	62	414	124	[Joined Keppel *before* the action.]
Fame	600	174	316	110	B.
Sultan	600	169	321	110	B.
Europe	500	177	247	76	Newfoundland.
Ruby	500	67	343	90	West Indies [Jamaica].
	4000	944	2312	744	

' SHIPS INCLUDED IN THE 35.'

[June 1778].

[In Lord Sandwich's writing.]

74 Centaur .	.	Has had a small repair.
Mars	.	Paid off.
Torbay .	.	Burnt.
Terrible .	.	Disabled by sickness.
P. of Wales	.	Sailed to the West Indies.
Resolution	.	Refitting.
64 Worcester	.	Gone to Gibraltar.
Asia	.	Gone to the E. Indies.
Ardent } Trident }	.	Gone to America.
Europe .	.	Gone to Newfoundland.
70 Boyne } 64 Ruby } ·	.	Gone to the West Indies.

II.   T

[70] Burford . . Destined for the E. Indies.
      Belleisle . . Gone to St Helena.
      Exeter . . Going to Gibraltar.

At Spithead under Admiral Keppel   20 ⎫
In Plymouth Sound with Admiral Byron 13 ⎬ 49
                                   16 ⎭

Mediterranean . . . . [Panther] 1
E. Indies . . . . . [Rippon] 1
Leeward Islands . . . [Yarmouth] 1
N. America   [Eagle, Nonsuch, Raisonable, St Albans,
                                  Somerset] 6 [1]

NOTES V.

[In Lord Sandwich's writing.]

Bringing Admiral Keppel to a Court Martial.

Could not be avoided : a formal charge brought by an officer of high rank could not be resisted : never refused in any instance.

Captain Powlett [Duke of Bolton] and Admiral Griffin : captains accusing Admiral Knowles : Clements's exaggerated case.

Mr K. would have been undone if the court martial had not been held : to refuse would give the Admiralty a power to try only whom they pleased : necessary to be done instantly as some of the witnesses were under sailing orders.

For further particulars, *vide* Paper 50.[2]

---

[1] Lord Sandwich overlooked the fact that the Augusta had been lost in the Delaware River the previous autumn. There were now five of the line in America, besides the Ardent and Trident.

[2] See below, p. 275.

*Not sending a fleet to the Mediterranean to intercept
d'Estaing to reinforce Lord Howe.*

Principal object: home defence. State of war
different to former times. French fleet disabled
in the last war: their attention and money employed on the Continent.

Explain what I said about having always a
superiority to the House of Bourbon.

Great extent of coast to defend: French
fortified everywhere.

Have however contrived to be inferior only
in the Mediterranean. Were so in the last war,
and must always be so from the vicinity of France
and Spain.

Though Spain is, I hope, a friendly power,
their armaments must not be passed over without
a watchful eye.

As to intercepting the Toulon squadron, everything was done that was advisable: their destination unknown: supposed to be meant to come to
Brest: could do no more than to have a superior
fleet ready to follow them wherever they went.

As to Lord Howe, he was sufficiently reinforced.
If d'Estaing had not gone to America, he had
more force than he had occasion for; as he did
go to America, he was pursued by Byron, who
(without the storm) must have fallen upon him
and destroyed him.

PAPER 50.

[In Lord Sandwich's writing.]

Charge: court martial ordered precipitately.

Constant custom to order courts martial when
a charge is exhibited: can find no instance of a

court martial refused. Clements's case : order signed by Admiral Keppel.

Would be very dangerous, as it would give the Admiralty a power of stopping justice entirely, the time for trial being limited.

Attention to Admiral K. not to let such a charge be concealed from him.

Necessary, as some of his witnesses were under sailing orders.

Admiral Griffin and Captain Powlett both sent their charges the 31st of May 1750, and they were told the next day that courts martial would be ordered on each of them.

The four captains delivered their charge against Admiral Knowles 31st March 1749, which was sent to him the 4th of April.

At the motion of an inferior officer.

How can a superior officer be complained of otherwise ? Examples without end.

Recrimination : Powlett and Griffin ; captains and Knowles ; Clements's case ; purser against Arbuthnot when Keppel commanded ; lieutenant against Captain Hood under Sir E. Hawke—all these cases of recrimination.

POINTS RAISED IN DEBATE

[In Lord Sandwich's writing. His answers are in the right-hand column.]

23 April 1779.

Lord Bristol

24 millions expended since 1771.
Deficiency of magazines.   Differ totally.
Stated that he should have a
    fleet superior to France and
    soon to Spain.

Declaration about the having a superiority over the House of Bourbon.	
Should have sent a fleet to the Mediterranean.	
Trade abandoned.	No one convoy taken.
Declaration about 35 ships.	False.
Naval review detrimental.	Did good.
Byron should have been sent away.	What ! before you knew d'E s t a i n g's object.
Admiral Keppel was assured his fleet of 20 was superior.	Not true.
Intelligence in the Licorne.	Got their anchoring order.
French primely manned, ours otherwise.	False.
Admiral Keppel praised for coming home.	Was ordered to do so.[1] Not applauded.
Ships ill manned.[2]	The reverse is true.
French out ten days sooner than us after the action.	Proves that we were more beaten than they.
Absurd instructions to Admiral Barrington.	

[1] See the secret instructions of 25 April 1778, Appendix A, pp. 369–73.

[2] One of Lord Bristol's criticisms was the reduction of the war complement of 74-gun ships from 650 to 600. This order, dated 20 October 1770, was given when fitting out the fleet at the time of the Falkland Islands affair, and signed by Hawke (as First Lord) and Charles James Fox. It remained in force till nearly the end of the century, when the complement was reduced again to 590, though the armament remained unchanged.

Inferior in the East Indies. — Not true.

114 ships of the line in 1759. — Includes 50-gun ships.

91 ships of the line in commission. — Must include 50 guns : his papers must be erroneous.

Could not get Sir J. Ross to sea. — I don't understand what is meant. Contrary winds.

Stephens the only man at the Admiralty. — LordM[ulgrave].

I have included 50-gun ships as of the line. — In no reasoning or expression have I ever done so.

Captain Walker [an intelligence agent praised by Lord Bristol]. — Tampering with spies : intelligence futile and always too late.

Good ships broke up. — Jobs on the other side.

12 ships will fight their way through anything.

Admiral the Duke of Bolton : Duke of Richmond.

5 guardships ; Culloden ; Canada ; Formidable.

83 French navy. — Ours on that idea about 140.

Admiral Keppel's returning right. — I thought so.

I did not think the French superior.

It was a matter very doubtful to me whether they were so or not in readiness. He was right if he thought so.

More beaten than the French.

Playing upon words: I think the French fleet was beaten ; we kept the field and they retired. Meant that our ships had suffered more than theirs.

FROM THE KING

Queen's House, [Wednesday] 28 April 1779.

I have kept the list of the peers that attended on Friday at the House of Lords, as it is declared to be exact.

I had received a copy of Lord Bristol's protest on Monday, therefore return the one that came yesterday from Lord Sandwich. Allegations unsupported with proofs, and many of them proved to be void of truth, seem to pervert the idea of transmitting to posterity authentic reasons for what has been proposed, though rejected, in Parliament.

The Earl of Bristol's Protest

Friday, 23 April 1779.

Dissent :

Because, having made the motion alluded to in the above dissent, I think it incumbent upon me to let posterity know the particular grounds I made that motion upon.

1st. Because, since the year 1771, there has been £6,917,872, 5s. 0¼d. granted for naval purposes more than was granted in an equal number of years between 1751 and 1759 for the use of the Navy, although we had then been four years at war with France within that period.

2nd. Because the Navy of England appears to be reduced from what it was in the year 1771, when the present First Lord of the Admiralty succeeded to the head of that Board, notwithstanding the immense sums granted for its support and increase since that time.

3rd. Because it appears that after having received such repeated intelligence, as has been acknowledged to have been received from the 3rd of January 1778 to the 27th of April following, of the equipment and progress of the Toulon squadron to their sailing the 13th of April 1778, the not sending a squadron into the Mediterranean to watch the motions of and endeavour to intercept the said French squadron from passing the Straits, nor sending any reinforcements to Lord Howe, or even dispatching Vice-Admiral Byron till the 9th of July [June] 1778, was exposing the fleet as well as the army of England then employed in America to a very superior force of France.

4th. Because it appears the sending of Admiral Keppel off Brest the 13th of June with twenty sail of the line, when the Lords Commissioners of the

Admiralty knew or ought to have known that the French fleet then actually at Brest and fitting for sea consisted of 32 ships of the line besides many heavy frigates, might have been productive at that time of the most fatal consequences to the only considerable naval force this kingdom had then ready for its protection, but also to the trade and even the ports of these kingdoms. And if Admiral Keppel had remained with his twenty ships of the line off Brest, he must with those twenty have engaged the French fleet of thirty sail of the line who sailed the 8th of July, as Admiral Keppel could not get the reinforcement of even four ships of the line to join him till the 9th of July, although he was then at St Helen's for that purpose.

5th. Because it appears that we lost that valuable island of Dominica for want of timely reinforcements and proper instructions being sent to Admiral Barrington.

6th. Because, for the want of the smallest naval force being sent to the coast of Africa, we have also lost that valuable station of Senegal, which might in time, with proper attention, have opened new markets for our drooping manufactures.

7th. And because it appears that the Admiralty, without any deliberation whatsoever, having precipitately ordered a court martial upon a commander in chief of that great rank and character which Admiral Keppel bears in his Majesty's fleet, was frustrating the salutary intentions of that discretionary power so wisely lodged by the Constitution in the Lords Commissioners for executing the office of Lord High Admiral of Great Britain, whereby all malicious and ill-founded charges, by whomsoever exhibited, may be avoided and the union and discipline of the service not interrupted.

CHAPTER IV

NORTH AMERICA
February-December 1778

INTRODUCTION

I

THE instructions to Lord Howe and Sir Henry Clinton for the North American campaign of 1778 will be found in Volume I.[1] The whole situation in North America was dominated by the imminence of war with France. Instead of the grandiose offensive of 1777 there is now a defensive campaign against the Americans, and a large force is detached to fight the French in the West Indies (see Chapter V).

The menace of d'Estaing's squadron from Europe held up the sailing of this offensive force until November, and endangered New York and Rhode Island with the armies based on them.

Philadelphia was evacuated on June 18, Howe taking the refugees, and Clinton marching overland to Sandy Hook, where they rejoined forces on July 1. The army was ferried up to New York and Howe prepared to receive d'Estaing, who had reached the Delaware on July 8.[2] The strength of Howe's defensive line and the danger of the bar decided d'Estaing to wait until he could

---

[1] Pp. 324–6, 363–5.

[2] The ships preparing for sea at New York and Sandy Hook were the following :

Eagle (flag), Trident (Com. Elliot), Ardent, Nonsuch, St. Albans, Somerset 64s ; Preston (Com. Hotham), Experiment, Isis, 50s ; Amazon, Apollo, Pearl, Phoenix, Richmond, Roebuck, Venus, frigates ; Vigilant, armed ship, and some sloops, bombs and fireships.

Several frigates and sloops were already at sea :

Greyhound on passage to Halifax (and to cruise off Cape Sambro to look for Byron) ; Maidstone, Zebra, Mermaid, Daphne, Swift, Solebay, looking for d'Estaing between Sandy Hook and the Chesapeake ; and a number of vessels employed on subsidiary services. There were also several ships at Halifax, some of them refitting (Howe's disp. July 6).

D'Estaing had two 80s, six 74s, three 64s, a 50 and three or four frigates (Lacour-Gayet, 629–30).

obtain American pilots.   These decided unanimously that
there was not enough water for his larger ships, and
d'Estaing sailed for Rhode Island on July 22, where he
conducted a combined operation with the American
General Sullivan.   On July 30 the first of Byron's
squadron (the Cornwall) arrived at Sandy Hook, and
Howe learned that he could no longer hope for a fleet
superior to the French.   On August 8, d'Estaing and
Sullivan began their attack on the British force at Rhode
Island.   When Howe arrived next day d'Estaing went
out to meet him.

THE OPPOSING FLEETS OFF RHODE ISLAND [1]

Ships	Guns	Ships	Guns
Eagle	64	Languedoc	80
Trident	64	Tonnant	80
Preston	50	César	74
Cornwall	74	Zélé	74
Nonsuch	64	Hector	74
Raisonable	64	Guerrier	74
Somerset	64	Marseillais	74
St Albans	64	Protecteur	74
Ardent	64	Vaillant	64
Centurion	50	Provence	64
Experiment	50	Fantasque	64
Isis	50	Sagittaire	50
Renown	50		
		Frigates	
Phoenix	44	Chimère	
Roebuck	44	Engageante	
Venus	36	Aimable	
Richmond	32	Alcmène	
Pearl	32		
Apollo	32		
Sphinx	20		
Vigilant, A.S.	20		

Sloop, Nautilus; fireships, Strombolo, Sulphur, Volcano;
bombs, Thunder, Carcass, and two tenders; galleys, Philadelphia,
Hussar, Ferret, Cornwallis.

[1] The British force is from Howe's dispatch of August 17, the
French is from Lacour-Gayet, 629–30.
   The Chimère took M. de Rayneval to Philadelphia, and may
not have rejoined the squadron by August 11.   When the Cornwall
arrived she 'struck several times, it being near low water,' while
crossing the bar.   (Master's log.)

During the next two days Howe manœuvred with great skill, but on the evening of the 11th, as they were about to join battle, both fleets were scattered by a storm. Ten days later Howe's shattered fleet had all reached Sandy Hook. Curiously enough the French sighted Byron's flagship on the 18th, and this fact added to Howe's tenacity and the damage wrought by the gale determined d'Estaing, in spite of the most urgent entreaties from the Americans, to give up the attack and to refit his squadron at Boston. He arrived there on August 28.

We must now turn for a moment to the adventures of Byron's squadron. He had sailed from England on June 9 with thirteen ships of the line and a frigate. The fleet was dispersed, and most of the ships severely damaged, by a gale on July 3. The Russell had eventually to return to Plymouth ; the Invincible and Guadaloupe reached St. John's, Newfoundland ; the Albion, after refitting at Lisbon, arrived at Sandy Hook in October ; the Cornwall, as we have seen, arrived there on July 30 ; the Monmouth in the middle of August ; the Royal Oak, Conqueror, Fame, Sultan, Bedford, and Grafton at the end of that month. Byron's flagship, the Princess Royal, sighting d'Estaing on the 18th, bore up for Halifax, where she found the Culloden ; the two ships sailed for Rhode Island in September.

Howe's squadron refitted in excellent time and was ready for sea on the 25th. He sailed first to Boston, where he saw the French, and thence to Rhode Island (Sept. 4) where he learnt of Sullivan's retreat. He stayed five days and then returned to Sandy Hook (Sept. 11), where he found six of Byron's ships under Admiral Hyde Parker. His work was finished, for he knew that Byron would arrive shortly. He therefore turned over the command to Gambier, called at Rhode Island, where he met Byron, and sailed for home on September 26, narrowly escaping capture in the Channel.

Howe's difficulties during his command were great. He was always short-handed, and he had only Halifax as a dockyard, with New York as an auxiliary ; Germain, the Secretary of State, was an old enemy, and Lord Sandwich was a political opponent whom he often distrusted.[1]   In spite of these handicaps, he successfully defended New York and Rhode Island.   His frigates enabled him, by their accurate observation, to outwit a superior enemy force, and his tact contributed to the success of all his combined operations with the Army.

There is little else to record.   Byron made one more attempt to find d'Estaing, but his fleet was again scattered by the weather.   At long last the St. Lucia expedition, under Commodore Hotham and General Grant, sailed on November 3, and on the following day d'Estaing sailed for Martinique.

At the end of November a successful expedition was undertaken by Captain Hyde Parker and Colonel Campbell in Georgia.   Finally Byron left Rhode Island for Barbados on December 14, and, needless to say, encountered heavy weather.

II

Sandwich wrote to Howe on 4 February 1778 :

'In consequence of your requisition for at least two flag officers (exclusive of Commodore Hotham) to serve under you in the next campaign, Vice-Admiral Byron and Rear-Admiral Gambier will shortly join you, the former in the Europe and the latter in the Ardent ; I flatter myself they are both persons who will be agreeable to your Lordship, which idea has been a principal cause for their being selected for this service. . . . I believe, that at the close of the next campaign, your Lordship will be directed to send Mr Gambier to England, I could wish therefore that you would employ him in such manner as you think most proper for allowing him to leave America when the winter is fairly set in.'

Howe replied on April 23 : 'I am equally sensible of your Lordship's indulgent consideration of the motives

[1] But not always, ' No wonder then that Lord Howe cheerfully accepted a seat at the Board, in 1763, under the able administration of Lord Sandwich, a man of first-rate abilities, and one of the most active and well-informed that ever filled the high office of First Lord of the Admiralty ' (Barrow, p. 72).

which influenced your choice of the flag officers for the American service, though my impaired state of health obliges me to hope for the earliest concurrence in my request to be relieved in this command.'

On March 10, Admiral Gambier was ordered to proceed to New York in the Ardent, taking under his convoy a large fleet of storeships, victuallers, etc., and upon his arrival to put himself under the command of Lord Howe. He sailed on March 16. Howe did not treat Gambier as a second in command, but instead left him at New York to act as Port Admiral—a post of some importance, since he had to repair the ships in a home-made yard, and maintain communications with the army; but one with no opportunities of winning either prize-money or renown. Moreover, Gambier was treated in a summary fashion, and had always to refit Howe's and Byron's shattered ships at the expense of his own small squadron. Throughout his letters Gambier complains of this treatment, and it may be assumed that he would not have consented to leave his post as Commissioner of the Yard at Portsmouth to take up what became a similar post at New York, if he had known how he was to be employed. He expected to succeed Howe, who had asked to be relieved of the command in November 1777, but had decided to stay on when he heard of the approach of a superior French fleet. Moreover, Sandwich appears to have shared Howe's low opinion of Gambier's competence, and the appointment was probably made because it was necessary to make room for Sir Samuel Hood at Portsmouth, either to placate his political connection or because an able officer was needed to get Keppel's fleet to sea. Gambier could hardly have been dismissed without another command, for his sister was married to Charles Middleton and his family was connected with the Pitts.[1] So long as he was engaged in refitting the fleets at New York he could do no positive harm, but if Howe had left him in chief command, the result might have been catastrophic.

Howe turned over the command to Gambier on September 11, but continued to interfere with the arrange-

[1] *Barham Papers*, I., xxiii.

ments until he sailed to meet Byron on the 24th ; and as Byron arrived at Sandy Hook on October 1, Gambier never enjoyed the chief command. When Howe left, Gambier was not made a member of the Commission, and this was a further cause of complaint.

His private letters to Sandwich are very long and full of repetitions. They are ill-written and seldom punctuated.[1] We have copied his letter of July 6 in full, but we have felt compelled, for the sake of clearness, to omit large portions of the other letters, and in some cases to express his views in our own words.

III.—NEWFOUNDLAND, 1778

Admiral Montagu's orders (dated May 2) were to capture the islands of St Pierre and Miquelon as soon as he should hear that hostilities had begun. Notice of war was sent to him on July 27. The islands were 'the constant rendezvous of all the little privateers that infest Newfoundland,' and our fisheries were still suffering heavily at their hands. An expedition was despatched in September under Commodore Evans, one of Byron's officers, whose ship had been driven to St John's, and the islands immediately surrendered. His purpose accomplished, Montagu left Captain Robert Linzee to transport the captured inhabitants to France, and himself sailed for home on November 1. He arrived at Spithead on November 19, and was immediately appointed one of the members of the court martial (see above, pp. 216–7). He did not serve again during the war, and was succeeded at Newfoundland in 1779 by Rear-Admiral Richard Edwards. The few letters amongst the Hinchingbrooke papers are unimportant and are summarised in this note.

---

[1] '[The dispatches] from Gambier extremely tedious, and show him little calculated to cope with difficulties though most ready to point them out.' From the King, December 17. See also *Corr.*, 2440.

TO LORD HOWE

Admiralty, 24 February 1778.

My Lord—The letter, of which the enclosed is a copy, has been communicated to me by Lord North, and in consequence of it your Lordship will have leave from the Board to return home, if the state of your health or any other cause should make you desirous of quitting the command in America. Had the intimation come from any less authentic or respectable quarter, I should not have thought of paying any attention to it, but should have waited till your Lordship had told us your wish upon the subject in question ; however the case is altered by the receipt of Lady Howe's letter, and I should think myself guilty of a great impropriety if I did not leave it entirely in your own option to remain in the command or to return to England : and you will consider your leave of absence as conveying no wish of the Board that you should come home, unless you should choose to do it.

I am very certain that his Majesty wishes you should not think it necessary to leave the command ; and for myself, I can with the utmost truth assure you, that I shall consider it as a very additional misfortune if we are to lose the advantage of your able assistance in the present critical state of our affairs both civil and military on your side of the Atlantic. I hope therefore that no use will be made of the leave you now receive from the Office, and that you will continue to direct our naval concerns in America, as long as the present unfortunate contest exists. I am [etc.]

LADY HOWE TO LORD NORTH [1]

Grafton Street, 18 February 1778.

My Lord—As I understood a Commission is intended to be sent out to treat with the Americans, which must supersede that Commission which Lord Howe and General Howe have been honoured with ; and as I am convinced His Majesty cannot wish Lord Howe to receive any mortification ; I beg leave to submit it to your Lordship's consideration, whether it may not be proper to ask his Majesty's leave for him to quit his naval command, in case he should wish to do so ; and that that permission may be sent out by the frigate ordered for America, which I understand is to sail forthwith.   I have [etc.].

TO ADMIRAL GAMBIER

Admiralty, 13 April 1778.

Dear Sir—Since you have left us the face of affairs is so much changed, and everything is now in such uncertainty, that I know not how to write to you either upon public or private business.   The original destination of your having the command at Halifax and Lord Howe's remaining about New York with a considerable naval force is at an end ; for I conclude that as General Howe

---

[1] North, in forwarding this letter to Sandwich on February 23, wrote: ' It is most certainly the earnest desire of his Majesty that Lord Howe should neither receive nor have any reason to think he receives a mortification ; if, therefore, he consents to Lady Howe's request, he hopes that any leave of absence that is sent to him may be done in such a manner as to leave no doubt of the King's approbation of his conduct, and of his wish that his Lordship would continue in his command, unless it is really and entirely his own desire to return.'

is on his passage to England, and the greatest part of the American fleet called home, Lord Howe will avail himself of the leave sent out to him and will return soon after, possibly before, the arrival of the Commissioners. If this happens, you will remain commander in chief, it is true, of a small naval force but of what I hope will be adequate to the services expected from it. Your being a commissioner, which will devolve to you if Lord Howe leaves America, will be so honourable and advantageous a situation that I conclude you will not think it a hardship to remain where you are till the great and important business between England and her colonies takes some consistency ; your return, therefore, at the end of the campaign, and your appointment to the government of Newfoundland, must remain in a state of suspense till we hear the success of our attempts for a reconciliation with our rebellious subjects.

We are upon the point of a war with France, and perhaps with Spain ; an American war added thereto is, I fear, more than we are equal to. I give you this merely as a private hint, being well assured that if the power of treating devolves to you by Lord Howe's coming home, your own abilities will direct you into that path which is most likely to lead to the extricating this unfortunate country from the difficulties in which she now finds herself involved.

I believe Mr Manners will not come out to you ; for Admiral Byron's voyage to America is at an end,[1] and I understand that Manners is on board Admiral Keppel's ship and that there has been some mistake about his being borne on

---

[1] Byron was first meant to join Howe in North America ; then he was appointed to command in the East Indies, and finally he was sent in pursuit of d'Estaing.

any ship's books so as to give him a right to pass his examination. I shall therefore fill up the vacancy that was intended for him in your ship with a person now in America who has some connexions with the leading people in the Congress, which it is imagined will be a favour not misplaced.

I shall expect from you as particular an account as possible of everything that passes in this very critical scene, and remain [etc.].

FROM HOWE

Philadelphia, 10 June 1778.

My Lord—I received your Lordship's commands by the Ardent sent from New York, and by the Trident at the same time. The appointment of Lieutenants Hervey and Mr Ham will be immediately made ; and I am to address my acknowledgements to your Lordship for the attention you have condescended to show to the purpose of the letter, with which Lady Howe in her anxiety ventured to trouble Lord North ; founded as I find on her ignorance of the effect of my public application for the same conditional leave in November last of which I was not indulged with any notice in the official answer to that letter.

I am perfectly conscious how much I am indebted to your Lordship's civility for the flattering interpretation you would encourage me to put on the gracious sentiments of the King with regard to my stay in this country. But though ambitious in the utmost extent to have seen his Majesty's service prosper in my hands, the fruitless exertion of my endeavours is become conspicuous in too many instances for me to err in the just estimation of my claims to that distinction, or to the favourable opinion you have had the goodness to express of my Lord, [etc.].

FROM THE KING

Kew, 13 June 1778, 40 m. past 6 P.M.

Perhaps from no great expectations of prosperous events in North America, I am rather pleased at the little success obtained by the expedition to destroy the vessels in the Delaware.[1] Had that mode been more adopted during the contest, it must have greatly distressed the rebels and prevented their taking the number of ships with valuable cargoes which enabled them to continue their unjustifiable measures.

I trust our next accounts from Keppel will be from Cawsand Bay or Torbay.

FROM GAMBIER

Ardent, off New York, 6 July 1778.

My honoured Lord—This instant only I learn that a packet is to be dispatched and to sail this evening with the Viscount's [Howe] and General's [Clinton] letters, forgive then, my revered patron, a hasty scrawl.

Painfully circumstanced as I have been ever since my arrival here, ignorant totally of all that has passed from scarce ever hearing from the

[1] A small expedition up the Delaware commanded by Major Hon. John Maitland and Captain John Henry with some galleys, in which a number of rebel craft were destroyed. (Sir William Howe to Germain, May 11.) It was expeditions such as these which were recommended in the March instructions.

Delaware until now that Lord Howe has just arrived at Sandy Hook, and Sir Henry with his army through the Jerseys. Not a single line have I ever had of even the Commissioners' arrival in the Delaware, the evacuating Philadelphia, or the army's marching, until Lord Howe appeared off the Hook, so that what preparations I indefatigably prepared of transports, small ships, flat-bottomed boats, &c. to co-operate with and assist the army, and which were highly necessary, I undertook and perfected from the confidential intercourse and communication I had with the General Jones commanding here ; and nothing transpiring from Philadephia hither during the whole time, we could only pick up surmises and common reports, very insufficient to form any judgment or ground any opinion. The packets Lord Howe sent me after the arrival of the Trident at the Delaware, and announcing to me the evacuation and intended march of the army, were it seems put on board the Trident, who was to have proceeded hither long ago but unfortuitously detained up the Delaware a long time, so long indeed that she arrives but now with Lord Howe in the Eagle, and the packet sailing instantly, I have scarce time to acknowledge the having but just received your two kind letters of the 13th April that came in the Trident and to return you my sincere and affectionate thanks for your continued attention to my fate, which I feel sensible satisfaction in confiding to your friendship, assured and convinced that I shall be happy while my destiny remains in your hands.

Distressed in point of time I have not sufficient, at least by this conveyance, either to express my gratitude or, from being hitherto kept in ignorance in this Siberia, to form any judgment of what has been done or is likely to happen, yet wish to obey your commands whenever possibly in my power. In view to see his Lordship and to get some insight I requested to be permitted to come down to him, he having wrote me to continue as usual in the command and duties of the port as if he was not at the Hook. He not forbidding my request, I went down to him for some hours and am just returned, but little wiser than I was either as to what has or may occur—so totally reserved to all. I learned from him that, having heard of a supposed destination of a squadron of French ships of war expected on the coasts of this continent, he judged fit to assemble all the ships of his Majesty's fleet of the greatest force in readiness to put to sea on the shortest notice ; and as my stay will in that case be necessary to regulate the duties here and to co-operate with the commander in chief of the land forces in such measures as he may see proper to adopt for the King's service during his (Lord Howe's) eventual absence, he directed me to embark and move my distinguishing flag on board such ship of my division (composed of three or four small frigates and other vessels) as I should think fit, directing the captain of the Ardent to repair with that ship directly to the Hook to join him there.

When his Lordship mentioned a hint of intelligence of a French squadron's being expected here or hereabouts (however different my own idea from the state of the particulars of the information and its grounds for apprehending their destiny being hitherwards, I mean in *North* America or the continent, and which idea of mine I respectfully submitted to his Lordship) I nevertheless as humbly requested that if aught of opportunity of active service or honour was to be sought that he would indulgently and considerately allow me to claim a right to be employed ; but he replied that it was absolutely necessary that either he or I should stay here with the army to co-operate with and assist it.

The orders he was under being to govern his conduct, more he would not say, nor did he seem inclinable to communicate aught. Visibly so, in so much that my painful suspense and ignorance of my future fate was not one jot relieved, and all that I had to console or comfort my sensibly uneasy feelings was and is the kind contents of your Lordship's letters. They are my only balm, and on them will I rely until a little time shall develop what his Lordship takes pains to keep so profoundly secret, in the comfortable hope that your continued friendship will not let me be kept abroad a second in command at any rate, nor permit the promises that I was considerately honoured with be annihilated and unperformed to the distress and hurt of a devoted servant, honoured with your friendship, who wishes to deserve it, and who has quitted a certain subsistence for an amiable wife and five helpless children to endeavour under your auspices and protection to better support and educate them at the cheerful risk of his life and health on a remote service of unequalled fatigue, difficulty, and unremitting attention. Most kindly did your Lordship comfort me by empowering me to rest satisfied that, if I should from the vicissitudes remain abroad, that the disappointment of not coming home as was intended would be made up in some degree to me and mine by my remaining commander in chief in an advantageous and honourable situation, with being one of the Commissioners, for which purpose a new commission would be sent out.   This being the advice and wish of you, my honoured loved patron, was a balm to every corroding apprehension joined to the hoped idea and prospect that come what might of dangers, difficulties, and anxieties in the most *unpleasing untoward service*, and now I fear reduced to become only a *secondary* object of the State's attention, I might still have my pains and labours crowned with some profit and support for my wife and children ; and in this idea let me again entreat your patronage and protection, or a family that reveres you and depends on your kindness will be reduced to wretchedness.

Evacuating Philadelphia was unpalatable to many : I conclude it was judged at this time necessary.   Some wish it had never been occupied, or the needle pointed to the southward.   It will require I am told a very great body of troops to keep even this place alone—and a much larger force if Rhode Island also.

The answer from the C[ongress]—however strong—yet appears to some not still impossible, but that some time, and possibly not far off, that they may be more inclinable to treat—when the dispassionate shall have time to reflect, and those that do shall circulate and avail themselves of opportunities of communicating to the herd their opinion of the indulgent terms offered.   At present a few illiberal, greedy, passionate mendicants sway and infatuate the multitude, keeping them in a state of ignorance and irascible ebriety.   If such a fortuitous change of sentiments does not speedily happen, this distant and in itself globe of country is more, some fear, *now* unconquerable than Peru and Mexico were of old.   Our army as they are is healthy, brave, and zealous ; but an army must constantly be recruited.   Twelve hundred leagues with its natural difficulties demand a solemn thought—the means and expense ! Our ships, long out, want repair ; and a considerable number must ever be constantly here on this extensive coast, too extensive almost to guard anyhow and at all seasons.

[La Motte-Picquet] his little squadron alarmed. Whenever all our cruisers are called in from the stations 'tis inconceivable what groups of supplies have been daily poured in, La Motte's few ships making such to have been found advisable. D'Estaing's reported visit or suspected mission causes the same to continue : they know all this, and they most sensibly avail themselves of it, astonishingly so ! Small ships, small good-sailing vessels and numbers of them, are not only indispensably necessary on this coast, but 'tis also impossible to do without : 20-gun ships coppered, sloops, cutters, and small vessels, are of the greatest utility here ; some ships of force are necessary likewise. The rebels can now muster threescore sail from their different ports from 36 to 20 and 18 guns ; and yet I will venture to affirm that a third of that number of our frigates would take them all, would each party agree to meet, but we have such a range of coast and such a multiplicity of various services, convoys, army requisitions and attendances, that it is an Augean labour to attend to and find means to encounter such a variegated choice of numberless difficulties.

Pardon my honoured Lord so undigested and hasty a scrawl, let want of time, want of matter from cruel banishment hitherto, and being kept in ignorance unaccountably so, be my apology for not being able to obey your commands. I only pray for ability and opportunity in future, for I want not zeal or inclination.

Reports are various, and only reports can I learn. Lord H[owe] did tell me that Admiral B[yron] was expected. Lord Carlisle confirmed the same. And yet your Lordship's kind letters are my balm and banish every painful apprehension, and I comfort myself that you will not let me stay here, at least without having the command in chief and being in the Commission ; and even then I fear there will be little possible field for your devoted servant to acquire either credit and honour to his zealous wishes of distinguishing your election or of getting subsistence and support for his wife and children. Monsieurs Picquet and d'Estaing have hitherto totally prevented the latter.

The General's messenger waiting for my letters, I must conclude a scarce legible scrawl with heartfelt thanks for your friendship and kindness to me and those most justly dear to me. If I live, my honoured Lord, I will most cordially act through life gratefully acknowledging what I owe your friendship. I appointed Mr Ham to act here in my nephew's room : I should hope Lord Howe will confirm him a lieutenant. I most sincerely wish every blessing to attend you and yours, and remain [etc.].

P.S.—Mrs Gambier's letters remind me of more obligations I owe your Lordship's friendship ; and she bids me to hope that, through the continuance of it, she may have her husband happily restored to her and her children with a degree of comfort by Christmas.

FROM GAMBIER

Eagle at Sandy Hook, Sunday morning, 12 July 1778.

. . . The Viscount repeated his former answer that either he or I must stay up here with the Army, and I must therefore return back to my station directly. . . . If they face the Hook I think they will fail ; for I don't in the first place believe there is water for their Languedoc and Tonnant. . . . We have sent through [Long Island] Sound two days ago reinforcement of troops to Rhode Island. I hope and believe they have arrived thither and none of the French frigates waylaid them round the Island. . . . Lord H. this moment *only* has given me some packets, viz. copies of orders, regulations, etc. in case he unexpectedly should sail and I remain in the command. . . .

FROM GAMBIER

Emerald, off New York town, 19 July 1778.

My honoured and revered Lord—The packet sailed unexpectedly we find yesterday ; from my friend Sir Henry, I this moment learn another will probably be dispatched to-morrow if not this evening. I hasten to embrace the opportunity to tell your Lordship that affairs at and without the Hook remain as they were in my last except that the F[rench] fleet have been ever since watering at the mouth of Shrewsbury River near the Navesink, where they appear to do it with great convenience and dispatch. A certain corroborating proof to my early opinion that they meant no attempt to force the harbour after their knowledge of our force within, as on the bar there is at spring tides bare water for their large ships and if intended to pass it they would endeavour to lighten their ships instead of getting them down still deeper.

If Admiral B[yron] *did* sail, or at the time we hoped, is it not odd that d'Estaing should run the risk he does of being caught. Admiral B. being equal to his force we conclude without our junction, and we here almost equal (had the Raisonable and Centurion joined us) even without the expected addition of Admiral B., a deep game he appears to play, unless *he* has *better* information than *we* have. In the meantime 'tis said he has already sent in 30 prizes to the Delaware, taken on his passage out and on the coast, and takes daily others even since his arrival off here, some we have been eyewitnesses of. I never longed in my life to see the finest of women more than I do to see Admiral B. ; and his nephew [Lord Carlisle] as well as E[den] and the rest of our friends here join me in the same wish, for 'tis an important crisis !

We hope he *did* sail and came *direct* hither ; if not and first to Halifax it may be fatal. The southerly winds at this time of the year bring the Trade winds here ; and the Eagle, a single ship, three weeks getting thence hither.

On my last visit down to the Hook, to again repeat my offer and importunate request on the vicinity of the F[rench] F[leet] to be employed on the more active and honourable service, I was again told he or I must remain up here to co-operate with the army, at which time he was pleased to put into my hands large packets containing the counterparts of official orders, arrangements, &c. which were for my government on his suddenly leaving the command in chief to me :

the first *item* I have ever had from *him* of such an event likely to happen. I acquainted your Lordship with my repeated offers and requests of the most active employ on the earliest appearance of the French fleet and refusals. It was not only my duty but what was my wish, after coming twelve hundred leagues from my family. I presumed also most respectfully to advise fitting the Leviathan with borrowed lower-deckers from the Army, and making half a dozen of the empty transports into temporary fireships on this very critical emergency, should they attempt to force their entrance or we by any fortuitous change be in condition to go out to them. Early I thought such my duty— I wrote your Lordship confidentially, trusting that what I communicate will remain in your own bosom. We are in a very critical situation indeed. The appearance of Admiral B. would relieve us and turn the tables.

Perusing, my honoured Lord, the several orders and arrangements and secret instructions put into my hands I cannot but feel too painful sensations (should they take place) at the certain prospect of my being left here with a force (it scarce merits the name of force) obviously and notoriously inadequate not only to the service expected from it but to any service at all, when the shattered state and condition of almost all the ships and vessels (numerous as on paper they may appear) is duly considered. Exclusive of the French, the rebels have by our last certain accounts not less than between twenty and thirty sail of armed Congress ships, completely manned and fit for sea at Boston, from 36 to 20 guns—and a nigh equal number in South Carolina—besides belligerent ships and vessels vegetating in every harbour and creek daily all along the coasts ; ours, though at this time numerous, are all foul, out of repair in hulls, masts, and yards, and in want of stores.

The several various *arrangements*, drafts, and *deductions* from this debilitated number that are directed by the arrangements in the secret instructions will leave but little behind of *serviceable*, or of force and consequence to act hostilely and offensively, or indeed to show their heads *out of port*—exclusive of that distress-completing paragraph : ' to send the remainder also to E[ngland], including those which may be in the River St L[awrence] &c.' The *previous* arrangements and sundry many appropriations would reduce this force to a very inoffensive one, foul, out of repair, and in want of stores, joined also to the several convoys likewise pointed out and directed ; and should I not then, my revered friend and honoured patron, be left with very *inadequate* means to do my duty ?

That *conclusive* paragraph would, I fear, make me poor indeed by robbing me of the power of doing service, few remaining and unconditioned ships and vessels and without possibly an asylum or port. Deign then, my dear Lord, as you bid me write confidentially everything, to commiserate my prospect as to situation, nor suffer my fate to be so wretchedly changed from that which I was given to be assured of when I quitted my dockyard. My fate is in your hands, and I am happy in that confidence and contented.

Soon after the receipt of your favours by the Trident the Commission appeared in print here, wherein Sir H. C[linton] was included. The Viscount it seems declined acting, giving for reason his going shortly home—no mention of his successor in the command in chief's being likewise to succeed him as Commissioner—and was I to succeed him as commander in chief but not in the Commission, could I, my honoured patron, with any degree of aught but misery live and serve as commander in chief with the stigma of being left out of the Commission, and at the same time that one of the members of it is a junior captain in the Navy [George Johnstone], and whom I took raw from Scotland to sea myself *since* I have been a *captain*. And is the land commander in chief's successor to be joined in the Commission and the sea not—a degrading circumstance I am sure the justly honoured patron of the Navy will not suffer. I can, my dear Lord, be content to live without honours, but never can submit the un- merited disgrace. . . .

I have received directions to try to get lower- deck guns for the Leviathan and to send her down, and also to endeavour to make a transport a temporary fireship ; you may believe I shall exert in the equipping what I early requested to be adopted.

That health, honour, and happiness may attend your Lordship I hope I need not repeat being my wish. As letters are *at* this *critical* time uncertain as to *whose* hands they may fall *into*, I subscribe no name : your Lordship will decipher your faithful, affectionate and obliged Servant.

New York, July 21.

The packet not being yet under sail, I have time to tell my honoured that this moment Sir H. C[linton] shows me a written intelligence just received that d'Est[aing] and General W[ashington] 'tis said meditate a general attack here at the same time. We here are all happy at the idea, as it will bring affairs to an issue ; the Army holding them- selves ready and equal to the whole force they can possibly bring, and the Navy as clearly deeming it impossible, but that they must lose their ships if they should attempt the harbour. Some fishermen escaped from them and deserters say they give out they only wait the spring-tide and pilots ; we fear 'tis only a gasconade, and that 'twill end in a Spithead fight.

If Admiral B[yron] does but appear 'twill be glorious ; we hourly pray for it as the most fortunate event that Heaven can bless us with. I send the Leviathan down to-day with a lower-deck tier of 32, 24, and 18, being what I could borrow from the Train. I hope the fireship will be finished before the day after to-morrow that the tides lift, although I have no ideas that *now* they mean *that* attack ; up here I think they may attempt something, but without success. But, my honoured Lord, I am more apprehensive that if they remain here, and we not relieved, we shall be distressed for provisions : that is a serious matter with such a multitude as here, and if the Cork fleet should be intercepted, the consequence dreadful unless we are relieved. . . .

FROM GAMBIER

Thames, off New York, 31 July 1778.

. . . My particular fate and destiny remains in your Lordship's hands. I am contented in that consoling thought amidst the gloomy sky that composes this transatlantic horizon. Admiral Byron's appearance would gild the face of affairs resplendently ; God send him to heave in sight. . . .

FROM GAMBIER

Leviathan, off New York, 6 September 1778.

My Lord— . . .

[Complaints of his inactive but responsible position without ' a possibility of acquiring the least glory or emolument . . .']

The French and rebels are most cordially sick of each other, a most reciprocal enmity and contempt ; so truly so that I think affairs might mend here, and the people brought to their senses. Pity, some say, we did leave Philadelphia *at the time* we did ; and numbers that going to the southward was banefully productive of what has happened. The war as it has been carried on and still continues benefits but too many individuals whose interest is its prolongation, having made and continuing to make amazing fortunes. A sea warfare here would long ere this have reduced them to a proper sense, natural to our own country, and carried at a twentieth tithe of expense.

When the Viscount, in view to the chapter of accidents, did condescend on his sailing to deliver to me (as his successor) the general orders and arrangements I found great appropriation of frigates to be detached from hence, more than, believe me, would leave a single serviceable frigate behind for the variegated duties of this amazingly expanded coast ; our frigates almost all worn out and shattered and at that time five or six lost, since which we have lost numbers, no less than five fine ones burnt and sunk lately at Rhode Island and also two fine sloops there and the galleys, the Mermaid, Liverpool, Syren, Mercury, and Repulse, and Senegal, so that considering those deductions with the universal rotten condition of the rest of the frigates and sloops the present whole remaining force is very inadequate without appropriations. For 'tis small ships that are useful here and small vessels : coppered cutters would be of amazing utility, and if sailing schooners and sloops were ordered to be purchased here it would be of inconceivable benefit to the service.

Terribly distressed are the newly arrived ships of Mr Byron's squadron, all their masts almost sprung, ships shattered, and above 1200 men sick in these six ships, chief part with putrid epidemic fevers that run through their whole crews ; some were obliged to be assisted in getting into the harbour. Would to Heaven they had gone to the southward ; it is notoriously the safest, healthiest, surest, and most certain passage. Everything that has crossed in northern latitudes universally demonstrate and acknowledge this fact. Had Mr Byron practised it, they would have arrived in time fatal for d'Estaing, who made a pleasant, safe, and healthy passage with his ships arriving in perfect order. We have 900 men sick here before the arrival of these 1200. I am distressed how to adopt modes for their relief and recovery, yet I meditate and order everything possibly in my power.

Having exerted every endeavour to the utmost of my power to give means for the variegated operations and convoys here, I am reduced to hoist my flag on board a storeship. My last unappointed frigate, the Lizard, having run on the iron chevaux de frise and forced to be hauled on shore. The debilitated Amazon with jury masts to be sent home, as also the Tartar rotten, similarly intended, and likewise the Brune. . . . We have likewise few or no stores remaining, yet the ships all in great want of them and repair.

I am this moment informed the Lioness and most of her convoy are off the bar, and some Cork victuallers in the offing. The rebel corsairs are so numerous we cannot expect all will arrive safe. I am obliged to send my only remaining frigate to convoy this packet off the coast. The next arriving one, I trust and live in hopes will bring me my welcome orders of release from so *painful* a servitude, in justice and equity to the arrangement under which I came out hither, and in the wish of early having the happiness to kiss your Lordship's hands [etc.].

FROM GAMBIER

Ardent, New York, 12 September 1778.

My Lord—

['Yesterday the Viscount Howe returned' and sent me a 'commission from the Admiralty to be Commander in Chief, not a word or hint previous from his Lordship.']

Your Lordship will expect me to say something of the late nigh junction of the two fleets and their separation without coming to action. I feel it necessary that I should, lest my silence after being unconfidentially kept constantly at a distance, and totally uncommuned and unadvised with, should give to imagine resentment [which] might class me in the minority synonymous to Opposition in the naval administration here, and my total silence be construed a total disapprobation of conduct and measures. However I may have at times felt myself humiliated by want of being treated with that confidence I thought due to my rank as second in command, and offers and repeated requests to have my flag fly in the line of battle after spontaneously coming twelve hundred leagues to serve under his Lordship, nevertheless candour is ever the menstruum I dip my pen in, and unimpassioned impartial truth guides it.

Rhode Island besieged it was, I believe, judged necessary to relieve it even at the risk and hazard of a battle, in view to which the Viscount collected all the force he thought could be of service. It was numerous, but inferior in point of weight of metal and calibre. Fireships and frigates were if possible to be made to avail by being opportunely employed so as to make up for the manifest inferiority in weight of ships. Chiefship, jockeyship, and superiority of skill in manœuvring was therefore our reliance for victory in case the fleets should engage.[1]

On his Lordship's appearing off the port the French fleet came out spiritedly, with a fair wind through a heavy fire reciprocally from the batteries and their own ships, to avoid being cul-de-sac'd in the harbour. My friend, from whose information I learn all, tells me that to first relieve the island appeared the Viscount's design. He therefore drew them off : they followed. His next object seemed to get the advantage of position in coming to action, so as to compensate by his fireships and frigates for his inferiority in weight of metal, by variegated masterly evolutions, signals, and manœuvring which to the honour of the captains were attentively observed and executed. His Lordship in the course of that remaining part

---

[1] The value Howe attached to fireships may be judged by his appointing the Phoenix 44, Experiment (a *small* 50), and Pearl 32, all important ships in so weak a force, to support the fireships in the expected battle. He ordered the Experiment "to keep to windward and to use the fireship as [Captain] Sir James [Wallace] thought necessary." (Master's log, Experiment.) See above, p. 177*n*.

of the day and the succeeding one had so successfully jockeyed and manœuvred that he had nigh
almost the wind of them, and would have been
able, and intended, to give them battle the next
day under the acquired advantageous circumstances of superiority of position by seaman- and
officership when the elements suddenly interfered
and unexpectedly declared themselves auxiliaries
to the enemy.

I was not there myself ; but this I believe to
have been the genuine fact. I had it from a friend,
a good officer and a man of honour, who was there
and saw every evolution.

Inadequate as my treatment has been to the
exerted merit in spontaneously quitting my dockyard, an honourable lucrative safe post, a loved
and amiable wife big with child of a fifth produce
of our conjugal happiness, to come 1200 leagues
to serve here, I never but will render justice to
every man. I shall have opportunity by the Eagle
of writing your Lordship on the subject of the
commissions and my given expectations of favour
from my Sovereign for my family. I conclude this,
which with all its faults you will excuse, and
believe me ever [etc.].

I find from the Viscount that, though the
Admiralty have been pleased to appoint me to
succeed him, I have nothing to do with the Commission, which must every hour appear more
humiliatingly awkward by the sea commander-in-
chief's now knowing nothing of what passes or is
intended in the upper Council ; for though the
Viscount would not act in the Commission, nevertheless they communicated to and consulted him
upon every move or intended evolution for his
previous approbation, whilst at present your Lord-

ship's representative is a cypher, and who most evidently ought to know everything in order to be a judge how to act, and can never be intended to serve as a hoodwinked commander in chief, unconsulted and uninformed. My reliance for due support of my honour and credit is wholly in your Lordship, who I am persuaded will never suffer any indignity to be offered to the Corps you patronize and superintend. The Viscount will of course give your Lordship's Board the true state of the ships in these seas, which are all in a mutilated decayed state indeed, besides our having lost no less than fourteen frigates and small vessels. Your Lordship will pardon this long postscript. Your Lordship will understand that my account of the naval evolutions is confidential from my friend Commodore H[otham].

FROM GAMBIER

September 22, Midnight.

My honoured Lord—You was so kind to permit, when you directed me to write, that I should confidentially communicate any occurrences. I availed myself of your indulgence, trespassingly I fear, on the 12th instant on the Viscount's giving me suddenly my commission as commander in chief. And the next morning on my requesting his advice on some critically circumstanced and important articles in the Admiralty instructions, which being long before meditated might and were to me to admit of a doubt now, and his declining my request and saying he had furnished me with all my instructions &c., and had given me my commission, therefore he would give no opinion ; and at the same time directed me to announce such to the General, commander in chief of the army, and to the Commissioners and other departments, and himself went directly to the General and announced his having relinquished the command and would no longer act. From all this I had to conceive he would sail directly, finding my commission to be dated that day (the 11th) immediately on his arrival. I therefore caught a few minutes to obviate being thought inattentive, taking for granted his Lordship in the disposition he appeared to be in would have sailed directly.

His Lordship choosing at times of giving orders to be supposed to continue to command until his flag disappeared, though contradicting that in various instances and in the most *material* ones making me responsible while in others contradicting, I am to expect and suppose him to give your Lordship's Board an account of everything to the time of his sailing, by whom this comes ; I can have therefore only by the next conveyance to begin giving an account of my official conduct.

Your Lordship will pardon my last hasty scrawl. The little expedition so lately successful was meditated and carried into execution by Sir Henry and myself during Lord Howe's absence towards [Boston]. They are the kind of spirited exertions that can only and but benefit our cause : 'tis amazing how even that alarmed and dispirited the people at large, giving them to expect continual depredations, and they are heartily sick I believe of the contest. Our first view was New London, but on reconnoitring found the small assemblage not an object. My colleague is spirited, liberal, and communicative, and has the service much at heart ; we have two good months more to operate in, and much may be done and probably will. Spirited exertions to destroy their trade and craft along the coast is the only real mode of distressing and bringing them to reason.[1]

I fret every hour and must increasingly do so : the humiliating situation of the naval commander in chief in point of being at present only a subaltern to the Commission, and trust a relief from that painful insufferable situation is at hand. I have been humbled enough lately and had occasion for all my philosophy, and determined to bear almost anything sooner than it should be known that the King's officers in command disagreed ; a hard trial have I had, in the midst of which I consoled myself with the consciousness that *I* acted *consistent* and was not to *blame*, and in spite of every frown from a Capulet avow myself a Montagu. Your Lordship will hear much—will see much. I have seen what has been both surprising and painful.

When Mr Byron joins, I apprehend what he will require, and will demand and order to reinstate his *reduced* force, *will disable me from possibly complying with the intended requisition for St Lucia*. I wish to act exceedingly well and spirited. Strange he [Lord Howe] never would give me an opinion as to that, yet kept the command to the last in other matters, puzzling and vexatious.

All our frigates are mutilated and disabled, 14 lost or taken or destroyed, the line of battle ships out of repair, no stores in the yard.

I think we shall hold our own here, and I hope more. We long to receive your Lordship's commands what we are to do.

In a day or two after the Viscount shall get

---

[1] Early in September forces under Major-General Grey and Captain Fanshawe, of the Carysfort, raided New Bedford and other privateer bases near Rhode Island.

from the Hook, I hope to get officially into the saddle and begin my arrangements exertedly meditated for the best advantage.

The boat waits to catch Lord Howe at the Hook. Pardon my honoured Lord all the faults of my pen : my heart is with truth and gratitude [etc.]

I trust to receive your Lordship's authority for continuing the same extra officers and appointments that my predecessor had. I am sure I need them, inadequate as I confessedly am in abilities. May I therefore hope to receive early your indulgent assent to so equitable a right, for hitherto here no Montagu has had one single favour or indulgence granted, but on the contrary every mortifying insult on that account ?

FROM GAMBIER

23 September 1778.

. . . The moment the Viscount's flag is out of sight from hence (although still at the Hook) the Commissioners intimate to me that they purpose to issue a proclamation to authorize the exporting of goods and to legalize the bringing in and exporting of prizes and prize goods ; and as such measure would obviously tend to make our seamen desert, they shall desire to hear from me so soon as I have taken whatever measure I think right, either by collecting the fleet at the Hook or elsewhere, to obviate that inconvenience. Certainly when such a move was first meditated and debated the commander in chief of H.M.

ships should be one of the council in the originating such. His Lordship I learn was averse and opposed to the taking off the embargo, and warmly remonstrated against the idea . . . of granting letters of marque. . . .

It must be small ships and numbers of small vessels that can do the business here with them this range of coast would soon be humbled and reduced.

FROM GAMBIER

11 October 1778.

My honoured Lord— . . .

[Complaint that Howe had only left him in chief command ' in the absence of a superior officer,' and still ' sent away ships and gave orders, with the which I was unacquainted.']

From hence on the 24th [Lord Howe] sailed for Rhode Island to join Vice-Admiral Byron, to whom more early I had communicated my credentials and copies of everything I thought could best inform him, and begged to receive early the honour of his commands on every matter for his Majesty's service. Vice-Admiral Byron informed me that he had convened with the Viscount, who had made known to him my having a commission as commander in chief *during the absence of a superior officer*, at the same time desiring the utmost dispatch might be executed in the continuing to refit the disabled ships and that I would supply frigates to Rear-Admiral Parker, to whom he enclosed a packet with orders for him to repair to Rhode Island as soon as possible with the above ships, a copy of which order the Rear Admiral sent me. Every exertion was, your Lordship may believe, continued to be made, when a day or two after the Vice Admiral arrived himself in the Princess Royal over the bar, and the Culloden, and as superior flag to me commanded in whatever he pleases. Very far from my wish of the King's service suffering by even an appearance of any disagreement between the King's officers, I have conducted myself in every shape to avoid it, however painful and humiliating my situation has been for a long time, nay indeed ever since I have been in America : a mere laborious fitting admiral or rather superintendent of a port, refused every active service repeatedly in Lord Howe's time, and now since whilst that I am now labouring to send out the ships in quest of the French and then to remain here to obey orders and attend flat-bottomed boats, unconsulted, and in a manner uncommuned with in aught material, as officially the Commissioners and General must act with the commanding officer in the first instance, yet obliged to live at an enormous expense though in a humiliating manner. . . .

[Complaint that the naval commander in chief is not consulted by the Commissioners but must obey their orders. ' In many instances this is the case, recently in the material one of granting letters of marque *ad libitum* and opening the port and taking off the embargo laid on by the Viscount, an evolution that has and does every hour most sensibly distress the fleet, and was what I had to conceive my predecessor most constantly was averse to and even reprobated.'

Lack of frigates and ' terrible condition ' of the few he possesses.]

When the Vice Admiral shall sail (as I hope to God he will get away to-morrow) he will have carried the far greater part of our force with him, and unmanned the major part of our ships, even not excepting several of Mr Hotham's squadron, to recomplete which I apprehend the greatest difficulty (even if practicable) without laying the remainder by the walls ; and I have within this two hours a requisition from the General that, unless I can undertake to guard the Eastern Sound and prevent constantly this winter any descent on Long Island, he shall not have force here enough without evacuating Rhode Island, for after detaching the above 11,000 men to the different places ordered we shan't have that number left here. Had the season been not so far advanced, I could have wished all, both army and navy, had gone against Boston with d'Estaing in it, and by a spirited effort *Delendâ Carthago.* As it is, if they bolt not, it will be bad cruising off there in the month of November and after.

'Tis astonishing how our seamen desert, and to complete our misery the sick of Mr Byron's squadron above 2000, that with the utmost difficulty I could man his ships ; to do it I am forced to lay up some frigates and unman my own. Thus is your obedient servant perplexed with choice of difficulties, many unsurmountable.

I fear our Commissioners' proclamations will have as little effect as their former letters. Nothing would have conquered or brought this country to reason but active and various expeditions by water, and small accompanying bodies of troops to distress the shore trade. Obvious how serviceable to that end was the little expedition Sir Henry and I carried on at Bedford during the Viscount's going off Boston, and we have now one at this instant operating against Egg Harbour and the rebels' considerable salt works there, the successful issue of which I hourly expect to receive account of.

Admiral Byron is going off Boston. I should have to apprehend cruising too late in the year off that port will not be advisable from the danger of the north-westers' driving off and disabling our ships, and the French availing themselves of the consequence. It might be more eligible to keep the fleet in constant readiness at Rhode Island, and with a chain of frigates to watch their motions and follow them. I have to fear the rebels and French have or may meditate taking Bermudas, that key of the West India and North America trade, especially as when our frigates were last there the majority of the inhabitants were disaffected, and a frigate of force building and rebellion vegetating quick. The General is now sending troops; and though I am distressed for want of frigates I think it highly necessary to send two frigates thither, and dispatch therefore the Galatea and Camilla.

I was happy to see the Vice-Admiral's ship safe out over the bar again I own. He took the Trident, Somerset, and Raisonable to replace the Russell, Albion, and Invincible, and also the Diamond, Renown, and the best of the frigates; the Albion has also since joined him in good order and healthy, having, as I take for granted Admiral Byron has informed the Board, re-masted at Lisbon. The other occurrences are doubtless communicated by Admiral Byron.

'Tis astonishing how mutilated and deficient in men and stores did those ships arrive here. We have not a single coil of rope left, and have

dismantled all our ships almost of men in order
to complete that squadron. We have even been
obliged to take men from the ships of Commodore
Hotham's squadron, which I fear to find difficulty
in replacing from the great dearth of seamen here
and baneful effect of taking off the embargo ; and
from the sense and spirit of the secret instructions
and the Vice-Admiral's determination I am bound
to obey that requisition. Commodore Hotham
will carry all therefore I have left of force, viz. the
Preston, Nonsuch, St Albans, Isis, Centurion, and
Venus, and bomb. The Vice Admiral gave me to
hope he would not long keep the Renown, but
send her after Mr Hotham. The enclosed list
will clearly demónstrate the state of the ships
and vessels here : how inadequate, my honoured
Lord, to the variegated numberless stations,
duties, and requisitions ; what a number lost,
burnt, and destroyed ; how few remaining, and
what a terrible state and condition ! The weak
Ardent will, however, I trust carry her flag safe
home to England and be repaired against the
Newfoundland season, much she wants it, being
crazy.

I have had extreme difficulties about our
numerous sick—about 2000 men—circumscribed
hospitals and means ; I have acted to the best of
my judgment to save what lives I could, and at
as little expense as possible to Government. With
equal precision and attention have I acted in
everything *in which I have been permitted to act*,
but really, my Lord, I have been and still am a
Duke and no Duke. Cheapest have I gone to
work in furnishing all the numberless requisitions
of the army and King's Commissioners in sending
and circulating their various manifestos and
proclamations, sending advices and expresses, and

this in a place where every man is either in his heart inimical or ostensibly attached from motives of self-interest and collusion. Uncovetable, Oh Lord, must such a painful scene be! Amazing also the number of officers of the Navy invalided from long, hard, unremitting services and fatigues, worn down to death, and indeed scarce within hope of quiet and their native country's restoring them; yet have I been cautious whom I permit to quit, none but where absolute necessity has required.

By the Brune, who must go shortly if she goes at all, I shall have the honour of informing your Lordship further. The notoriety of my unremitting labours and exertions will I flatter myself come from other hands; I have the heart-felt satisfaction to know I have done my duty, though at the expense of the remainder of my constitution.

I shall have difficulty in finding means of furnishing convoys for Pensacola, Florida, the Bahamas, and St Augustine; and rebel privateers swarm on the coast.

Admiral Byron doubtless informs you of the several occurrences. The Experiment and Unicorn have brought in the Raleigh, a fine new Congress frigate, in such excellent order and so well stored that she will want little to make her the finest frigate in America of 28-gun establishment. I purpose, therefore, forthwith availing myself of so welcome an acquisition in our present distressed state.

The constant attendance on the army in manning flat-bottomed boats, gunboats, galleys, &c. incessantly disables and diminishes our seamen surprisingly; and the enormous number it has taken to re-man Vice-Admiral Byron's fleet, and the embargo taken off, completes our distress. I shall nevertheless continue to exert every nerve to carry on the service, in whatever shall be left to me, to the utmost of my power whilst I remain, which I trust will not be long. The Otter I hear is lost, though not informed officially, or of any particulars. In the great hurry of re-equipping Mr Byron's fleet and dispatching the England convoy, that to Halifax also and Commodore Hotham's, I fear I shan't until by the Brune have time to write every particular to the Admiralty of the minutiæ of this department as fully as I could wish.

I sincerely hope health and happiness to be your Lordship's constant attendants, being [etc.].

A circumstance this moment happening gives me reason to think d'Estaing bound to Europe forthwith. A young officer of his, taken some time ago and returned from his parole to be exchanged, brings a proposal to me from d'Estaing for exchange of prisoners, charged with a power to adjust it. Wishing to return directly, I have by various pretences detained him until Admiral Byron should be sailed. Out of all patience he just now writes me, repeatedly demanding and urging to be dispatched, as I had from day to day promised : Nous sommes au douze du mois, et l'escadre françois peut partir. Il serait fort dur pour les officiers Anglais d'être mené en France, et pour moi d'être obligé à passer mon hiver en Amérique. J'imagine que c'est pour cette raison que M. le C. d'Estaing m'a ordonné de faire diligence, et j'ai déjà dépassé le temps fixé.

As I am informed they are exerting every means to get refitted and perhaps nigh ready, and provisions and flour particularly scarce at Boston, they from what I can very lately gather certainly mean not to remain there but forthwith to sail, and most probably to Europe. I don't think they are in condition or stored for the West Indies. I thought it proper to open my cover to communicate this fresh incident to your Lordship. I wish the Vice-Admiral was at this time off Boston.

FROM GAMBIER

New York, 23 October 1778.

[Expedition against Egg Harbour, ' a seminary for little rascally privateers,' under Captain Henry Colins of the Zebra sloop, with other small craft and 300 soldiers under Captain Patrick Ferguson.]

On the return of that numerous little squadron I hope to be furnished with men sufficient to re-man the ships I have been obliged to dismantle in order to complete Admiral Byron's fleet, and since that Commodore Hotham's—whose expedition (pardon my presumption in giving my opinion) I could wish or an equal force would in my humble idea be of great service in the Chesapeake, where if five or six thousand men were to act the Delaware counties would very well furnish them with provisions. The complexion of the people was last time demonstrable by the ready supply of provisions to the army. . . . We have much to guard and hold, and scanty pittance to do it with, yet I look up to some fresh instructions from *home* ; for if a war with France does take place, we cannot I apprehend carry on one here in force on *shore, offensively*, at the same time. May I say I could have wished to have heard finally resolves of Admiralty before Commodore Hotham's expedition had sailed, to have formed some idea of what is to be the grand plan.

FROM THE KING

Kew, 25 October 1778, 10 m., P.M.

The cast of Lord Howe's dispatches contain nothing but disasters.   I am sorry to see he takes so much to heart the not having got the Red flag when those that had the White one were promoted.   Lord Sandwich must remember I suggested his feelings would be kindled at the time.[1]

The reason is very plain why he does not mention the West India expedition, as it cannot take effect whilst d'Estaing is in North America.

Keppel must now soon arrive at Spithead.

FROM THE KING

Windsor Castle, 26 October 1778.

I have read the dispatches from Lord Howe and Admirals Byron and Gambier, and seen Captain [Henry] Duncan, who seems to be a sensible though very cautious man.

The private letters from Gambier makes me think he will not be sorry at receiving permission to return home.   As to his application to me for

[1] In the general promotion of 29 January 1778, the five senior vice-admirals of the White were advanced to the Red squadron.   Howe, the seventh and junior in this rank, received the step later in the year.

his family, it was in case he should be killed ; but I see he is desirous of turning a civil, though I am certain not pointed, answer into a promise of support ; but he will not succeed by that very common trick.[1]

TO GAMBIER

Admiralty, 1 November 1778.

I have a volume of your letters by me which remain till now unanswered. Indeed, I could have said nothing effectual to you till we had heard the conclusion of Lord Howe's arrangements, and could then determine what orders to give relative to the future management of the fleet in America. Things have changed their face relative to that business so often since you left England that there was no possibility of pursuing any fixed plan with regard to yourself, or to anything else ; but you might be assured that your interests were always in safe hands with me, and that I wanted no solicitation to keep my attention fixed on doing you every service that times and circumstances would admit of.

By what I can collect from the tenor of all your letters, your most favourite object is that of returning home and having the command next year at Newfoundland : that point I have steadily adhered to, and the orders that go by this conveyance will enable you to be with us time enough to allow you to take about a couple of months' repose at home, and then enter upon that honourable and advantageous command.

[1] Lord Sandwich sent these dispatches to the King the same day. He also ' ventured to send ' Captain Duncan to Windsor, ' lest your Majesty should wish to ask any questions relative to what has lately passed in America ' (*Corr.*, 2440–41).

The moment that it was found necessary to send a large fleet in pursuit of Monsieur d'Estaing, the command became too large for a rear admiral, therefore the idea of your continuing commander in chief ceased of course ; and though it may happen that Admiral Byron may leave America, and that only a small force may remain behind, still I thought it better for you to pursue the original arrangement, and to bring you home in order to go to Newfoundland, than to leave you in a precarious situation at New York, with almost a certainty of having a senior officer sent over you as soon as the winter is past. These are the motives upon which I have acted as your friend, and I shall be very happy to find that they coincide with your own inclinations.[1]

Many thanks for the minute and instructive communications which you have sent me in your several letters. They contain a most curious history of the late campaign, which has been big with events though nothing very decisive has happened on either side. I am sure you know that I have not time enough on my hands, nor indeed have I a turn for entering into the same sort of detail with regard to affairs on this side the Atlantic. I will therefore detain you no longer than to convey the fullest assurances of the truth and regard [etc.].

P.S.—Captain Fielding's friends in England are very desirous that he should come home ; therefore, if you find that he joins with them in the same wish, you will contrive if possible that the Diamond may be one of the ships first ordered to England.

[1] Gambier did not go to Newfoundland : see above, p. 290.

TO GAMBIER

Admiralty, 13 November 1778.

Dear Sir—I cannot as a friend help giving you a hint that the postponing, and much more the putting a stop to, the expedition to the West Indies seems to me an ill-judged measure, as it subjects you (and very justly in my opinion) to the blame and clamour that will be the consequence of the loss of our islands.

You will observe that though I make use of the word *you*, I do not mean that the naval commander alone can be found fault with upon this occasion, as it is obvious that there is an unwillingness in every department in America to the making this detachment, which I conclude arises from your considering only your own immediate wants, and not thinking of our distresses at home.

If you can't send the whole force (pointed out to you in the original orders) to the West Indies, send what you can ; for believe me that this is an object that all sorts of people here have set their hearts upon, and upon which they are much in earnest.   I am [etc.].

TO GAMBIER

Admiralty, 1 December 1778.

The convoy for America having been detained till this time by contrary winds, I have the opportunity of acknowledging the receipt of your letters of the 11th and 23rd of October ; but there is nothing in them relative to yourself that is not answered in my former letter.

I am very happy at the sailing of the expedition to the West Indies.   You cannot conceive the sudden alteration that news occasioned among us, as the West India merchants had had a meeting and agreed to make a very hostile representation to the Throne, stating that the defence of their property had been neglected, and requesting that immediate reinforcements might be sent from hence, without which the loss of our West India islands would shortly be added to our other calamities. Whatever representation now is made will be in a different style.

I am much vexed at your list of promotions, and at the disagreeable necessity you have put me under of refusing confirmation to some of them. How could you think it was the intention of the Board to continue the novel and strange introduction of such an officer as an adjutant general to the fleet, and of two additional lieutenants to the flagship ?[1] But what I am most hurt at is your making Mr Byron a post captain, who was then only a lieutenant and not then in America. This arrangement seems particularly calculated to set me at variance with Admiral Byron ; for there is an end of all regularity in business if these sort of appointments are ever confirmed at this Board. I am [etc.]

Captain Byron is coming out as a master and commander, and I shall have no objection to the giving him a new commission to a post ship on his arrival, though I can on no consideration confirm the former one.[2]

[1] On this matter see vol. i., pp. 294–5, and Gambier's letter of September 22 above, p. 316. Gambier also wrote on September 23 : ' I trust that your Lordship will do me the justice to patronize my having the equal assistance, in carrying on the service, of additional appointments allowed to my predecessor.'

[2] George Anson Byron, a lieutenant of 30 May 1776, and captain 3 April 1779.

FROM SIR GEORGE RODNEY

Sunday night, 10 January 1779.

Sir George Rodney presents his most respectful compliments to Lord Sandwich, and has the honour to acquaint him that the vessel arrived at Nantes is an American packet dispatched to Doctor Franklin, of 14 guns and commanded by one Jenkins, who left Count d'Estaing's squadron on the 11th of November, 160 leagues east of Cape Cod. Two of the ships had lost their masts and were very much shattered; that when they left Boston the French fleet had but two months' provisions on board. Sir George humbly presumes that by the course of the French fleet their destination was for Europe; for they could not have been in that latitude at that distance from Cape Cod, had they been bound to the West Indies with a fair wind at north-west.

Captain Jenkins reported at Paris that an English man of war of 74 guns was in the midst of the French fleet, and between their two squadrons on the 7th of November; that on the 11th of November, when he parted with them, it blew a very heavy gale at north-west.

If Count d'Estaing has been obliged to push for the West Indies, it must have been from distress; he cannot be in any condition to annoy his Majesty's islands before Mr Byron arrives in that part of the world.

CHAPTER V

THE
CAPTURE OF ST. LUCIA,
December 1778

INTRODUCTION

THE inception of the plan to seize St Lucia has been described in the sixth chapter of the first volume of these papers.[1]

On 3 May 1778 the Admiralty addressed secret instructions for the expedition to Rear-Admiral the Hon. Samuel Barrington, who was about to take command in the Leeward Islands. Five thousand infantry, with artillery and engineers, were to come from North America, escorted by ships under Commodore Hotham to strengthen the small force on the station. In the meantime the Admiral was directed ' to assemble in Carlisle Bay [Barbados] such of the ships of the Leeward Islands squadron as you shall judge may be necessary to add to those which may be expected to come with Commodore Hotham . . . and so soon as the said Commodore shall appear off the Bay, you are to go out to join him ; and having taken him and the several ships, transports [etc.] under your command, you are to make the best of your way with them to the island of St Lucia . . .' The original orders for sending ships and troops from America had been dispatched in March ; and the Government hoped that Barrington would not have long to wait at Barbados, but that the business would be finished before the hurricane season. Nevertheless, ' if any unforeseen accident should prevent the fleet from sailing from North America so soon as might be expected ' Howe was told to inform Barrington ' that he may not be detained unnecessarily at Barbados in expectation thereof ' ; and if Hotham should not find Barrington at the place of assembly, he was to begin the attack himself, sending word to the Admiral, who would join him as soon as he could.

[1] Pp. 325-6, 357-67. The command of the troops was given to Major-General James Grant.

Barrington left England in the Prince of Wales within a week of receiving his instructions and arrived at Barbados on June 20 ; his second line of battle ship, the Boyne, joined him on July 15, having stayed behind to bring out the trade. Except for a short visit by the Boyne to Prince Rupert's Bay in Dominica to fetch wood, the two great ships stayed at Barbados till the middle of September, while the rest of the squadron—half a dozen small frigates and sloops—cruised to protect the trade. On September 12, however, the Admiral heard from Lieutenant-Governor Stuart of Dominica that the French had attacked him on the 7th (the day he wrote) ' with a very considerable fleet of several line of battle ships with an admiral, supposed to be from Toulon ' ; the Governor was afraid the island must fall, and indeed he capitulated the same day. The enemy was really but three frigates and a corvette with a landing party of 2500 soldiers from Martinique ; this Barrington learnt on the 15th, and he then wrote to the Admiralty : ' I cannot help regretting my being confined here in obedience to their Lordships' secret instructions, as it was my intention, when at liberty so to do, to have lain in Prince Rupert's Bay, as the most proper station for watching the motions of the French ; and had I fortunately been there with the Prince of Wales and Boyne I think the French would not have ventured to attack Dominica without the assistance of some ships of the line.' [1]

This remonstrance must be due in part to natural distress at the loss of the island. The importance of being ready to move against St Lucia immediately the troops arrived is obvious ; and a look at the chart leaves little room for doubt that Barbados was the best point of assembly. In some ways the situation resembles Rodney's, while waiting for the expedition to Havana in 1762. [2]

[1] Barrington's journal and his dispatch of September 15 ; Lacour-Gayet, 181–2.

[2] It is possible that Barrington suggested Prince Rupert's Bay as the rendezvous before leaving England, but was overruled by the Admiralty. See Corbett, *England in the Seven Years' War*, ii. 235–45 and 255–61 for Rodney's case.

PLATE IV.

THE CARENAGE, ST. LUCIA, 1920

A. Martinique, 30 miles away in this direction.
B. Gros Islet Bay.
C. Anse du Choc.

Lord Howe had not been able to send word that Hotham and the troops were delayed; but when Barrington received the second report from Dominica on September 15, and a call for help from Antigua at the same time, he made up his mind to disregard his instructions. The Boyne and the frigate Aurora were with him at Barbados; and after consulting with their captains and with Benjamin Hill (his own captain), the Admiral decided to go to Antigua, taking the three ships of war and some victuallers, and leaving orders for the rest of the squadron to join him. He sailed the same day and arrived in English Harbour, the dockyard, on the 18th. There he found the storeship Supply, which Howe had at last managed to send with a message that the expedition was held up; he also learnt that Dominica had fallen. On October 11, ' the hurricane season being over and the apprehension of the people of [Antigua] a little subsided' the squadron sailed to cruise to windward of Martinique, ' as the most probable means of preventing the French from getting possession of any other islands.' His water and provisions being spent, Barrington returned to Barbados on November 18, heartened by news he had received from Stuart that his cruise had kept the privateers at Martinique in harbour.[1]

On the 23rd the frigate Venus arrived, sent ahead by Hotham to report that the expedition was on its way, though she added that the ships of war were very bare of stores and short of complement. They entered Carlisle Bay on December 10; two ships of 64 guns, three of 50, the Carcass bomb, and ten regiments in fifty-nine transports—the generals in the Charming Nelly, the staff in the Roman Emperor. The plan of attack was settled by Barrington and Grant the same afternoon, Hotham's arrangements for the landing being taken over as they stood. Barrington would have sailed next

[1] Barrington's journal and his dispatches October 8 and November 19. The cruisers were the Prince of Wales 74, Boyne 70, Aurora 28, Boreas 28, Ariadne 20, Ceres sloop, and Pelican armed vessel.

Barrington met Stuart early in November, the dispossessed governor being on his way to Barbados in a flag of truce.

morning, but the General begged a day's grace, so the expedition set forth on the 12th and anchored off the Grand Cul de Sac in the afternoon of Sunday, December 13.[1]

The story of the capture is told in the long letter from the master of the Boyne, Mr. Charles Stuart. Apart from one or two muddled dates, perhaps copied straight from the log without changing the nautical date to the civil, it agrees well enough with the Admiral's journal.[2]

The interruption by the French fleet was not altogether a surprise, for the governors of the British islands were diligent in collecting information and sending it to Barrington, who thus had several reports that d'Estaing was coming from America or Fabry from the Mediterranean. The Frenchman's task was far from easy, notwithstanding his greatly superior force; wind and current were against him, and he gave up more than one attack owing to calms. On the other hand, his landing to attack our men on shore was welcomed by Grant, whose sanguine messages to Barrington were justified by the prowess of the grenadier and light companies under Medows on December 18. The risk of being interrupted in his turn was always in d'Estaing's mind, as it had been in North America in the summer; he left St Lucia to its fate as soon as he heard that Byron was on his way.

Byron joined Barrington on 6 January 1779, having called off Carlisle Bay without anchoring the day before. His coming made the British squadron stronger than the French: fourteen sail of the line against eleven. On February 12 Commodore Rowley arrived from England with seven more, closely followed by an eighth, while the Comte de Grasse joined d'Estaing on the 19th with four.

---

[1] Barrington's journal. The regiments of Foot were the 4th, 5th, 15th, 27th, 28th, 35th, 40th, 46th, 49th, and 55th. They were organised in three brigades under Generals Robert Prescott, Sir Henry Calder, and William Medows.

Valentine Morris, the Governor of St. Vincent, who did not know of the plan to seize St Lucia, proposed it independently to Barrington in October.

[2] There is nothing in the letter to prove the identity of the writer, but the only C. Stuart, Stewart, or Steward in the Boyne's muster book is her master.

GENERAL GRANT TO GERMAIN

[Copy.]

Philadelphia, 24 May 1778.

Sir Henry Clinton has honoured me with the command of a corps of troops which is to be sent I believe from New York to the West Indies. As I have not received his Excellency's instructions, I am not at liberty to trouble your Lordship with a public letter ; but I venture upon a private one, as I have had the honour to be known to you for many years and have always been favoured during that time with marks of attention from you.

I took possession of the place of our destination last war, which was then reckoned the most sickly island in the West Indies, the harbour good, the water remarkably bad. I should therefore be sorry to remain there with troops which are equal to anything if they are not got the better of by sickness. The number intended for the expedition is small, as more than a half is not to be counted upon as fit for service after they have been a little time in the West Indies : I write from experience. But don't think I despond : everything your Lordship is pleased to point out shall be attempted, and I hope with success, but I could wish not to be confined to a particular spot.

Money, provisions, and ammunition, as far as I can judge, may be wanted : additional numbers if you think proper.

Your Lordship knows that, with an independent fortune, I have had some small share of zeal and perseverance in reaching the rank with which the King has now honoured me. But though my expense during the American war has always

II.   z

exceeded my military appointments, I am not anxious about emolument ; but I flatter myself his Majesty in point of powers will put me upon the same footing with other officers who have had the honour to command in America and the West Indies. The service, 'tis to be hoped my Lord, will not suffer by such a trust being reposed in me ; but I should be sorry to ask for anything which is not intended by his Majesty, and therefore submit the whole to the King's pleasure. Having [etc.].

GERMAIN TO ADMIRALTY

Whitehall, 29 July 1778.

My Lords—In addition to my letter to your Lordships of the 25th inst., I am commanded by the King to signify to your Lordships his Majesty's pleasure that you do instruct the commander of his Majesty's ships in the Leeward Islands to co-operate with, and give all the assistance in his power to, the commander of his Majesty's troops there in carrying into execution any attempts which they shall concur in opinion are proper to be made upon the French possessions in the West Indies in consequence of the discretionary orders contained in my letter of this day to Major-General Grant, extract of which I have the honour to enclose herewith for your Lordships' information. I am [etc.].

[Enclosure.]

GERMAIN TO GRANT

Whitehall, 29 July 1778.

Sir Henry Clinton, in his letter of the 23rd May, has acquainted me that he should put the detachment of 5000 men he is ordered to send upon an expedition for the reduction of the island of St Lucia under your command ; and I have the satisfaction to inform you that the King approves of your appointment to the command of that very important enterprise, his Majesty having the greatest reliance upon your zeal, ability, and experience ; and it is with equal pleasure I add that his Majesty, as a further testimony of his Royal confidence in your conduct and as an encouragement to the troops serving under you to distinguish themselves in the execution of your orders, is graciously pleased to allow you to post to all vacancies that may happen in the corps under your immediate command and to permit me to assure you that the greatest attention will be shown to your recommendations when those vacancies come to be filled up by his Majesty.

Our accounts from some of the King's servants in the West Indies represent the strength of the French garrisons in Martinique and Guadeloupe as very much reduced by sickness and desertion, and that the troops which remain are greatly discontented and suffer much from the scarcity of provisions and the want of other necessaries. And we are further told that the inhabitants are very desirous of coming under his Majesty's government, and that should our cruisers be successful in intercepting their supplies their distresses, co-operating with their inclinations, would induce them to capitulate upon the first appearance of a body of the King's forces if assurances were given them of their not being restored by treaty to France, and their property secured to them.

I confess I am not sanguine enough to give entire credit to these accounts ; but I am inclined to think they are so far authentic as to afford good ground to expect little opposition would be given by the militia to any attempt we might make to reduce those islands, if proper means were employed to assure the inhabitants that they should be continued in the full enjoyment of their properties and free exercise of their religion under the British government, and that although no promise could be made, the performance of which must depend upon the successful issue of the war, yet that they might rely with the utmost confidence on his Majesty's gracious disposition to comply with their wishes and that all possible attention would be shown to their interests when peace is made.

Whether the troops under your command that could be spared from the defence of the King's possessions would be adequate to the reduction of either of those islands under such circumstances cannot be determined here ; but as the getting possession of the country of either and securing a port for communication with the shipping, even without reducing the principal forts on the sea coast, would be very advantageous for the King's service and of great utility in distressing the enemy, his Majesty is pleased to leave it to your discretion to employ such part of the troops under your command as you shall think may be spared, after the expedition for the reduction of St Lucia has had its issue (which I trust will be a successful one), in any further operations against the other French islands that you and Rear-Admiral Barrington or the Commander-in-chief of his Majesty's ships in the Leeward Islands, upon a full consideration of all circumstances, shall be of opinion is proper to be undertaken and that there is sufficient ground to expect will be attended with success.

The Lords of the Treasury have ordered a

supply of provisions to be sent to you from Cork on board armed victuallers, and advice is received of their having sailed from thence the 24th of last month. It is proposed to keep the troops supplied in this manner ; and as the speedy return of the ships is absolutely necessary to secure a regular and constant succession you will give the strictest orders for their immediate dispatch.

Their Lordships will also take care to send out money for the payment of the troops whenever a ship of war can be spared for that service ; and I shall signify the King's commands to the Board of Ordnance to provide and send out a proper supply of ammunition as soon as a return is received of the ordnance you take with you.

I wish I could also send you an augmentation of your force ; but unless peace is made with the colonies I cannot encourage you to expect it at present.

I have further only to express my sincere wishes for your success and that the command you are entrusted with may prove as advantageous for the King's service as I am convinced it will be honourable for yourself. I am [etc.].

TO NORTH

Admiralty, 30 October 1778.

His Majesty ordered me to inform your Lordship that he wished you would communicate the intended expedition to the Chairman and Deputy Chairman of the India Company, and know from them whether they would assist in the measure, before it was mentioned in the Cabinet or to any other person except those who are already informed of what is in agitation.

I have directed Mr Stephens to inform the West India merchants that orders have been long ago given to send a very considerable naval force with troops from America to protect their settlements, and that if any misfortune has happened it is owing to the unexpected though probably necessary delay of that reinforcement. If your Lordship disapproves of that communication's being made, you will be so good as to send to Mr Stephens to countermand it before Monday next, at which time he will, if he hears nothing to the contrary from your Lordship, follow my directions. I am going into Huntingdonshire early to-morrow morning, which is the occasion of my giving you this trouble. I am [etc.].

FROM PALLISER

Pall Mall, 9 November 1778.

Having no opportunity of making enquiry of Lord Howe about the state of the expedition from New York to the West Indies, I submit it to your Lordship whether Lord Howe should be written to to attend the Board to require from him any information in his power to give.

I should hope ere long we shall have some farther advices from New York. At all events, will it not be right to have a squadron ready in all respects for foreign service equal to that preparing at Brest (which consists of 7 ships of 74 guns and 1 of 64), and an admiral ready to proceed with them in case they should go to the West Indies ? If there should be reason to think they are for the East Indies, we ought to lose no time in fitting an equal force ready for that quarter ; those ships will be fit for either East or West Indies. In the meantime, the force already at the Leeward Islands surely is sufficient to stop the progress of so small a force as is doing mischief there.

If I remember right, Lord Howe was directed to dispatch a frigate to Admiral Barrington at Barbados to advise him of the time he might expect the ships and troops or to advise him if anything happened to prevent them coming. If this was done, Admiral Barrington was not confined, as *he says in his letter*, to stay at Barbados nor obliged to go to Antigua instead of going to the relief of the place attacked, the sure and only way of preventing the same forces doing any farther mischief.

Lord Mulgrave is to call upon me to-morrow morning to consult what can be done towards raising more men and securing those we have from deserting. I am [etc.].

MR CHARLES STUART TO [?]

[Copy by several hands.]

Boyne, Grand Cul de Sac in the Island of St Lucia,
8 January 1779. [Finished February 3.]

Dear Sir—My last was dated, or rather finished, the 16th September at English Harbour in Antigua, and sent per a ship bound from that island to England. I now take the liberty of troubling you with occurrences since.

On the 11th of October, having refitted for sea, we sailed with Admiral Barrington in the Prince of Wales and three frigates on a cruise to windward of Martinique. This cruise ended November 20th without anything material except the taking two French prizes, one a snow from Newfoundland the other a privateer, which though of little value to us was of singular consequence to our country.

On Thursday the 19th November [really Wed. 18th] we anchored in Carlisle Bay, Barbados, intending to complete our ship and return with the greatest expedition to our station ; we found here the Winchelsea and her convoy from Cork etc. for the islands. Monday 23rd arrived his Majesty's frigate Venus from America with advice that she had left on their passage Commodore Hotham and other men of war with a convoy of transports etc. and 5000 troops destined for Barbados etc. Here finished the thought of a second cruise : nothing being talked of but revenge on the French and the retaking Dominica, which they had basely surprised. Thursday in the morning, the 10th December, the signal was made for a fleet in sight to windward, which proved our expected reinforcement. Short were our councils. On Saturday the 12th by ten in the morning we were all clear of Barbados and steering for St Lucia, full of health, full of spirits and wishes for our country.

At Sunday's dawn we saw the island of St Lucia, and passing round the northernmost end, having our ships cleared for action and everything necessary to bring our broadsides to bear on the batteries that might oppose the landing of our troops, though we assured ourselves of no opposition and that we should at most only have an opportunity to *smell* powder, being certain there was no power in the West Indies the French had could oppose us. There was but one small four-gun battery that annoyed us, and this we silenced in about half an hour. We instantly manned our flat-bottom boats and began disembarking ten regiments of the finest fellows that ever drew a trigger ; no sooner were they landed than they began with the Regiment of Martinique, the militia, mulattoes, negroes and inhabitants, who attempted to make a stand but soon broke and flew into the woods. Our people secured the four-gun fort and also the adjacent heights. The next day the whole of our troops were landed ; our people pushed on and secured the town and harbour called Grand Carenage.

The bay we chose for anchoring and landing etc. was about 4 miles or more to the southward of this called Grand Cul de Sac, the which by Captain Sawyer's order I took a plan of, and the line of battle, from which several drawings have been done.

Perfectly easy with regard to our own safety, having landed our troops, we were praying for their success when to our utmost astonishment our frigates looking out made the signal for the enemy's fleet. This happened about three in the afternoon of Tuesday 15th December [really Monday 14th (Barrington's journal)]. Fancy our confusion and hurry when we counted from our masthead a French fleet of 13 sail of the line and 12 frigates standing in for us ! Our squadron consisted of one seventy-four, Prince of Wales, one sixty-eight, Boyne, two sixty-fours, Nonsuch and St Albans ; three of fifty guns, Preston, Isis, and Centurion ; the Venus of 36 guns, the Aurora 28 guns, the Ariadne of 20 guns. To fly was impossible : we resolved to die a thousand deaths rather than leave our troops. The whole night was employed to secure our defenceless transports within us, and then dispose our little squadron to make them as capable of resisting the enemy as possible. This done, we cleared our ships for fighting and patiently waited the approach of morning. When it was well daylight we saw the enemy close preparing to attack us, and a fearful odds it was, but were resolved and hoped for the Almighty assistance in our trial. The enemy's fleet commanded by d'Estaing consisted of the Languedoc of 84 guns (and 16 additional guns she had taken from a prize made 100 in all), the Tonnant 84, eight seventy-fours, two sixty-fours, and one fifty, besides three frigates from 36 to 40 guns and 9 lesser frigates, with twenty-nine transports full of troops.[1]

Guns of the enemy				*English line of battle*			
	Guns		*Men*		*Guns*		*Men*
Languedoc	100	42 pr. and below	1100	P. Wales	74	32 pr. and below	620
Tonnant	84	,,	1000	Boyne	68		520
8 seventy-fours	592	32 and below	7200	2 sixty-fours	128	24 ,,	1200
2 sixty-fours	128		1400	3 fifty	150		1500
3 large frigates	108		1050	Venus	36		240
9 different size	180		1620	Aurora	28		200
	—		—	Ariadne	20		160
	1192		13370		504		4440
	504		4440		—		—
French superior in guns.	688		8930	French superior in men.			

I have given all our ships their full complement of men whereas many of them were exceedingly deficient, viz the St Albans, Nonsuch, Centurion, Venus etc.

Our ships being anchored in a line extending along the harbour's mouth with our transports

---

[1] Besides the Languedoc and Tonnant, which were both rated at 80 guns, the French actually had six 74s, three 64s, and one 50-gun ship. In the English squadron, Stuart has allowed 600 men to each 64 and 500 to a 50-gun ship; the complements of these classes were 500 and 350 respectively. He has over-manned the French ships in the same proportion.

moored within, we waited the motions of the French. At 9 on Wednesday morning [really Tuesday 15th], d'Estaing, having got his fleet in a line of battle ahead, bore down upon us, and passing along our line discharged their broadsides and continued a hot fire as they passed, which I believe they will own we returned with equal warmth allowing for the great disproportion of strength. This cannonade lasted a long hour ; the whole fleet having passed us hauled their wind to the northward, and making several tacks to gain to windward closed their line, and at 3 o'clock they stood in again and engaged something more than an hour and a half. The ardour of our people is not to be described nor conceived ; they forgot every idea of a superior force, and as the French hauled off would have gladly pursued them. As d'Estaing had by sailing by us sufficiently reconnoitred our strength and position, we expected his second attack would have been a bloody and decisive one, yet nothing was heard but Our dear country, England for ever, and a general resolve to sell our little fleet as dear as possible. Down he came and seemed to be resolute and come closer. Many of his shots that flew over us were found half a mile in the country : I myself brought on board a 42-lb shot that had lodged a quarter of a mile from the sea inland.

In this action we had some of our rigging shot away and twice hulled, but very fortunately nobody killed nor wounded except two of our men burnt by their own powder. The Prince of Wales had two killed and seven wounded, and that was all that suffered in the men of war. The unhappy transports, though far within us, lost twenty people, amongst which was two women killed. We received from every intelligence the

French upon an average lost twelve killed out of each ship and many wounded. At the second attack, which was made like the first only nearer, the sternmost of the French fleet suffered much, especially a rear admiral's ship which was almost wholly becalmed ; and the perpetual fire of our guns seemed to gall him very much, and to incapacitate him farther from getting away we luckily shot away his main topsail yard etc. This ship did not make sail for two hours after she was clear of us.

In the night [of the 14th] the Boreas's boat (which frigate Admiral Barrington had sent to Antigua when we left Barbados to bring some victualling ships for the use of the army) came on board the Admiral, and acquainted him in her way to Antigua she met the Pearl, one of Admiral Byron's frigates from America, who had been to Antigua in search of Admiral Barrington to acquaint him d'Estaing had left the coast of America and supposed sailed to the West Indies. Admiral Byron's letter said to be brought by the Pearl contained or was reported to contain : d'Estaing has left America, I suppose for the West Indies ; I send the Pearl to acquaint you therewith and will follow her in two days with 16 sail of the line etc. The Pearl had been in the West Indies ten days when the Boreas spoke to her, from which everybody concluded Admiral Byron would appear every hour. At daybreak this news was public, and every eye was turned to seaward in anxious expectation of Admiral Byron.

The French, having got their fleet in a line, at 8 in the morning [of the 16th] stood towards us again. I had forgot to say our whole night had been employed in new-berthing our ships, making our line closer and nearer inshore, as the Admiral thought the rear of our line was in danger of being cut off ; and indeed it was by being too much extended. However, we were ready at dawn to receive Monsieur. He changed his mind in the moment we thought him coming in and stood off to sea, and continued standing off and on till 4 in the afternoon when d'Estaing and the whole fleet anchored off Gros Islet Bay, about six miles (and in sight of us) to the northward of us.

Our valuable army, who had entertained the utmost anxiety for our safety, had made us many offers of assistance which however we could not benefit by, as it was impossible in so short a time to have their artillery ashore or throw up batteries in this mountainous and inaccessible country. The French by their anchoring giving us time to breathe, we set about throwing up batteries and in two days with infinite labour opened two, one of 4 twenty-four pounders and one of 3 twelve-pounders upon the points of the bay, which added to the 4 twelve-pounders taken from the French we thought ourselves (wrapped as we were in a resolution to defend ourselves) pretty secure, although d'Estaing and the French line of battle had anchored. His frigates, and frequently a line of battle ship or two, were employed watching our motions and to keep a good look out that we did not run away. Had they but known our minds this had been needless ; for the instant Admiral Barrington saw him coming in the third time, himself and his little fleet struck their topgallant yards, a signal to Monsieur that we intended not to run but fight it out.

However, his frigates, by keeping so close to us, had the advantage to surprise at daylight one of our transports, that had weighed to stand within us but unfortunately fell to leeward in the night.   She was said to be the Lord Shuldham, and had on board the baggage of the 55th Regiment.   By the same means they surrounded a man-of-war sloop of 18 guns that was coming in, and took her ; she was called the Ceres.[1]

The boats of our fleet were employed every night rowing guard to watch the French and prevent surprise and the mischief of fireships which might be sent amongst us.   Our people spent a fortnight laying by their guns upon the deck, hammocks being up night and day to barricade the ships.

We soon learned the design of the French in coming to an anchor was to force our army and possess the ground round the bay wherein we had moored our ships, and by cannon on shore drive us out, and the fleet then to have fallen upon us and subdued us.   We were conscious of the issue of this plan if they succeeded in it.   Our brave army had however possessed the heights around us, and assured us they would be cut to pieces to a man before they would give way.   During the night of the 17th the French landed 4000 troops, which with the mariners of the fleet who were also landed, the regiment on the island, the militia and inhabitants under arms, who universally joined them, at daybreak they were 10,000 strong.   All night long we heard the French cleaning their arms, and did not doubt they meant an early attack—ever since we have been here it has rained, and this night particularly hard, and in the morning during the engagement also.

At 2 o'clock [A.M. 18th] we heard the random

---

[1] The Lord Shuldham was taken on the 17th, the Ceres on the 19th (Barrington's journal).

firing of field pieces and some musketry which the French discharged at the fires round which our poor soldiers, dripping wet, were solacing themselves and chiding the lingering night. At 4 the firing of small arms grew hotter, the French clearing the woods as they advanced. At daylight the 46th Regiment, of which only five companies were together, found themselves closely pressed by the Regiment de Martinique and the militia of the island, which they routed at the third fire, but were themselves obliged to fall back as the columns of the main body of the French army had nearly surrounded them. When daylight and the showers of rain permitted, our troops saw the design of the French was to cut off our grenadiers and light infantry, who had taken post (under the gallant General Medows) upon a hill between the French and English armies. What operated them to this was that our grenadiers and infantry had no retreat without passing the harbour of the Grand Carenage, a thing without boats impossible. This body of heroes of ours amounted to 1400, and determined to defend themselves, naked as they was (not having time to entrench themselves), till the last. At 8 the whole French were in motion and advanced in three heavy columns to the attack of the grenadiers and infantry, and began a fire so hot that no drum could equal its perpetual noise. Our troops stood with the greatest composure (having placed detachments down the hill to flank them) until they could hear them speak, when they began a very heavy and incessant fire.

The French sustained this ill fortune and great mortality like men, were routed, rallied again, were again routed, rallied again, were again repulsed, and again rallied and advanced as to a third attack but wheeled, broke, and fled with the greatest disorder : they left 403 killed on the field, and the average of wounded is generally allowed 4 to 1 killed—they acknowledge 1200 wounded.

A five-gun battery of ours, which we had taken from them, flanked and cut them to pieces. They were aware of the mischief of this battery and sent two line of battle ships to attack it ; but so successful and intrepid were the artillery and soldiers stationed at it that they obliged the first ship to cut her cable, having hulled her seven times running and set her on fire. The second ship stayed about 20 minutes and made off. Our troops, notwithstanding the fire from the ships, had turned their cannon at intervals and fired upon the flying French army to their total discomfiture. Our loss was 12 killed and 124 wounded, two of which have died since. Among the latter was the brave General Medows, who was grazed in the arm but is perfectly recovered.

D'Estaing made a feint to get on the other side (to the southward) of us, but finding that impracticable he afterwards seems to have acted like a villain in despair, intent upon nothing but dishonourable mischief. Nothing but abuse and wrangling was heard in their councils, the land forces saying the fleet was sufficient to have devoured us and should have done it, their navy on the other hand complaining of the troops' not forcing ours and defeating them.

In the night of the [23rd-]24th an American frigate of 22 guns (doubtless dispatched to d'Estaing with news of Admiral Byron) stood in with our fleet by mistake, and being towards daylight becalmed within our guns. At daylight, seeing her mistake, she attempted to make off ; but our shot soon made her strike, she being hulled between wind and water and in danger of sinking.

She struck, and we sent the boats of the fleet armed and towed her in. She was called the Bunker's Hill, and by Admiral Barrington received into his Majesty's service.[1]

The taking this ship close to the French seemed to rouse them : they immediately got under way, and d'Estaing promised that day should be our last. He got under way, and after manœuvring his fleet, forming into two divisions (the only way we feared an attack), he came down ; and when he *should* have come in, dastardly put about and came to anchor. How he can excuse himself to his country is to me amazing.

This behaviour increased the tumult and murmur ashore ; they compelled him to get under way the next day, when after parading he came to anchor again without attempting anything. Resolved on every possible mischief he gave orders for his soldiery three days before this embarkation to plunder the island, which they did, taking away 300 head of cattle, shooting those on shore they could not catch, and destroying every species of furniture etc. they could not remove. And to crown the whole of this infamous behaviour to his country, on the 29th at 9 in the morning, having previously committed every species of cruelty to the wretched inhabitants, he left them (loaded with their curses) to make what terms they could with us ; and I rejoice with them that they met with more tenderness and clemency than they really expected or conceived, having notwithstanding their opposition everything secured to them that could make them happy as prisoners to an honourable and forgiving people. Our people were

---

[1] ' I commissioned her by the name of the Surprise (being expressive of the manner in which she came into our possession) ' (Barrington's journal).

under the necessity of burying the French dead, the French having abandoned and left them to rot above ground though frequently summoned to this last office of humanity. Our flag of truce was twice fired at, and when he arrived at their camp insulted with accounts of the disgrace and defeat of Admiral Keppel etc., reproaching the English with being beat in America and their loss of that continent etc.

Notwithstanding the capitulation and surrender of the island we still kept watchfully on our guard, having everything to apprehend from the machinations of a man of d'Estaing's complexion. Our little army and fleet struggled during this cessation to outdo each other in mutual civilities, and never I believe had any people more confidence in each other than we had.

On Wednesday the 6th January 1779, our long expected Admiral Byron joined us with eight sail of the line [1] and one frigate in a shattered condition, having most of them sprung and carried away masts, yards, anchors, and exceeding sickly etc. We are now busily employed watering and refitting the fleet, and hope to move in a few days. D'Estaing we hear is in Martinique fortifying himself. Dominica is by the French accounts impregnable, but the report is we shall try it. What Admiral Byron's delay could be owing to I know not ; no doubt he did all that man could do, but had he been so fortunate as to appear ten days sooner than he did d'Estaing I think would have been our own, and ere a second force could have arrived, the whole of this part of the West Indies. As it is we have taken St Lucia, and by engaging d'Estaing's attention prevented the success of his expedition, which when he saw us was intended against St Vincent, Grenada, Tobago, and Bar-

[1] Really nine, followed by a tenth a few days later.

bados, all which he would with the force he had probably have taken in a fortnight, and there might have fallen Antigua, St Kitts, etc. Indeed it is not to be said where he would have stopped, for until the arrival of our troops there was scarce a regular soldier in the islands, their fortifications in the most wretched condition and not a ship of force in the country but the Prince of Wales and the Boyne.

The Marquis de Bouillé, Governor of Martinique, conscious of the advantage to be taken of us, on the instant of d'Estaing's arrival (having previously provided everything necessary) proposed to him the reduction of our islands, which he readily embraced and sailed from Martinique with an absolute force in forty hours from his arrival in the country.[1] You will perceive we at Barbados used the same expedition, not knowing d'Estaing was arrived in the West Indies. Nor did d'Estaing know of the arrival of our troops etc., although it is certain the two fleets sailed within 40 or 50 leagues of each other all the way from America to the West Indies ; for Commodore Hotham thinking himself not far enough to the eastward as he intended for Barbados tacked in the night, a brig with horses for his army not minding the signal kept on, and the next morning d'Estaing took him.

Thus by our little endeavours we have taken St Lucia, and I hope rendered our country more service in preventing the mischiefs intended by d'Estaing. We were surprised to see him, and he was astonished to see us, though he pretended on our first appearance to rejoice at the sight of us, especially as we were at an anchor, for by that he

[1] D'Estaing reached Martinique on December 9, and sailed on the 14th, having heard that the English were at St. Lucia the day before (Lacour-Gayet, 185–6).

would make sure of the fleet, saying if they were under sail as he was sure they'd run away some might escape, but as it was he'd ruin the English by a total defeat. But the Almighty struck with us and we conquered. Had Byron luckily come, no doubt we should have procured to our country the whole West Indies or an honourable peace ; as it is we have nothing left but to hunt d'Estaing, who is now in Martinique, and if possible compel him to battle or prevent him doing further mischief by a blockade.

The famous (or rather infamous) Conyngham was attending d'Estaing in a Yankee privateer sloop of 14 guns, and had the impudence to fire at us, but he took care to do it out of gun shot. There were two other Yankee brigs with him who constantly paraded before us with their colours hoisted. We hear that d'Estaing received advice of Admiral Byron's sailing from America by an American frigate the day before Monsieur ran away from St Lucia.

The day after Admiral Byron arrived the Weasel sloop of war had orders to sail in 24 hours for England, by which I send this, and not having time to write a second letter I must trouble you to communicate this to all enquiring friends, particularly Mr Champion's family, to whom remember me with the greatest respect and esteem, as also to Mr Brittain, Mrs and Mr Croom, etc. I am with sincere affection, Yours etc.

A cartel that sailed from hence to Martinique with the French which became our prisoners is just returned and brought the captain and crew of the Ceres etc., who informs us amongst many particulars that the several times d'Estaing got under way it was with a determination to attack us ; and so resolved was he to carry our admiral's ship that he got 100 additional men from several ships, increasing his own crew to 1800 with which he intended to board the Prince of Wales, but he now pretends to excuse himself by saying he could not depend upon his other ships to second him in a proper manner. People of Martinique are enraged with d'Estaing to madness, abusing him in the open streets. They also blush at their own credulity ; to such a degree was their assurance of his success against us that they sent and petitioned him that *all* the English prisoners might not be brought to Martinique, but that they might be divided amongst the French islands.

Being much hurried in mooring our ship etc. I missed my opportunity of the Weasel, who unexpectedly sailed in the night and most unfortunately was taken by the French on the third day after her departure from us, which occasions the Admiral's sending another express by which conveyance this comes.

Occurrences since the 8th January to the 3rd February are as follows. Busily employed refitting this shattered fleet, erected tents and got the sick on shore, who are very numerous, particularly in the Conqueror, Royal Oak, Fame, Trident, Grafton, Monmouth, some of them having from three to four hundred unable to come to quarters in case of action.

On the 11th January in the evening our frigates in the offing made the signal for a fleet in the N.W., which we knew must be the enemy's. Our admiral (Byron) made the signal for everybody to be on board, made the signal to weigh, little winds nearly calm, counted from our mastheads six sail of large ships ; at 6 the Admiral furled his topsails and continued at anchor till 3 in the morning

[12th] when the signal was made to unmoor. Many were for sailing at sunset and standing over to Martinique in the night, by which it was thought we might get between d'Estaing and the land by morning and compel him to action. This though a very (nay the most) eligible plan was not pursued. Indeed this might prejudice our commanders against it : there was little wind and they might apprehend by the current to be drove to leeward. However, I humbly think it might have been ventured because it is common, nay almost constant, to have calms in the night under the lands while there is a very sufficient breeze in the offing or in the channels between the islands ; and what makes me believe it was so this night is that our frigates who sailed at 8 o'clock in the evening were sufficiently to windward in the morning ; and had we luckily been where they were, or closer inshore than they perhaps cared to venture, I think we should cut the French fleet off from the land and either compel them to run away to leeward or engage us on the spot.

At the next morning [12th] most of our fleet were under sail, consisting of thirteen sail of the line, two frigates and one 50-gun ship under the command of Vice-Admiral Byron and Rear-Admiral Parker—leaving the Delight of our Hearts, Admiral Barrington, behind, who shifted his flag from the Prince of Wales to the Isis 50-gun ship, his own ship being ordered to follow Admiral Byron, and also all Admiral Barrington's squadron except the Isis and Preston and two or three sloops of war, which were left with Admiral Barrington in the Cul de Sac with the transports belonging to the army.

At 9 o'clock saw the French fleet, something to leeward and near the land of Martinique, standing

offshore to the southward. Our Admiral Byron
made the signal for the line ahead, which we formed
at 2 cables length asunder, and in this position
gave chase ; but as we were obliged to keep our
stations in the line the good-sailing ships, to keep
their distance with the bad, were under the
necessity of not setting their mainsails, lowering
their topgallant sails, and bracing up their main
topmast-staysails etc. It blowed fresh and smooth
water, rate of sailing about 6 miles (or knots) per
hour. About 10 the French, perceiving our line
and knowing it must be Admiral Byron, tacked
and stood towards Fort Royal Harbour, three or
four of them without topgallant sails. There were
I apprehend from the time of their tacking and
getting in (which was till $\frac{1}{2}$ after 12) four leagues
from the land, and so much to leeward that though
close-hauled two or three of the rear were obliged
to make a tack and stand offshore before they
could reach in.

During this time we were chasing in a line ;
and I am sorry to say it is the almost universal
opinion that had we, when the French fleet tacked
to stand into Martinique (which indicated their
fear and disinclination to come to action), made
a general chase, as we could being so much favoured
by our situation to windward, set studding sails
etc., and steered for the point or entrance of
Fort Royal, which bore N.N.W. westerly with the
wind E.b.N., the rear of the French fleet being
about [one ?] point before the beam of our van,
we might have cut them off. I had an opportunity
of certainly knowing this as the Boyne was the
second headmost or next to the leading ship of our
line, which was the Grafton, and I verily believe
the Boyne if permitted to crowd would have
brought some of d'Estaing's rear to battle ; those

the French admiral must have supported, which most probably would have brought on a general engagement. I sincerely wish (though perhaps I may be wrong) this had been tried because had d'Estaing found that the rear of his fleet were so closely pressed by the headmost of the English as to be in danger of being cut off, he must have formed to support them (for sure, bad as he really is, he dare not have left them), which if our head-most ships had seen and thought themselves too weak to begin the attack they had nothing to do but shorten sail or lay to for the rest to come up ; and so happy is this country for an exploit of the kind that, as the wind was certain not to change (being a constant trade) so as to separate our ships or permit the French to get between the chasing ships and the fleet, we had little to fear, especially as Martinique could not become by any means a lee shore. I am heartily sorry that we didn't push them harder, since we then should conclude ' all had been done that could be done ' whereas there seems now something wanting ; but this I speak with infinite deference to the better judgments of my superiors, and own that the old proverb may be with justice retorted upon me, 'when there is much warmth there is less prudence.'

At noon the Diamond Rock near Martinique bore N., 2 miles ; at ½ past, the French being within the point of the harbour of Fort Royal, the Admiral made the signal for the fleet to tack and hauled down the signal for the line. A French frigate stood off to reconnoitre us ; two of our frigates chased but she got in. At 7 o'clock came to anchor off Gros Islet Bay, St Lucia.

Two of our line of battle ships and a frigate (the Venus) daily looked into Fort Royal where they saw d'Estaing unrigging his fleet to over-haul and refit them. Many of them had their masts out; this relaxed our attention, and no ships appearing off their harbour for four or five days.

On the 2nd February the Venus and Centurion being ordered out they made the signal for four sail in the N.W. The Prince of Wales with Admiral Barrington, who has again hoisted his flag on board her, the Boyne, Nonsuch, Cornwall, St Albans, were ordered by Admiral Byron to slip and give chase. They were three ships of the line and a frigate of d'Estaing's, who on our appearance went into the harbour again.[1]

It is reported d'Estaing has no provisions at Fort Royal but that six months' is arrived for him at St Domingo, whither it is expected he will quickly sail; and we doubtless shall follow him and I hope come up with him ere he arrives there (though it is rumoured the Boyne if possible will stay behind, as Captain Sawyer is very desirous of continuing with Admiral Barrington). The report is that the French have a squadron of eight sail of the line and 10,000 troops actually sailed from Old France, and that as soon as they are well on their passage, that is within 10 days' sail of the islands, d'Estaing intends to run to leeward for Hispaniola, by which he will draw the whole of the English fleet after him and expose to the uncontrollable power of the forces now on their passage all the Windward Islands etc. This seems a plausible story, but we have the comfort to hear from the Pomona frigate, which arrived the 1st February, that six sail of the line are on their passage hither. If they

[1] Barrington also had the Albion, and was joined at sea by the Centurion and some frigates (Barrington's journal).

arrive safe and soon I am to think we shall yet give a good account of Mr d'Estaing.[1]

During our stay here accounts have been received that some American and French privateers have landed in Tobago, murdered several of the inhabitants and plundered the island. The Aurora and Surprise are sent in pursuit of them.

FROM COMMODORE HOTHAM

English Harbour, Antigua, 14 February 1779.

My Lord—I did myself the honour to write to you from St Lucia by the Weasel sloop, which was dispatched to England with advices of the reduction of that island, but was unfortunately taken by a French frigate off of St Eustatius.

The Pearl, having accidently put in here and being substituted in her room, furnishes me with another chance of paying my respects to your Lordship. At the same time that I lament you should have been so long in obtaining the news of our success, the particulars of which will be so fully related in the public accounts of our transactions to the Board that I shall observe no farther upon them than that, until the arrival of Admiral Byron at St Lucia, our situation was not altogether the most eligible, but since that time we have been upon velvet. I take the liberty, however, to enclose a rough sketch of our position, which will enable your Lordship to form at least some idea of it; and if it proves in any degree satisfactory will answer every

[1] Commodore Rowley's reinforcement of seven sail of the line arrived on February 12; and the Lion, Captain Cornwallis, arrived on the 21st (Barrington's journal).

intention of mine, besides that of assuring your Lordship how very sincerely I have [etc.].

TO ADMIRAL BARRINGTON

Admiralty, 14 March 1779.

Dear Sir—As we have received no official account of your very distinguished behaviour in repelling the attack made upon St Lucia by a very superior fleet and army, no public approbation can as yet be sent to you from this office. I cannot, however, in justice to your merit avoid telling you how much your conduct is approved by your Royal Master and by all ranks of people in this kingdom. We should indeed be very ungrateful if we did not feel the obligations we owe to you ; for you have done the most essential service to your country and rescued a considerable and very valuable part of the King's dominions from imminent destruction.

We are in hourly expectation of the news of your farther successes, and you will not be surprised that much is expected from you because you have already given so good a sample of what you can do.

I will not at present trouble you any farther than with my most sincere and hearty congratulations upon the credit you have so justly acquired, and with the assurance of that truth and regard [etc.].

TO BARRINGTON

Admiralty, 5 August 1779.

I have received your private letters of the 20th May and 10th of June, and will begin by answering the postscript of the former, though indeed I find it difficult to answer it to my own satisfaction, as an acknowledgement of negligence and inattention is but a lame excuse for an impropriety in serious business. I will, however, state the fact and tell the truth, and leave the rest to your determination whether the mode now taken may be allowed to compensate for the former error.

It is certain that this Board and all mankind must highly applaud your behaviour at St Lucia. My private letter of the 14th of March fully speaks my sentiments upon that subject. After I had written it I gave directions to the Secretary in the usual manner to write to Admiral Barrington to tell *him how highly the Board approved of his conduct*, concluding that he would not confine himself to the dry expression I had made use of, but would have conveyed that approbation in suitable language and more extended terms. To be sure, I ought to have seen the letter before it went, but hurry of business and want of thought prevented me; and Mr Stephens in the same hurry trusted to another to draw up the letter, which was sent off without being examined, the packet being then being upon the point of sailing and waiting only for our dispatches. This is the naked fact: all then that can be done is to acknowledge our fault and to apply for your assistance to set it right. In this idea an ante-dated letter goes by this conveyance, expressing the real sentiments of the Board, and I hope in proper terms. If you will allow this well-meant fallacy to pass, and will conceal our inattention from your brother officers, I shall consider myself as under a great obligation to you, for I really feel very awkward at what has passed.

I lament the distresses you labour under, and as far as it is in my power will relieve them. You have before this received a considerable supply of stores and provisions ; and our official dispatches will apprise you of what farther assistance you will receive in these particulars. It has been very difficult to supply you properly till now, as we did not know at first where to send to you, as your motions were uncertain, depending entirely upon those of your adversary ; for this reason we were obliged to send the stores at first round by America. I hope in the beginning of the winter to send you a relief of ships, but till then nothing of force can be sent from home ; for while we are struggling for the sovereignty of the seas with the combined force of France and Spain, you will easily conceive that we have full employment for everything we can trust afloat. As coppering our line of battle ships is now become almost general, I hope to send you some ships so fitted, which will be particularly suited to your seas as they will not want to be hove down, and will thereby be kept free from sickness and desertion and always clean.

As to sending you a recruit of men, I see the necessity of it, but I own I know not how to do it. If we send men from hence we cannot fit out so many ships as we hope otherwise to get to sea. The press, though at this time exerted to the utmost, does not afford a sufficiency for what is now in readiness ; and if we send away the men we have we shall man your disabled ships, but be thereby prevented from sending you those coppered and completely fitted which, if circumstances will admit, I hope to send to you as soon as the present campaign is over.

I think what you say about a commissioner at

Antigua is very proper, and you may be assured that that matter will be duly considered.[1]

I am much obliged to you for your kindness to young Swan, who I took the liberty to recommend to your protection. I would not wish to have him sent home, as he will be in much better hands where he now is, especially if you have the goodness to take him into your own ship, where he will see nothing but what will give him useful instruction.

I cannot conclude without offering my services in everything in which you think I can be useful in this part of the globe, and repeating the assurances of that high esteem [etc.].

[1] John Laforey was appointed Commissioner at Barbados and the Leeward Islands, and to reside at Antigua, on November 26 of this year. His letters to Middleton, the Comptroller of the Navy, are in *The Barham Papers*, vol. ii.

APPENDICES

APPENDIX A.

[Both Appendices are from papers at Hinchingbrooke. We have compared them with the complete letters in the Public Record Office.]

SUMMARY OF ORDERS TO ADMIRAL KEPPEL 1778

April 25.[1] The great armament making in the ports of France, and the late offensive proceedings of that court, giving the strongest reasons to apprehend that their intentions were hostile and that the squadron at Toulon might be designed to join that at Brest, he was ordered to proceed to sea with such of the ships put under his command (see the number of those of the line in the margin)[2] as were in readiness, making the following services the particular objects of his attention :—

To see the Mediterranean convoy and the reinforcement of troops going to Gibraltar into the latitude of Ushant, and to send a detachment further with them if necessary.

To cruise at such distance, and on such station, off Brest as he should judge most proper to prevent the junction of the French squadrons, and to intercept any ships which might sail from Brest to interrupt the above-mentioned convoy, using his best endeavours to take or destroy them, and pursuing the Brest squadron should it slip by him and there be any probability of overtaking it without leaving Great Britain or Ireland

---

[1] Lord Sandwich laid these instructions before the Cabinet on April 21, and they were approved. Members present : Lord Privy Seal, Lord North, Lord Sandwich, Lord Amherst, Lord Weymouth (Minute of Cabinet).

[2] Ships of the line put under the command of Admiral Keppel :

18 Mar. when he was ordered to hoist his flag	20
11 Apr.	1
18 ,,	8
	29

II. 2 B

exposed, the protection of which was to be the principal object of his attention.

To take any French ships of the line or East India ships during the cruise, but not to take frigates unless watching his fleet or merchant vessels except those already mentioned.

To give battle to the Brest squadron, though joined by that from Toulon, if the superiority of their combined force should not be too apparent ; but if it should be manifestly superior, then to return to St Helen's for a reinforcement.

To seize any Spanish ships of war of the line he might discover or meet with acting in conjunction with the French, and to intercept such as might be attempting to enter or evidently bound to any of the ports of France ; in all other cases to consider the ships of Spain as those of a power at peace and in friendship with Great Britain, affording them every assistance and protection they may stand in need of.

To protect the trade of His Majesty's subjects which might fall in his way, and to take or destroy all ships or vessels belonging to the rebellious North American colonies and all ships and vessels going to or returning from trading with those colonies.

April 29. Ten ships of the line having been taken from him to serve under V. A. Byron, and one to go to the East Indies, and those in his squadron being consequently reduced to 18, he was directed not to sail from Spithead till further order.

May 25. Ordered to put to sea with as many ships of his squadron as might be in readiness and to proceed off Brest in execution of his instructions of the 25th ultimo, calling off Plymouth for V. A. Byron and taking him and the ships under his command to sea with him. And, in case it should appear by good intelligence that d'Estaing's squadron was sailed from Toulon and gone to North America or the West Indies, to detach the Vice Admiral in pursuit of it agreeable to his instructions ; but if the said squadron should not have left the Mediterranean to detach the Vice Admiral to Gibraltar in quest of it, with directions, if it should have passed the Straits bound out of Europe, to follow it agreeable to his said instructions.

May 27. He was further ordered, if he should find it necessary to detach V. A. Byron as before mentioned before he should have received a sufficient reinforcement to enable him to give battle to the Brest fleet unless with a manifest inferiority in point of strength, to return to St Helen's for a further reinforcement.

June 5. Intelligence having been received that the Toulon squadron had passed the Straits, and as there was reason to believe left the European seas, and V. A. Byron having been directed to pursue it agreeable to the instructions he had received, he was ordered (instead of calling off Plymouth for the said Vice Admiral) to put to sea as soon 20 ships of the line of his squadron should be ready and to proceed directly off Brest and cruise agreeable to former orders.

June 12. Sailed from St Helen's (where he had been ever since the 31st ultimo waiting for a wind) with 20 ships of the line out of 22 then under his command (see margin).[1]

June 20. Orders were sent to his rendezvous directing him, in case he should have taken or should take a French ship of the line or Indiaman, immediately to take and send into port all French ships of war or merchantmen he might meet with.

June 25. In consequence of a letter this day received from him by Lieutenant Berkeley, dated at sea the 21st, setting forth that he was convinced from the information found on board a French frigate, which he had thought proper to take possession of as attending and watching the fleet, that the squadron then in Brest was manifestly

---

[1] Remaining

29 April	18
Added since, viz. :	
30 April	2
12 May	1
7 June	1
	22

superior to him (see margin) [1] and that he should therefore return to St Helen's for a reinforcement, orders were immediately given for six more ships to be put under his command.

June 26. Orders were sent to meet him at St Helen's directing him, so soon as he should be joined by any four of the six additional ships above mentioned, to proceed again off Brest with the utmost dispatch and continue to cruise in that station agreeable to his former instructions till further order. [2]

June 27. He returned to St Helen's.

July 3. Orders were sent to him, in case the French should have committed hostilities against his Majesty's subjects by their ships of war or in consequence of commissions granted to privateers or letters of marque, to commit all acts of hostility against that nation, and to endeavour to seize and send into port all their ships and vessels as well those of war as merchantmen which he might meet with. [3]

July 9. Sailed from St Helen's with 24 sail of the line out of the 30 under his command (see margin), [4] leaving orders for the remainder to follow, all of which had joined him on the 17th except the Terrible, and she joined him on the 21st. [5]

N.B. Before he sailed he was authorized to extend his station from between Brest and Ushant as far as

[1] In Brest Road 27
  To be added 5

                 32

Besides an extraordinary number of frigates.

[2] Founded on a resolution of the Cabinet of the same day (S.P. Dom. naval).

[3] This order is founded on a resolution of the Cabinet sent that day by Lord Weymouth to the Admiralty (S.P. Dom. naval).

[4] Under his command on 12 June 22
  Added since, viz. :
   25 June 6
   27 June 1
   6 July 1

                 30

[5] P.M. 19th (Master's log, Foudroyant).

Scilly and the Lizard, he having represented such latitude to be necessary to be allowed him whenever he should see occasion for protecting of the trade of his Majesty's subjects coming into and going out of the Channel.

July 19. Orders were sent to his rendezvous directing him to seize or destroy all ships and vessels belonging to France or French subjects he might meet with, the French court having given similar orders with respect to those belonging to British subjects.

July 23. Discovered the French fleet.

    27. Gave battle to it.[1]

    31. Returned to Plymouth.

August 7. Ordered, as soon as a sufficient number of the ships of his squadron should be ready, to return with all possible expedition off Ushant, and to cruise on such station as he should judge most proper for carrying into execution his former instructions.

August 23. Sailed from Plymouth with the whole of his squadron, now increased to 33 sail of the line (see margin),[2] except the following, which joined him at sea on the days against each expressed :—

Terrible	26 August.
Egmont	5 September.
Defence }	
Resolution } . . .	11 ,,
Suffolk	25 ,,

October 26. Returned to Spithead with the greatest part of his squadron, the remainder coming afterwards to that place or Plymouth.

---

[1] It consisted of 30 ships of the line, including two of 50 guns; our fleet, though equal in number, had a considerable superiority in the number of guns and size of the ships. (Marginal note.)

[2] Under his command on 9th July 30
    Added since, viz. :

      3 Augt. 1
      6 ,, ... 1
     14 ,, ... 1

                              —
                            33

By the most authentic accounts the French fleet did not consist of more than 27 sail of the line.

APPENDIX B

SUMMARY OF SECRET INSTRUCTIONS TO ADMIRAL BYRON 1778

May 3.[1] Intelligence having been received of the sailing of Monsieur d'Estaing's squadron from Toulon, and of its probable destination to Boston or some other port in the revolted colonies, instructions were given to Vice-Admiral Byron to put to sea with a squadron consisting of 13 ships of the line and a frigate and proceed directly to Halifax in Nova Scotia acquainting Lord Howe with his arrival.

If upon his arrival at Halifax he should learn that d'Estaing's squadron had put into Boston or was elsewhere on the coast of North America, to proceed immediately in pursuit of it, taking with him any of the King's ships he may find at Halifax or which may join him there or in his course afterwards, and conducting himself as he should judge best for effecting the destruction of the French squadron until he should be joined by Lord Howe or receive his Lordship's orders.

If he should learn that the French squadron had not appeared in the North American seas, and have reason to suppose that it had proceeded to the West Indies, then to follow it thither and do his utmost to attack and destroy it, and to cover and protect his Majesty's possessions.

N.B. He was not only to use his best endeavours to take or destroy d'Estaing's squadron but any other French ships of war he might meet with.

May 13. To remain with the ships under his command in Plymouth Sound until further order, advices having been received that d'Estaing's squadron (whose real

---

[1] These instructions are almost word for word the same as a letter from the Secretary of State to the Admiralty, dated April 29 (S.P. Dom. naval and Secret Orders and Instructions).

destination was unknown) had not passed the Straits of Gibraltar.[1]

May 18. Instead of going directly to Halifax, conformable to his first instructions, to proceed in the first place to Sandy Hook for intelligence relative to d'Estaing, and to pursue him according to the information he might receive and the judgment he might be able to form of the place to which he might be gone.

If on his arrival in North America or the West Indies, he should find it impracticable to bring the said squadron to action and should learn that the whole or any part of it had quitted the North American and West Indian seas to return to Europe, in that case to return to England with the whole or so many of his ships as from the disposition of the French squadron he might judge best for his Majesty's service, taking care, if any of the French squadron remained, to leave a superior force to watch their motions and if practicable to attack and take or destroy them.

June 5. Advice having been received that d'Estaing's squadron had passed the Straits of Gibraltar, to put to sea without one moment's loss of time (notwithstanding former orders to join Admiral Keppel) and carry into execution his former instructions for proceeding to Sandy Hook etc. in pursuit of that squadron.

November 6. A commission having been signed appointing him Commander-in-chief of his Majesty's ships in North America from the North Cape on the Island of Cape Breton to Cape Florida and the Bahama Islands, in the room of Rear-Admiral Gambier called home, instructions were sent to him : to use his utmost endeavours to bring d'Estaing's squadron to action if it should remain on the coast of North America when these instructions came to hand ; and if it should elude his vigilance, and leaving that coast proceed to the West Indies or return to Europe, then to detach Rear-Admiral Parker with at least an adequate number of line of battle ships and a suitable number of frigates in pursuit of it.

But if Monsieur d'Estaing should have found an

[1] See above, p. 58.

opportunity to escape from the said coast with his whole force before these instructions come to hand, then to select the number of ships and vessels of the classes mentioned in the margin which are in the best condition; [1] and considering them as the squadron to be employed for the future under his command within the limits above-mentioned, to send the remainder (except the Trident and such as may have been appointed to proceed to the West Indies with Commodore Hotham) to England. But if Monsieur d'Estaing should remain in North America, or have sailed with only a part of his force leaving some of his line of battle ships behind, then, and in either case, to retain such a further number of ships as with the squadron above-mentioned he may judge proper to enable him to watch the motions of the French ships, to attack them if they come out, and to carry on the other services entrusted to him.

[1] Line of battle 3
Of 50 guns 2
44 ,, ... 2
32 ,, ... 2
28 ,, ... 4
20 ,, ... 2
Sloops 10

And all the fireships, bomb vessels, schooners, armed ships, and galleys, and such of the storeships and hospital ships as may be necessary.

INDEX

The titles of peers and the ranks of officers are those held on 23 April, 1779; later advancements in the peerage are given in square brackets. Entries in round brackets following a person's name show the post he held or the ship or regiment in which he served. The names of American states are those used in 1778. The names of his Majesty's ships are followed by their rate and number of guns in brackets or, in the smaller classes such as sloops and the like, by the name of the class. Merchant ships, transports, and so on, have their description in brackets. Foreign ships have their nationality and guns or description in brackets. E.I.C. means East India Company.

ADAIR, Captain Jesse, the Marines (Duke), 161 *n.*

Adams, John, 117

Admiral, number in fleet and position in line of battle, 28–9

Admiralty, the Board of, 4, 5, 81, 102–3, 161, 162 *n.*, 195–7, 212, 213, 231, 246, 248–9, 278; orders and instructions from, 8, 9, 194, 196, 268–9, 270, 277, 280–1, 285, 333–4, 369–76, to, 42 *n.*, 259, 338, 369 *n.*, 372 *n.*, 374 *n.*; responsibility, 255, 259

Affleck, Captain Edmund, 46 *n.*

Allen, Captain John Carter (Egmont), 151, 228

American ships of war and privateers, 33, 35, 92, 117, 290, 295, 300, 304, 310, 315 *n.*, 322, 324, 352–3, 356, 362

Amherst, General Jeffery, 1st Baron, K.B. (Lieut.-Gen. of the Ordnance), 38, 110; present at Cabinet, 23, 58 *n.*, 369 *n.*

Amiel, ——— (Am. sea officer), 117

Anonymous letter, 101

Antigua, 335, 343, 348, 366

Aranda, Pedro, Conde d' (Span. Ambassador at Versailles), 117

Arbuthnot, Vice - Admiral Mariot, 194, 239, 244, 247 *n.*

Army, the, 66, 73, 304; in N.A., 53, 64, 83, 285–6, 288–9, 295–9, 302, 306, 314–315, 319–20, 322, 324; expedition to St. Lucia, 285, 319, 325, 328, 333, 335–6, 337–41, 344–5, 349–52, 355

Astley, ———, 211

BAILLIE, Captain Thomas, 235 *n.*

Barbados, 333–4, 343, 354–5

Barrington, Vice-Admiral Hon. Samuel (C. in C. Leeward Is. as rear adm.), 29, 277, 281, 333–6, 340, 343, 348, 349, 353, 358, 361; letters to (two), 363

388 *THE SANDWICH PAPERS*

SCOTLAND

Scotland, volunteers from, 73, 76

Secretary of State, instructions to Admiralty, 42 *n.*, 52, 259, 374 *n.*

Senegal, loss of, 281

Shipbuilding, 5, 262

Ships :—

Actaeon (V. 44), 164 *n.*
Actif (Fr. 74), 11
Actionnaire (Fr. 64), 11
Aimable (Fr. 30), 286
Alarm (V. 32), 8 *n.*
Albion (III. 74), 20, 22, 40, 272, 287, 320, 361 *n.*
Alcmène (Fr. 30), 286
Alert sloop, 9, 74, 95, 119, 122, 124 *n.*, 125, 127, 134, 134 *n.*, 141
Alexander (III. 74), 245, 245 *n.*
Alexandre (Fr. 64), 10
Amazon (V. 32), 309
America (III. 64), 11, 20, 21 *n.*, 59, 75, 79, 79 *n.*, 168, 171, 245, 247 *n.*, 271 *n.*
Amphion (Fr. 50), 10
Andromeda (VI. 28), 109, 113, 119, 122, 127, 134, 134 *n.*, 149, 163
Antelope (IV. 50), 30, 31 *n.*, 37, 48
Apollo (V. 32), 285, 286
Ardent (III. 64), 272, 273, 274 *n.*, 285, 286, 288, 289, 294, 321
Arethusa (V. 32), 9, 11, 57, 65, 73, 94, 95, 109, 113, 149, 217 *n.*
Ariadne (VI. 20), 335 *n.*, 345, 346
Artésien (Fr. 64), 11
Asia (III. 64), 19, 21 *n.*, 43 *n.*, 272, 273
Augusta (III. 64), 274 *n.*
Aurora (VI. 28), 335, 335 *n.*, 345, 346, 362

SHIPS

Ships (*continued*) :—

Bedford (III. 74), 19, 21 *n.*, 272, 287
Belleisle (III. 64), 20, 22, 272, 274
Belle Poule (Fr. 30), 9, 95, 118
Berwick (III. 74), 10, 20, 21 *n.*, 59, 73, 75, 79, 80, 82, 92, 169, 171, 271 *n.*
Bien-Aimé (Fr. 74), 10
Bienfaisant (III. 64), 11, 19, 21 *n.*, 55, 57, 146, 149, 171, 272
Blenheim (II. 90), 70, 73, 119, 121, 122, 128, 133, 134, 136, 136 *n.*, 145, 219
Boreas (VI. 28), 335 *n.*, 348
Boyne (III. 70), 20, 22, 44, 56, 272, 273, 334, 335, 335 *n.*, 336, 345, 346, 355, 359, 361
Bretagne (Fr. 110), 11, 128, 154
Britannia (I. 100), 177, 178, 186, 194, 205
Brune (V. 32), 309, 322, 323
Buffalo (IV. 50), 57, 60
Bunker's Hill (Am. sloop) [Surprise], 353, 362
Burford (III. 70), 20, 22, 271, 272, 274
Camilla (VI. 20), 320
Canada (III. 74), 278
Carcass bomb, 286, 335
Carysfort (VI. 28), 315 *n.*
Centaur (III. 74), 10, 20, 21, 70, 82, 107, 113, 113 *n.*, 119, 121, 122, 123, 168, 171, 247 *n.*, 272, 273
Centurion (IV. 50), 286, 303, 321, 345, 346, 361, 361 *n.*
Ceres sloop, 335 *n.*, 350, 350 *n.*, 356

Printed in England at THE BALLANTYNE PRESS
SPOTTISWOODE, BALLANTYNE & CO. LTD.
Colchester, London & Eton

THE NAVY RECORDS SOCIETY

———

THE Society has already issued the following volumes:

For 1894: Vols. I. and II. *State Papers relating to the Defeat of the Spanish Armada, Anno* 1588. Edited by Professor J. K. Laughton. (30s.)

For 1895: Vol. III. *Letters of Lord Hood,* 1781–82. Edited by Mr. David Hannay. (*Out of Print.*)

Vol. IV. *Index to James's Naval History,* by Mr. C. G. Toogood. Edited by the Hon. T. A. Brassey. (12s. 6d.)

Vol. V. *Life of Captain Stephen Martin,* 1666–1740. Edited by Sir Clements R. Markham. (*Out of Print.*)

For 1896: Vol. VI. *Journal of Rear-Admiral Bartholomew James,* 1752–1828. Edited by Professor J. K. Laughton and Commander J. Y. F. Sulivan. (10s. 6d.)

Vol. VII. *Hollond's Discourses of the Navy,* 1638 and 1658. Edited by Mr. J. R. Tanner. (12s. 6d.)

Vol. VIII. *Naval Accounts and Inventories in the Reign of Henry VII.* Edited by Mr. M. Oppenheim. (10s. 6d.)

For 1897: Vol. IX. *Journal of Sir George Rooke.* Edited by Mr. Oscar Browning. (*Out of Print.*)

Vol. X. *Letters and Papers relating to the War with France,* 1512–13. Edited by M. Alfred Spont. (10s. 6d.)

Vol. XI. *Papers relating to the Spanish War,* 1585–87. Edited by Mr. Julian S. Corbett. (10s. 6d.)

For 1898: Vol. XII. *Journals and Letters of Admiral of the Fleet Sir Thomas Byam Martin,* 1773–1854 (Vol. II.). Edited by Admiral Sir R. Vesey Hamilton. (*See* XXIV.)

Vol. XIII. *Papers relating to the First Dutch War,* 1652–54 (Vol. I.). Edited by Dr. S. R. Gardiner. (10s. 6d.)

Vol. XIV. *Papers relating to the Blockade of Brest,* 1803–5 (Vol. I.). Edited by Mr. J. Leyland. (*Out of Print.*)

For 1899 : Vol. XV. *History of the Russian Fleet during the Reign of Peter the Great. By a Contemporary Englishman.* Edited by Admiral Sir Cyprian Bridge. (10s. 6d.)

Vol. XVI. *Logs of the Great Sea Fights,* 1794–1805 (Vol. I.). Edited by Vice-Admiral Sir T. Sturges Jackson. (*See* XVIII.)

Vol. XVII. *Papers relating to the First Dutch War,* 1652–54 (Vol. II.). Edited by Dr. S. R. Gardiner. (10s. 6d.)

For 1900 : Vol. XVIII. *Logs of the Great Sea Fights* (Vol. II.). Edited by Vice-Admiral Sir T. Sturges Jackson. (*Two vols.* 25s.)

Vol. XIX. *Journals and Letters of Sir T. Byam Martin* (Vol. III.). Edited by Admiral Sir R. Vesey Hamilton. (*See* XXIV.)

For 1901 : Vol. XX. *The Naval Miscellany* (Vol. I.). Edited by Professor J. K. Laughton. (15s.)

Vol. XXI. *Papers relating to the Blockade of Brest,* 1803–5 (Vol. II.). Edited by Mr. John Leyland. (12s. 6d.)

For 1902 : Vols. XXII. and XXIII. *The Naval Tracts of Sir William Monson* (Vols. I. and II.). Edited by Mr. M. Oppenheim. (40s.)

Vol. XXIV. *Journals and Letters of Sir T. Byam Martin* (Vol. I.). Edited by Admiral Sir R. Vesey Hamilton. (*Three vols.* 31s. 6d.)

For 1903 : Vol. XXV. *Nelson and the Neapolitan Jacobins.* Edited by Mr. H. C. Gutteridge. (12s. 6d.)

Vol. XXVI. *A Descriptive Catalogue of the Naval MSS. in the Pepysian Library* (Vol. I.). Edited by Mr. J. R. Tanner. (15s.)

For 1904 : Vol. XXVII. *A Descriptive Catalogue of the Naval MSS. in the Pepysian Library* (Vol. II.). Edited by Mr. J. R. Tanner. (12s. 6d.)

Vol. XXVIII. *The Correspondence of Admiral John Markham,* 1801–7. Edited by Sir Clements R. Markham. (12s. 6d.)

For 1905 : Vol. XXIX. *Fighting Instructions,* 1530–1816. Edited by Mr. Julian S. Corbett. (*Out of Print.*)

Vol. XXX. *Papers relating to the First Dutch War,* 1652–54 (Vol. III.). Edited by the late Dr. S. R. Gardiner and Mr. C. T. Atkinson. (12s. 6d.)

For 1906 : Vol. XXXI. *The Recollections of Commander James Anthony Gardner,* 1775–1814. Edited by Admiral Sir R. Vesey Hamilton and Professor J. K. Laughton. (12s. 6d.)

Vol. XXXII. *Letters and Papers of Charles, Lord Barham,* 1758–1813 (Vol. I.). Edited by Sir J. K. Laughton. (12s. 6d.)

For 1907 : Vol. XXXIII. *Naval Ballads and Songs.* Edited by Professor C. H. Firth. (12s. 6d.)

Vol. XXXIV. *Views of the Battles of the Third Dutch War.* Edited by Mr. Julian S. Corbett. (20s.)

For 1908 : Vol. XXXV. *Signals and Instructions,* 1776–94. Edited by Mr. Julian S. Corbett. (15s.)

Vol. XXXVI. *A Descriptive Catalogue of the Naval MSS. in the Pepysian Library* (Vol. III.). Edited by Dr. J. R. Tanner. (12s. 6d.)

For 1909 : Vol. XXXVII. *Papers relating to the First Dutch War*, 1652–54 (Vol. IV.). Edited by Mr. C. T. Atkinson. (12s. 6d.)

Vol. XXXVIII. *Letters and Papers of Charles, Lord Barham*, 1758–1813 (Vol. II.). Edited by Sir J. K. Laughton. (12s. 6d.)

For 1910 : Vol. XXXIX. *Letters and Papers of Charles, Lord Barham*, 1758–1813 (Vol. III.). Edited by Sir J. K. Laughton. (12s. 6d.)

Vol. XL. *The Naval Miscellany* (Vol. II.). Edited by Sir J. K. Laughton. (12s. 6d.)

For 1911 : Vol. XLI. *Papers relating to the First Dutch War*, 1652–54 (Vol. V.). Edited by Mr. C. T. Atkinson. (12s. 6d.)

Vol. XLII. *Papers relating to the Loss of Minorca in* 1756. Edited by Capt. H. W. Richmond, R.N. (10s. 6d.)

For 1912 : Vol. XLIII. *The Naval Tracts of Sir William Monson* (Vol. III.). Edited by Mr. M. Oppenheim. (12s. 6d.)

Vol. XLIV. *The Old Scots Navy*, 1689–1710. Edited by Mr. James Grant. (10s. 6d.)

For 1913 : Vol. XLV. *The Naval Tracts of Sir William Monson* (Vol. IV.). Edited by Mr. M. Oppenheim. (12s. 6d.)

Vol. XLVI. *The Private Papers of George, second Earl Spencer* (Vol. I.). Edited by Mr. Julian S. Corbett. (12s. 6d.)

For 1914 : Vol. XLVII. *The Naval Tracts of Sir William Monson* (Vol. V.). Edited by Mr. M. Oppenheim. (12s. 6d.)

Vol. XLVIII. *The Private Papers of George, second Earl Spencer* (Vol. II.). Edited by Mr. Julian S. Corbett. (12s. 6d.)

For 1915: Vol. XLIX. *Documents relating to Law and Custom of the Sea* (Vol. I.). Edited by Mr. R. G. Marsden. (17s. 6d.)

For 1916: Vol. L. *Documents relating to Law and Custom of the Sea* (Vol. II.). Edited by Mr. R. G. Marsden. (15s.)

For 1917: Vol. LI. *Autobiography of Phineas Pett.* Edited by Mr. W. G. Perrin. (12s.)

For 1918: Vol. LII. *The Life of Admiral Sir John Leake* (Vol. I.). Edited by Mr. G. A. R. Callender. (15s.)

For 1919: Vol. LIII. *The Life of Admiral Sir John Leake* (Vol. II.). Edited by Mr. G. A. R. Callender. (15s.)

For 1920: Vol. LIV. *The Life and Works of Sir Henry Mainwaring* (Vol. I.). Edited by Mr. G. E. Manwaring. (15s.)

For 1921: Vol. LV. *The Letters of Lord St. Vincent,* 1801–1804 (Vol. I.). Edited by Mr. D. B. Smith. (15s.)

Vol. LVI. *The Life and Works of Sir Henry Mainwaring* (Vol. II.). Edited by Mr. G. E. Manwaring and Mr. W. G. Perrin. (12s. 6d.)

For 1922: Vol. LVII. *A Descriptive Catalogue of the Naval MSS. in the Pepysian Library* (Vol. IV.). Edited by Dr. J. R. Tanner. (24s.)

For 1923: Vol. LVIII. *The Private Papers of George, second Earl Spencer* (Vol. III.). Edited by Rear-Admiral H. W. Richmond. (16s.)

For 1924: Vol. LIX. *The Private Papers of George, second Earl Spencer* (Vol. IV.). Edited by Rear-Admiral H. W. Richmond. (15s.)

For 1925: Vol. LX. *Samuel Pepys's Naval Minutes.* Edited by Dr. J. R. Tanner. (21s.)

For 1926: Vol. LXI. *The Letters of Lord St. Vincent, 1801–1804* (Vol. II.). Edited by Mr. D. B. Smith. (20s.)

Vol. LXII. *Letters and Papers of Admiral Viscount Keith* (Vol. I.). Edited by Mr. W. G. Perrin. (17s.)

For 1927: Vol. LXIII. *The Naval Miscellany* (Vol. III.). Edited by Mr. W. G. Perrin. (20s.)

For 1928: Vol. LXIV. *The Journal of the First Earl of Sandwich.* Edited by Mr. R. C. Anderson. (17s.)

For 1929: Vol. LXV. *Boteler's Dialogues.* Edited by Mr. W. G. Perrin. (16s.)

For 1930: Vol. LXVI. *Papers relating to the First Dutch War*, 1652–54 (Vol. VI.; with index). Edited by Mr. C. T. Atkinson. (15s.)

Vol. LXVII. *The Byng Papers* (Vol. I.). Edited by Mr. W. C. B. Tunstall. (15s.)

For 1931: Vol. LXVIII. *The Byng Papers* (Vol. II.). Edited by Mr. W. C. B. Tunstall. (17s.)

For 1932: Vol. LXIX. *The Private Papers of John, Earl of Sandwich* (Vol. I.). Edited by Mr. G. R. Barnes and Lieut.-Commander J. H. Owen. (21s.)

Corrigenda to *Papers relating to the First Dutch War*, 1652–54 (Vols. I. to VI.). Edited by Captain A. C. Dewar. (2s.)

For 1933: Vol. LXX. *The Byng Papers* (Vol. III.). Edited by Mr. W. C. B. Tunstall. (21s.)

Vol. LXXI. *The Private Papers of John, Earl of Sandwich* (Vol. II.). Edited by Mr. G. R. Barnes and Lieut.-Commander J. H. Owen. (21s.)

Future publications contemplated are further volumes of *The Keith Papers, The Sandwich Papers,* and *The Byng Papers,* and also *The Letters of Robert Blake, The Papers of Sir Evan Nepean* and *Piracy Papers from the Correspondence of Admiral Sir Edward Codrington.*